HOUSE PLANTS FOR THE PURPLE THUMB

BY MAGGIE BAYLIS

PLANT ILLUSTRATIONS BY
E. D. BILLS
OTHERS BY THE AUTHOR

101 PRODUCTIONS
SAN FRANCISCO

TO DOUGLAS BAYLIS

whose insight and hindsight gave
my thumb its new color . . .

Printed and bound in the United States of America.

Distributed to the book trade in the United States
by Charles Scribner's Sons, New York.

Published by 101 Productions
834 Mission Street
San Francisco, California 94103

Library of Congress Cataloging in Publication Data

Baylis, Maggie.
    House plants for the purple thumb.

    Includes index.
    1. House plants.   I. Title.
SB419.B25   1981   635.9'65   81-11174
ISBN 0-89286-194-0   AACR2

CONTENTS

THE PURPLE THUMB SYNDROME

" I'VE GOT A PURPLE THUMB!"

Ever since Adam got kicked out of the garden without time to pack his pruning shears, man has been progressing in frustration to the age of plastic petunias.

These sad words, repeated over and over, touch the note of hopelessness: "Every plant I bring home starts dying the minute I carry it through the door!"

There is an increasing centripetal force pulling live plants into our environment today. Of course you *can* live without greening up, ecologists to the contrary, but why should you? With a modest amount of helpful information and a fertile imagination you can develop grow power in your personal paradise, be it mobile home or mansion. Admittedly it's not easy going for nonbelievers. But an old proverb from Kenya says that seeing for yourself is different from being told.

When you watch a plant thrive on the magic combination of personal interaction, adequate light, temperature, moisture and a happy location—and it comes up roses—you will learn what a living, growing thing can do for you.

Here's something you can talk to; a fern doesn't have to be walked twice a day. Here's the pet which will still look great after a three-day weekend alone—and you didn't have to worry about who opened the cat-food can.

House plants do their bit for ecology, too. They consume the carbon dioxide you exhale and hand back life-giving oxygen. There's also a good chance that some of the rarer plants which will grow inside may be destined for extinction, just like the wildlife. Swiss-based studies indicate 10 percent of the known species are dodo-bound. So the plant you save may be its own future!

WHERE DO I LOOK FOR PLANTS?

The increased demands of discount outlets, great retail stores like Sears, Wards and Woolworths, as well as nurseries, have forced the mass growing of house plants. With this development comes scientific know-how, stronger strains.

Today you can buy green livestock more resistant to disease. The content of each pot or tub has better shape, texture, leaf color and limberness. And there are more varieties to choose from.

For the bold adventurer, there's the open-sesame of growing your plants from scratch with rare seeds. Nurture a coffee tree, or the red-flowering bat-wing coral tree, or a telegraph plant (the leaves are in constant motion in the sunshine). They all make impressive tub plants, natural conversation starters. There's a list of catalog sources in the section Experimental Plants.

Consider growing vegetables at home, too. Transplant a young zucchini started in your own cold frame into a large wood tub or plant box, in the sun, just outside a window where you can watch it practically vault out of the soil. In six to eight weeks, you'll have a great show of huge leaves on thick hairy stems, and gay yellow blossoms

Procrastination is a house plant pest, too. There's no spray for that.

Raise a pot on a clean inverted pot for more visibility, better air circulation.

5

which will eventually grow into vegetables of jumbo proportions. The seeds from Chinese cabbage send up a huge bouquet of pale green, each crinkly leaf edged with dark green; the curly red cabbage makes a rounded mass of startling pinks, purples and blue, an awesome centerpiece for a Thanksgiving table.

Discover the rooting of cuttings, the dividing of overblown pots. You can end up with two or three dramatic long-bloom orchids on your coffee table simply by learning when and how to divide. Orchids can be grown without any more special care than African violets.

Try paper-white narcissus in a Delft blue bowl for think-spring-on-a-rainy-day. There are a host of plants which love the water routine.

As for cacti and succulents, these characters live agreeably without water for at least three weeks in the winter (which removes your built-in guilt about that ski trip).

TELL ME THAT YOU LOVE ME

Clue yourself in to fun with foliage, for soulfeeding. But remember, it's a two-way stretch. Mention of the cacti brings to mind that you may ignore the watering—but be sure you let the stay-at-home plant know you care! The past ten years have brought astounding disclosures about the documented sensibilities of growing things.

Luther Burbank, the geneticist in Santa Rosa, looked at plants in the desert and reasoned that every one was spiny, bitter or poisonous because of years of fighting for survival in a threatening environment. When he set out to make the spineless cactus (including the tasty prickly pear) he talked to his test objects: "You have nothing to fear. You don't need defensive thorns. I will protect you." He stated later: "The secret of improved plant breeding, apart from scientific knowledge, is love."

Even the prestigious Wall Street Journal put a story on its front page "Be Kind to Your Plants—You Could Cause a Violet to Shrink."

Purple paling? Velvet plant, zebrina, African violets need as much light as possible (without direct sun). Crotons lose their exotic patterning unless given full sun.

6

Fresh dates: If you can pick ripe fruit off a tree—and have patience—remove pulp, plant each seed in planting mix, moisten, cover with plastic bag and put in a warm bright place. Germination? A month or more and then transplant. Warmth is the key.

The reporter quoted experiments which showed plants possess feelings. When violence threatens, when an unkind word is spoken, something disturbs them—and sensitive instruments have recorded that.

Take the story I heard in San Francisco. A venerable Oriental grandmother carefully raised a Chinese grapefruit tree in her kitchen for 12 years. No fruit appeared although the tree seemed happy. Then one day a plumber, looking for a place to support an exposed pipe which went from floor to ceiling, drove a couple of nails into the trunk of the tree to hold a cross piece of wood. The nails stayed in the tree. And the following winter, the fruitless tree burst out with a heavy crop.

The explanation? Citrus horticulturists found, years ago, that piercing the trunks of trees produces a kind of systemic reaction to the steady plodding of growth. The wound becomes a catalyst, just as a splinter in the finger alerts all the corpuscles in the blood stream to do battle against bacteria. The enzymes and hormones in the tree sense it is in danger and they move into high gear to make the tree bear before it dies. Only, the grapefruit tree didn't die. It went right on producing.

7

WHY DOES MY PURPLE THUMB LUCK OUT?

Walking a cart down an aisle of your local supermarket and impulsively adding a pot of chrysanthemums on top of the Wheaties and peanut butter because the color caught your eye is fine. Its "special today" price tag means the store wants to move it out to make room for fresher stock. So don't count on that charming bouquet in a pot to keep proliferating as it might if you had bought a bedding plant or a six-inch pot and raised it lovingly to the blooming moment. Some plants are just good brighteners, timed for the quick TV-dinner scene, pushed and shoved into early bloom and short but merry life.

We live in an expendable society. Impulse buying is the take-off point and the $2.99 spent for instant sensory joy is peanuts compared to

Brown tips on spider plant, dracaena, ti? Florida Agriculture Experiment Station found these plants sensitive to fluorides in water. Use rain or spring water if you are allergic to brown spots.

Unusual "tears" or moisture dripping from ends of leaves? Plants like nasturtiums, impatiens, even strawberries do it. No problem—it's probably excess water naturally exuded by leaves. Just be sure surface below pot is protected from droppings.

plant for $2.99, but the mums are grown for a use-it-today, throw-it-away-tomorrow. The plant *may* go on for months, even years if you put it out in the garden, although it will probably never be so full of blooms again. But for $2.99, it's a bargain, whether it lives or not.

Incidentally, if you picked the pot with full open blooms, it was probably the best moment of that mum's life. A pot, perhaps partially opened or with tight buds, may refuse to bloom when you get it home. And the ones with signs of browned edges and built-in droop are already over the hill.

Now, consider another kind of plant selection. You buy a bottle of $4.95 wine some vintner has nursed through a couple of years in a French cave, and take it home. Its label and its vintage promise much; it's for one night, for now. Then, at a large nursery center, you pick out a handsome maranta for $4.95 with velvety sheen and dark purple markings for the centerpiece the night you open the wine. It has no fancy lineage, only a bright fresh aura which comes with a healthy normal growth. But if it likes the location and care and feeding you hand out, it will keep growing and glowing, perhaps adding pizzazz to the tapioca personality of your kitchen or the sterile basin counter of the bath for a long, long time.

The nice bonus is finally recognizing that plants *will* live for you and that you can keep most of them happy indefinitely. Don't worry about the rest.

TAKING UP A COLLECTION

In other words, start training your eye to select stable healthy plants. (There's nothing wrong with a one-night-stand bloomer, but buy with that understanding and don't let it bug you if the performance isn't repeated.) It is a good rule of green thumb to get the best your money can buy in this expendable world.

If there are many choices of one species of greenery when you go to select, start by looking at the leaves:

A top-performing plant will have a nicely balanced crop of leaves, fairly uniform in size, and alert. Scratch the plant with small ones, spaced far apart on spindly stalks—they haven't had adequate light. Avoid the pot with some leaves noticeably larger than others—it has probably been overfed and already has a handicap.

Look at the new growth carefully to be sure it is clean and free of the little footprints of pests; any curling or drooping of foliage is telltale, too.

Touch the leaves gently, sniff the plant (each has its own trademark).

If your plant choice is a flowering one, look for foliage which starts close to the base of the plant and buds which are about to open so you can enjoy the longest show of color (instead of choosing the pot of color forced into bloom which has a short life as mentioned earlier).

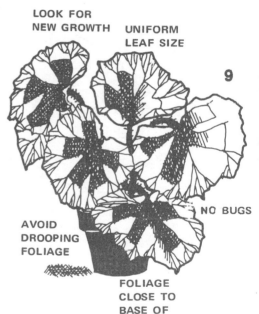

LOOK FOR
NEW GROWTH   UNIFORM
LEAF SIZE

9

AVOID
DROOPING
FOLIAGE

NO BUGS

FOLIAGE
CLOSE TO
BASE OF
PLANT

Once you start recognizing plants which may *not* respond to the challenge, you are on your way to success. The second-class plants, the ones which start out handicapped, with built-in shortcomings, have thin growth, twisted forms, limp leaves. The carelessness of a wet-nurse overwatering or forgetting to water, and the indifference of the potting-shed help whose mind is far away tinkering with his Honda can blight the adult life of any plant.

LET'S TALK ABOUT THAT PURPLE THUMB

If you have awarded it to yourself for the buffs and rebuffs (and even wipe-outs) you have taken in the past from greenstuff, perhaps it's time to give up Kick-A-Plant Week! *This syndrome can be cured.*

Start by finding out what has worked for the experts for the

SMALL FERNS

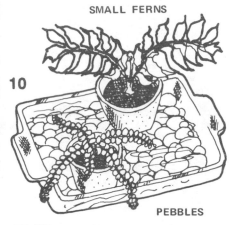

10

PEBBLES

GLASS BAKING DISH

Algae in a pebble tray? Use a weak solution of household bleach in the water: ¼ tsp. to one pint water. Keep water level below bottoms of pots so soil drains naturally.

variety you own or want to buy (some guidelines are included later in Plants to Nourish and Cherish).

Plants which like shade want light too; but do not set them in a sunny west window unless you want them cookie-brown by the time you turn around. Very few plants can live in dark corners, either, so look into special artificial lights designed to give plants a daily turn-on.

On chilly nights, slip newspapers or rigid plastic between window glass and the plants to ward off chilblains and keep leaves from freezing to the glass. Keep in mind, too, that plants like elbow room; don't try for too many in a limited space because you will not appreciate the nice forms of each if you juggle a jungle.

Start by accepting the fact that most environments inside the house, the apartment or the mobile home are too dry. A daily mist over ferns, using lukewarm water, will replace the water they exhale. A glass tray or a nonrusting metal one with a layer of gravel on which to set several pots of violets, with water added so it does not touch the pot bottoms, will give a pleasant relative humidity.

Plants just naturally like cooler temperature at night. There are thermometers which give the clue of maximum-minimum temperatures inside; if you are serious about plants, start looking into these gadgets. Controlled growing temperatures insure results.

Plants don't catch cold, but they do *not* like drafts. Greenery caught between an open door and window will keel over in agony. Ventilation and air movement is part of their requirements (particularly in interiors heated by coal or gas, where fumes linger). Air rooms of stale, high-pollutant contents for plants and for yourself.

There's the matter of hygiene, again. Greenery allowed to collect airborne dirt and grease is a natural for invasion by nasty little pests which suck out life juices. They multiply overnight, and before you realize, crippled falling leaves are candidates for socialized medicine.

Putting the whole plant under the shower once a week for a washoff is a friendly answer to housekeeping (not recommended for the desert group, please). If you live in a house where you can move a large tub specimen outdoors with a two-wheel cart, a fine spray with a hose is a great antidust system.

Foliage in offices, in planters, is particularly bugged by dust and dryness. (Protection, too is important against discarded drinks at the Christmas party and the dumping of window-wash water.)

Plants, to repeat, do not like cold water. Be sure it is lukewarm, close to the temperature of its location.

Finally, there is the problem of old age (if you can accept the fact that a plant does live long enough to require geriatric assistance). It is a kindness to that former giant with the huge glossy leaves to give it a decent burial in the compost heap or the trash container. When a plant is down to its last brown-edged leaves, a stump and a mat of roots, no repotting can revive the tired sap.

Right now is the time to replace it with another variety, another form, color and container. Whether you buy it, or bring up from your collection a plant grown too boisterous for its present spot, make the scene *new*. If you bring in Son of Ficus to replace the old fiddle-leaf fig, it will only remind you of what you once had.

SO MUCH FOR THE PURPLE THUMB

The cure is to get acquainted with your plants. Treat them as individuals and not just pots of dirt with something green coming out the top. Very simple treatment, indeed: It includes recognizing that *plants have personal needs, they are subject to disease, fright, mischief and loneliness—just as you are.* Plants thrive on attention, on love.

I hesitate to dig up your past, but if you persist in egging yourself into believing you'll never have luck with house plants, then all the suggestions in this book, or in any book, can't put Humpty-Dumpty together again.

True, curiosity exposes you to some risks, but any worthwhile catalyst should have nine lives! Get in there and *grow!*

11

WHEN AND WHERE TO ADD OR SUBTRACT

PLANTS ARE CHANGING THEIR IMAGE

Save the water used when you sprout eating seeds (alfalfa, beans, whole wheat) for watering house plants.

Archeologists have recorded finding decorated pots with holes in the bottom, quite possibly used to grow plants, dating from 1,000 B.C. In the Renaissance, middle Europeans cherished lemons and oranges brought back by ship, and learned how to keep the trees alive by protecting them in heated sheds through the cruel winters.

"Room" plants, as the English call them, were very "in" during the 1800's. Sophisticated greenhouses with complicated heating systems and lots of glass encouraged accumulating exotics (that's where the word "hothouse" originated).

The greenhouse was a natural evolvement, and there was no stopping the race to collect everything. In Victorian times, the glass conservatory was a sign of affluence, and plants like the Egyptian fig, the water-lily-leaved Indian fig, the great American aloe, croton from Hawaii, yucca from western deserts and palms of every variety appeared. (The poor had to be content with outdoor vines which grew through cracks in the roof.)

The good mass of the populace had another limitation besides money; with the increased use of coal to heat and gas to light and cook by, the choice of room plants dwindled to the iron-clad few which could flourish despite the fumes. The list was pretty much these six: aspidistra, ferns, ivy, palms, begonias and pelargoniums.

And so it stayed, even after Mr. Edison introduced the electric juice which has changed our lives. Some adventurous grew the small-leaf philodendron, darling of the 1930's when it climbed up thousands of walls all over America in never-ending tendrils or was lashed to a moss-covered post like a cat-scratcher. Others put out a lone pot of fiddle-leaf fig, or a broken-spout teapot planted with busy-lizzie. Amaryllis and Christmas cactus appeared every winter. And there was that stiff pillar of respectability, the sansevieria.

Today, right now, there is no limit, You spend $1.99 or $1,900. for a plant. You buy the right kind of potting soil and charcoal to keep it sweet, at your supermarket. Gadgets water for you, spread the food; bugs fight a losing battle with the systemic potions which you poke into the soil. You raise exotics and vegetables from seeds, you swipe a cutting from your doctor's orchid collection. Never has it been so easy for so many to have what the few had just a hundred years ago.

THE GREENING OF EMPTY SPACES AND PLACES

A house plant is for all reasons. Thumb through a favorite home-service magazine and every picture has one, two or a dozen casually stashed plants, containers of color or jars filled with weeds. This is a movable completion of a static scene: soft curves, living action to brighten the fixed furniture arrangement, the high-calorie cuisine or the low-key fashion.

The greenery performs a blooming miracle! It is a bargain compared to filling the same spaces with more furniture or fabric. It offsets the neon of civilization: you're watching nature's TV, in full color.

Plants screen out something you don't want to look at as well as

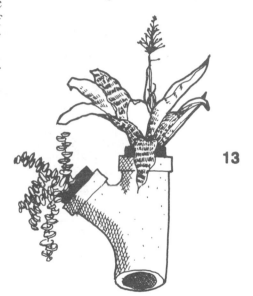

13

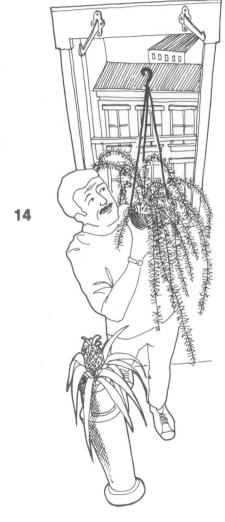

framing something you want to emphasize. They join leaves to make a single mass of half a dozen pots—the breath-taking kalanchoe in quantity is something to contemplate. Plants grow tall and dramatic like the *Dracaena marginata* to give important welcome at the front door.

They are window dressing, curtains in disguise—hanging pots of asparagus ferns and the sweat plant *(Selaginella)* camouflage a bleak back porch or a fire escape. They are rows of discarded amber syrup and liqueur bottles, each with a geranium cutting, on the windowsill.

They sit in baskets—three or four lush Kaffir lilies on the floor by the TV. Or they are an old fishbowl-turned-terrarium on the kitchen counter—the little rex begonias, a cryptanthus and baby tears rampant. Herbs sprawl out of small pots hidden in moss in a clay chicken roaster at the dinner party buffet. A spider plant hangs from the chandelier.

DON'T LIMIT YOUR IMAGINATION

If you like African violets, grow 20—or 200—if there's room for them and living too. Or bromeliads? There's probably an epiphytic society in your town already; you will be amazed to find kindred spirits all around you willing to share or trade secrets and the "offsets" left after the plant blooms.

Brick or stucco or wood planters built into houses in the 50's and 60's (often without thought for light source or drainage) were a cliché which often ended up the plastic-plant route. These can be brought to life with a layer of gravel over a sheet of heavy plastic; fill with a lightweight soil substitute, and sink several blooming pots of bulbs up to their rims in the material. Add a plant light to dramatize.

Pots or tubs aren't orphaned on the floor any more; give them a lift on a piece of driftwood, a section of flue tile, an upside-down wicker wastebasket. Or knock together a simple wood pedestal so you can eyeball-to-eyeball the fuchsia instead of bending over to talk with it. Even an old porch pillar with cap, repainted, elevates an ordinary asparagus fern to classic grandeur.

14

Hangers, plants suspended from brackets, have new water-drip answers: saucers cunningly attached. The slings are wire, macrame, leather—and even a Mexican donkey harness swings a hand-formed clay pot. They can hang singly, or in a chorus, from the wall, the ceiling, the window or door frame, over the shower, next to the washer or off the back-porch railing.

Terrariums, those see-through, glass-enclosed gardens are perfect homes for group encounters of small exotics. They need minimal care because their environment is pleasantly humid and free of pollutants. New man-made soils and a layer of charcoal plus small profile plants at modest cost make the bottle garden with terrarium intentions possible.

Window boxes have to be outside the glass? By a simple switcheroo of the imagination, bring the idea indoors. A long wood box intended for ammunition storage or tool shipment can be found at a surplus store. Line it with tin, raise it to sill level on footings of stacked loose bricks, paint the whole shebang a rousing yellow or orange and fill with pots of white-blooming cyclamen.

Or take an open laundry hamper (not plastic but woven wicker or split cane) and a tub of schefflera, raising its umbrella-topped arms (you may have to put an upturned pail under the pot to bring it level with that of the hamper).

Or find a secondhand piano bench. Renew the top with a mosaic of ceramic tile (another breakthrough for your new courage), add a neat metal or wood trim to the rough edge and you have a condominium for a family and relatives of the begonia family. You may have to experiment to find a happy combination of conditions because they're fussy about stuffy rooms and drafts.

Even a couple of bird cages from the Salvation Army holding (don't laugh) bird's nest ferns becomes another kind of window box. Hang far enough out from a north window so you pull the curtain.

If you begin to taste the sweet smell of success, you'll open up places you never thought of before for your collecting. The breezeway between the house and the garage, closed in with a framework of wood

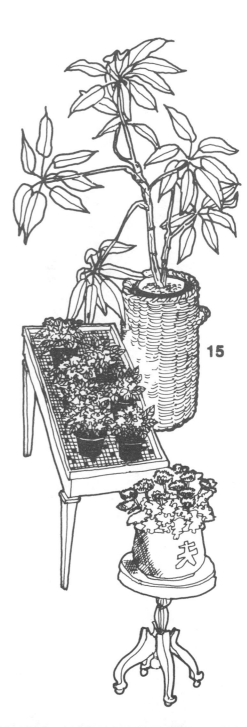

15

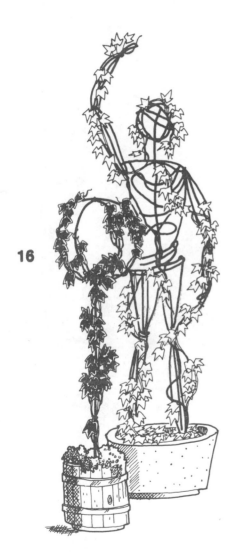

and glass or sheet plastic and a simple electric heater with waterproof cord, puts you in business. A bay window with glass shelves can be converted into a terrarium.

If you're ambitious, greenhouses are available commercially, which can be tacked on to the house.

A HOUSE PLANT IS NOT A HOUSE PLANT

Outdoor plants, pots which start to flower, can be brought in from the garden to display the best blooming time. Indoor plants enjoy a trip out when the weather is warm and humid. And there are hundreds of plants which like half-and-half.

Ivy, for instance, is a hardy ground cover. But, bring stringy small-leaf Hahn's rooted cuttings indoors and they can be trained in six to eight weeks to follow a decorative wire shape with the help of a few ties. There are spheres, tree forms, bird shapes in wire you can get from a florist which will give the ivy the same fun, less work. One such container makes the ivy important; three similar containers in front of a big glass wall or just outside on the patio makes *you* important.

WHAT PLANTS CAN LIVE WHERE

Say you have a space and you'd like to start a little windowsill gardening, or office landscaping to green-bower the straight walls—or your own national park in the family room. Try these lists on for size. If you start shopping for the right species for the spot you've plotted, you get two free moves to Green Thumb Street.

LOTS OF SUN

These plants thrive in south windows, especially in the winter months. During the hottest part of summer, try moving to east or west exposures, so they won't roast for lack of humidity.

Aloe, bougainvillea, crown of thorns, cryptanthus, dracaena, dwarf pomegranate, echeverias, flowering maple, gasteria, geraniums, haworthia, kleinia, firecracker plant, plumbago, shrimp plant, star jasmine, and most succulents and cacti.

SUN FOR FOUR HOURS A DAY

It is the pale anemic leaves which indicate a need for more light; make the move gradual so the plant can adjust. A flowering pot needs sunlight to encourage blooms; however, it should be kept out of the hot midday rays or blossoms will wilt down.

Azalea, basketvine, campanula, Christmas cactus, croton, fuchsia (morning), gardenia, gloxinia, impatiens, Kaffir lily, kalanchoe, osmanthus, pelargonium, poinsettia, pick-a-back plant, rosary vine, spider plant, strawberry geranium, wax vine and zebrina.

BRIGHT LIGHT

Light is a primary need. Rooms painted white and with good window walls have a cheerful effect on plants.

African violet, begonias, episcia, figs, false aralia, fatshedera, jade plant, kangaroo vine, philodendron, podocarpus, pothos, ti plant and wandering Jew.

FILTERED LIGHT

These plants need good light, but manage to survive if you've made a misjudgment in location. Keep moving them around to find a place you can both accept.

Air pine, aluminum plant, artillery plant, asparagus, aspidistra, anthurium, bromeliads, Chinese evergreen, dieffenbachia, ferns, fittonia, grape ivy, ivy maranta, Norfolk pine, palms and schefflera.

Jelly-Deli: The manufacturer of plain, unflavored gelatin suggests a high-protein diet for greens: Dissolve one package (one tbsp.) in one cup hot water to melt, then add three cups cold; use once a month to encourage healthy growth.

Grow lights: Some will fade rugs and drapes just as sun will (particularly those high in red rays). Use sheet of sunscreen plastic in area near plants, or replace lamps.

*Cold drafts and warm ges-
neriads: Plants left near windows during cold months won't
bloom. They need warmth, protected 60° nights. Water with
lukewarm; feed monthly with
fertilizer heavy on phosphorus.*

*Bromeliad—an antacid? No!
It's a family of "air" plants,
renting space from trees and
limbs instead of living on soil.
They are almost the most easy
house plant to own; they bloom,
have "pups" that will grow into
new plants. Look for billbergia,
aechmea, ananas (pineapple),
guzmania, tillandsia, cryptanthus, neoregelia, vriesia.*

*Ming fern: Polycias likes high
humidity (use a humidifier),
strong bright light. May defoliate if too wet—mist or even
shower occasionally. Pinch back
to encourage branching. Protect
from drafts, mealy bug.*

COOL ROOMS

These live well if both day and night temperatures are relatively low. They still need light, bright light.

Aucuba, cineraria, cyclamen, citrus, Jerusalem cherry, podocarpus, pick-a-back plant, primula and wandering Jew.

SOME LIKE IT HOTTER

The conditions which plague most plants are home games for desert plants. They store water in leaves and stems, like reservoirs. Take advantage of their peculiarities of form; decorators have made them suddenly important, particularly the huge specimens. They are hard to locate but once you have such a collection, the care is minimal, and the surprise blossoms are spectacular. They enjoy their noses right up to the glass; don't let the temperature drop below 40° or it's Death Valley.

Aeonium, angel wings, agave, chenille plant, burro tail, crown of thorns, Christmas cactus, echeveria, haworthia, hen and chickens, kleinia, lamb's ears, orchid cactus, ox-tongue and rhipsalis

MOISTURE SEEKERS

These plants adore dampness, warmth by day and cooler night—plus a steady light to prevent wilting. Root growth is speeded with this combination through the process of photosynthesis. The bathroom or the poolhouse are ideal places for the wet-feet families.

Acorus, anthurium, bromeliads, hanging orchids, kentia palm, umbrella plant and velvet plant.

PLANTS FOR STUDIOS, OFFICES, PUBLIC PLACES

The biggest brown-out of plants in places like these happens because no single person is responsible to nourish and cherish. Rental of plants is one strategic answer to those dusty plastic replicas of foliage which are the inevitable answer after many failures.

The list of plants which can survive the high mortality rate because of lack of light and care is brief. If display plants are handled by professionals, they know when to replace the plant which isn't doing well; the receptionist is usually too busy or too bored to play house with the plant stuck by the elevator.

Modern architecture is planned to give better light for people and plants, but the life span of the latter is still dependent on someone's personal attention and concern for weekend temperature drops, drafts, dust and humidity.

Clay pots dry out because they are porous. Containers which have moist moss between them and the plant pot and pots with a mulch on top help fight Friday-to-Monday droughts.

Bromeliads, Chinese evergreen, cacti and succulents, dieffenbachia, dracaena, fatshedera, grape ivy, kangaroo vine, palms, philodendron, podocarpus, screw pine, schefflera and wandering Jew.

Add seasonal flowering plants like azalea, clivia, chrysanthemums, wax begonias, primroses, to be brought in for color and removed later when the bloom is finished.

PLANTS OF ANOTHER COLOR

Green is green is green—and yet the contrast when blossoms open is always a pleasant surprise. But the leaves themselves change their spots, or edges, or the whole leaf is an offbeat color.

Variegated forms are familiar, the greens mottled with speckles of creamy white. One of the aucubas has yellow leaves edged with green; the dracaena has white lines drawn the full length of the leaf. Ficus decora has rosy red new leaf buds; philodendron evansi is an example of the lipstick contrast. Each of these plants needs some sun to keep the color at its brightest.

Aucuba, aurora borealis, begonias, caladiums, coleus, croton, tradescantia (wandering Jew) and velvet plant.

Growing under lights? Look for tiny wigglies when you water; these are larvae of fungus gnats that deposit eggs on soil. To eliminate, add one tbsp. of household bleach to one gallon of water and use mixture for a period of at least a month. Clean pots, trays in soapy water.

Coleus in a north light will sulk; it loses spunk and color.

Protect plants in window locations when temperature drops: pull shades or blinds at night.

INDOOR-OUTDOOR LIVING

Before bringing plants in from the summer garden, wash away dirt on pots. Gather them together in one place and spray to remove lingering pests. Bring in before it's time to turn the furnace back on. Go one step further to enhance the pots: Shop flea markets and garage sales for glazed crocks, deep bowls to set the pots in; rest plant pot on rocks to keep it above drain water.

If you live where you have space outside, consider that there are several plants which move outside to advantage. For the apartment dweller, moving plants to an open shady window or a roof deck will give greenery new hope.

Pots getting this vacation time should be sunk into the ground up to the rim, in partial shade where the drainage is good. If you unpot them, they may just revert to Mother Earth—and won't make it back to the house. Move them back in late summer in the pot, at least a couple of weeks before starting the furnace, to get adjusted. This is a good repotting time if the plant has outgrown itself.

Aralia, azalea, citrus, clivia, fatshedera, bougainvillea, hydrangea, plumbago and shrimp plant.

PARTY PROPS

The most imaginative party I remember was dressed up with dozens of large pots, all painted white and filled with vegetables. Lettuce, allowed to go to seed formed two-foot pale-green trees. The squash and the pumpkin had huge leaves on long stems, with yellow blossoms. Pots of parsley, solidly seeded, made great mounds of dark green. The cabbages added color, as did cherry tomatoes. (Some vegetables were bought and tied to plants which refused to cooperate.)

Tubs of small citrus trees can come indoors for an afternoon or evening; a barrel can contain a banana tree.

Growing for party use takes long-time planning. If there's an anniversary bash coming, allow yourself time to accumulate pots, bedding plants and the pleasure of urging them on. Your nursery will give you timetables and suggestions.

Impatiens, begonias, gloxinia, lilies, including the seasonal ones, like narcissus, Easter, crocus, giant onion, scilla and clivia. Indoor trees with bouquets tied to the branches.

Practice
Plant Parenthood

21

Maggie Baylis

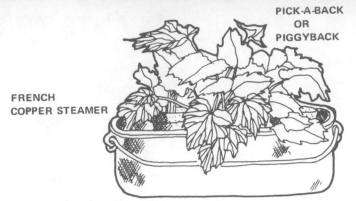

FRENCH
COPPER STEAMER

PICK-A-BACK
OR
PIGGYBACK

BIRD'S NEST FERN

ANYONE CAN GROW THEM

The following case histories are for the "easy" ones, hardy but handsome plants with textural contrast and simple needs. They will please in December as they do in June and can free you from the purple-thumb label once and for all.

Take, for instance, the size limits generally accepted: I have a corn palm (a sturdy dracaena Janet Craig), a tropical which resembles field corn. The books say it grows to 15 feet tall. This palm's grandfather came into our house as a five-footer, 25 years ago. It stood in a dark stairwell and grew to 16 feet to reach the light of a high window. Eventually, in a two-story south glass wall with filtered light it got to be 20 feet tall, and had to be cut back twice to keep it from pushing up the ceiling.

The present plant was the second cutting, moved to Pasadena 12 years ago. It was moved back, pot and all, to San Francisco and finally was refunded to the two-story window. In the final move, the ball of earth stayed in the pot when the plant was being lifted out—the roots came out bare! The poor plant was stripped of most of its leaves to reduce its growing pains and repotted. It is 17 feet tall now, recovered and full after a year and a half—and about to have blossoms, a rarity.

The rule of thumb is unproved by the exception.

The following 18 plants are cheerful, tolerant ones which will survive in almost any enclosed room; they adjust to the conditions of their location just as you and I when it's too hot or too cold. Until you are prepared to readjust the humidity and temperature to enjoy tropical exotics, temperamental light snobs and plants which challenge the player piano for space rights, I suggest you cohabit with Anyone-Can-Grow-Them plants.

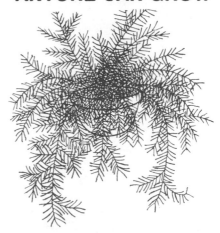

ALOE

An impressive succulent from South Africa, the aloe is a great bloomer with orange-red flowers loosely held on tall spikes. It grows to 15 inches. *Aloe variegata,* tiger aloe, is rich green marked with light speckles and a notable banding. *Aloe barbadensis* (formerly *Aloe vera*) is a fine bright windowsill brightener. It is also a good luck plant, hung above doorways in South America; it has healing power for burns in its juices and has been medicinally acknowledged for centuries.

They are ideal easy-growers in handmade clay bowls to match the rugged leaf rosettes. The aloe does best in dry, hot conditions and moderate to intense light. It likes a coarse, sandy soil with helpings of peat and leaf mold. Add fertilizer after April. This prickly-leaf performs best year after year if kept cool and dry through winter. These are the camels of the plant world; water only when the soil feels quite dry just below the surface, and then offer it a good drink. Do not let pot stand in water.

Propagation: by offsets. Allow a couple of days for callus to form before potting.

ASPARAGUS FERN

Dainty as an old maid's wedding hanky, this hardy (not a real fern, incidentally) rarely gives problems. Florists dote on *Asparagus asparagoides,* smilax, for bolstering bouquets.

Asparagus sprengeri, a lacy trailer, does well in a hanging basket or perched in an old brass fern pot on a pedestal so the branches can shower down to the floor. It has tiny blossoms when adult, followed by coral-red berries.

These ferns are greedy eaters and like rich soil and leaf mold intermixed with sand; they love humidity and can do with a daily misting. Allow a week between soakings. Try partial shade—no sun or the plant loses its cool green. Keep it dainty by regularly cutting back raggedy fronds.

Propagation: by division of roots, or plant the berries one inch deep in a two-inch pot.

23

Soap in the bug's eyes: Tests by Univ. of California researchers proved a soapy spray or bath provided better removal of sucking insects than pesticides; too much soap can damage leaves lacking waxy coating, so make a test first on a few older leaves. If no visible trouble, spray whole plant or spray and rinse-spray.

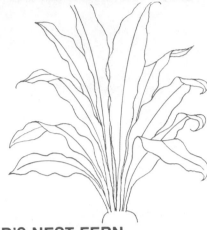

BIRD'S NEST FERN

This is the chartreuse broadleaf with a nonfern look which forms funnel-shaped rosettes of wide leaves; can tolerate forgetfulness except for feeding. *Asplenium nidus* has tall (up to three-foot) fronds with wavy, uncut edges instead of the pinked ones of its relatives; in house conditions it rarely grows over 18 inches.

The bird's nest likes being grouped with others of its kind for community transpiration (but doesn't go for hand touching). Pot up in light, rich soil and keep on the moist side except in winter, when too much humidity may start browning. Setting pots on trays of damp sand or gravel will furnish summer rainforest condition the bird's nest relishes. Give north or east light without direct sun. Move out to a cool shady patio or deck in summer. Discourage bug colonizing common to moist warmth by frequent showers in sink or bath. Never use an oil spray near a fern.

Temperature range should be 60° to 70°. Fertilize if you want to brighten up the green; add food with high nitrogen content.

BOSTON FERN

Venerable first lady of ferns, *Nephrolepis exaltata bostoniensis* arrived to please the Cabots, Lodges and little old ladies all over America in the 19th century; it continues as most durable though often in and out of favor because it gets too big, too shaggy.

Grow in limited sun or shade in pots, baskets and where the graceful cascading fronds can flow uninhibited. Discipline yourself to remove browning ones regularly so the plant will maintain its elegant cool. Water when soil starts drying; the Boston doesn't take dry air or much heat, so a daily misting will substitute for some of the more frequent watering ferns want. Feed monthly with diluted fish-emulsion fertilizer.

Don't let spoilsports tell you the Boston fern is temperamental—it just likes personal attention. Select a plant with sturdy fullness rather than one with feathery delicacy. A new patented Golden Boston, "Aurea," will thrive in high light.

Two other ferns which defy indifference are the *Davallia* (hare's foot) with lacy fronds like a maidenhair, and *Cyrtomium falcatum*, long glossy greens called holly fern which is ideal for city windows and warmer rooms.

Propagation: by spores from fertile fronds.

24

CHINESE EVERGREEN

These natives from Borneo, the Philippines and Asia have no illusions of grandeur; they are the original foolproof plant. They take dim light and over-heated apartments with the same results as if conditions were ideal.

Except in an impossible dark corner where *nothing* could grow, the *Aglaonema commutatum* puts up a fine show. Try it in a dish garden, a bottle terrarium or on the mantel. Or, you can bunch up several and crowd them into a 10- to 12-inch pot to produce a mass that will grow vertically at a fast pace as leaves reach for light. It is a handsome dark-green, long-leaf dependable with pale veins. It will grow 15 to 24 inches in height, have delicate green flowers with a calla lily resemblance, and later will produce yellow to red berries.

The variety *Aglaonema modestum* gets bigger—up to three feet. *Aglaonema treubii* is a variegated form with white markings that needs more light to emphasize the patterning. These all can be grown in water too; add a few bits of charcoal to keep the water from clouding.

All these evergreens ask is to be potted up in a good all-purpose soil mix and watered thoroughly between periods of almost drying out. Some plants release droplets from leaf tips; protect surfaces under the pot.

Propagation: use root division or stem cuttings.

COLUMNEA

This is a swinger out of the jungle which would ordinarily be listed under Hanging Plants but is included here because it is one of the "easies."

Columnea microphylla has long hanging stems with leaves neatly climbing like ladder rungs. Lovely red or pink flowers spurt out of the stems from fall to spring, making it a knockout of a plant for hanging near filtered sunlight, in an east window, a sickroom or by the kitchen sink.

Columnea likes warmth, up to 75° days, 65° at night. Give it moisture, both by watering and misting. This plant requires sure drainage so if it looks sick, check the bottom action first. To avoid a scrawny look, barber the longer stem ends when the plant is young to encourage more new growth in the center.

Propagation: those pruned-off stems can be rooted in moist sand or vermiculite. Insert stems an inch or two below the top of the sand and add a plastic or glass cover to make a terrarium for quicker rooting.

Using indoor lights, a mix of cool white and wide spectrum fluorescents will induce flowering plants like fuchsia to bloom their heads off.

25

ANYONE CAN GROW THEM

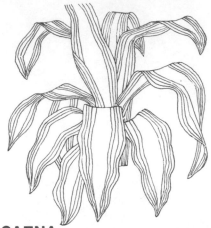

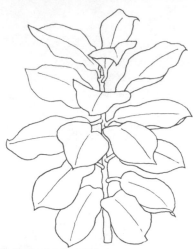

DRACAENA

Old ruggeds, the *Dracaena* family includes everything from corn palm to the dragon tree and all are practically indestructible.

Perhaps most common is the *Dracaena massangeana* with beanstalk pretensions; it will grow from 15 inches to 15 feet! Don't let this turn you off because you can lop off the top, let it root and have another trunk to pot at the base of the plant. (They are more interesting with multiple stems, anyway.)

The big tropical foliage has a light-green strip down the center of each long leaf. If it is plagued with browning of the tips, too much or too little water are at the root of your problem. Brown spots on the edges come from sun scald. Good drainage and a loose mixture will almost guarantee long life. Plants take on new interest if you strip the lower leaves of a tall plant so the stems show; this is particularly true of dracaena Janet Craig and other of the dragon tree group. *Dracaena sanderana* is a small variety with white-outlined leaves.

The corn palm is a great addition to indoor planters and bath gardens with overhead artificial light. Also, it is particularly bug resistant.

FIDDLE-LEAF FIG

Fiddle-leaf fig is named for its stiff, shiny dark-green leaves which are violin shaped with ruffled edges and almost as large. *Ficus lyrata (Ficus pandurata)* as it is botanically known, was one of the Victorian pets because it had a cast-iron constitution. Today it is most often found in offices or studios because of its height—six to 15 feet; but for the home nothing is more dramatic than this plant towering to the ceiling—and nothing more durable.

The mature fig likes light from any direction and will even produce small, hard, inedible fruit. It will survive in darker areas where others give up, but don't overdo the strain.

Dusty leaves respond to a sponging with soapy (no detergents) water; add a little Volck to give gloss and ward off scale. To water give a thorough wetting, then allow the fig to be almost dry for a couple of days. Leaves will fall if the roots dry out which happens in rootbound older plants where water can't penetrate. Repot if roots show signs of emerging from the drainage hole; otherwise, add a yearly top dressing.

If side branches make the plant too wide for its location, they can be removed and cuttings will root in water. Pinch back young plants to encourage branching. Too tall specimens need support sometimes; add a one-by-one-inch stake.

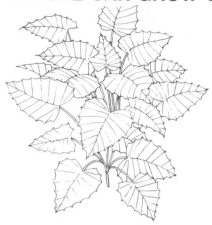

JADE PLANT

Crassula argentea, a succulent which will grow into the shape of a tree, is one of the oldest standbys in the house. It is a no-fuss plant and an uncommonly good friend to dry interiors because it doesn't demand humidity. Its rubbery green leaves grow on thick columns and the flowers in spring—not common when grown indoors—are fragrant and delicate, contrasting to the stout little leaves.

By playing with pruning shears, you can help a jade plant become even more tree-like in shape. The tip cuttings you remove will make new plants for windowsill or gifts.

With too much water or freezing conditions, rot takes over; never dunk a succulent but water from the top, sparingly from May through September, or if leaves show signs of leatheriness. Increase gradually to once a week, September through February. Fertilize only during these heavier watering times. Summering outdoors gives succulents a new lease on life. Warning: keep Malathion away from jade plants—they're allergic. Use rubbing alcohol on a cotton swab to deal with mealy bug threats.

Propagation: let a cutting form a callus by resting for a week or so in a shady warm spot. Then insert it into sand and add only enough water so it won't shrivel. Transfer to small pot when it has an inch of root, using sandy mix with good drainage or purchased cactus mix.

KANGAROO TREEBINE

Although not true ivy, these relatives of Virginia creeper have characteristics like ivy but are much more interesting. The firm stems and curly tendrils make it a good climber or trailer. Medium-green shiny leaves are two to three and a half inches both directions, with toothy edges.

Kangaroo treebine, or *Cissus antarctica*, will perform nobly in modestly lit archways or creeping up wires in bay windows (no hot sun, though). It can be trained on walls or partitions with simple vine tacks.

Cissus rhombifolia answers to the name of grape ivy. It is also a vine which tolerates low light or sun; it can be formed into pleasant rounded pot for the center of a table. It has diamond-shaped leaves which grow to four inches and have reddish hair on the underside. Control of the *Cissus* family is important because they outgrow your welcome if you have limited space; allowed to crawl, they will cover a whole wall with vine tracery.

The popular new variety, "Ellen Danika," oakleaf, is more compact than grape ivy, with darker, slightly dull leaves.

Water liberally during the summer but hold back in winter if brown patches appear. Watch for mealy bug and red spider. These vines also may take awhile to get used to a new position.

Propagation: cuttings.

MARANTA

Primarily, *Marantas* are true rain-forest creatures, taking more moisture and humidity than most foliage plants. They are shy of sunlight and can accept modest shade or artificial light.

Best known for indoor greening is the *Maranta leuconeura* or prayer plant (in England they call it husband-and-wife), which folds its broad but thin and brilliant leaves at night. Watch the stems that have been outstretched all day slowly lift themselves up at dusk; in the morning they bend back in place. *Maranta kerchoveana* has distinctive undersides on its leaves, gray, spotted red.

The young *Maranta's* velvety, light-green leaves have distinct markings which turn chocolate-purple as the plant grows; the less light, the darker the markings. It is low growing and spreading with white blossoms. As a plant it makes a nice foil for the vertical growth of Chinese evergreen.

Misting is important; a clay pot, double-potted with sphagnum moss around the clay will insure necessary dampness. Relax watering during the fall rest season. Filtered sun, behind shutters, or a steady north light, and 65° or warmer at night are prescribed. Cut back the stems to the surface of the pot in January to encourage new growth by March. If this cutback is too drastic for you, at least trim back all the older leaves which look tacky.

NORFOLK ISLAND PINE

Also called star pine, *Araucaria heterophylla* is a miniaturized evergreen (from a 200-foot giant!) for house growing. The soft, short needles grow on branches which appear at yearly intervals in tiers of six on the main trunk. It is a pleasant tree form, pyramidal but not too regular to be boring. Potted in a handsome sculpted container or tub, it is unusual enough to make a dull spot important.

Used as a living Christmas tree, decorated with tiny cookies or dainty wood ornaments from Scandinavia, its beauty brings portable joy to shut-ins.

Give this evergreen a medium light condition; if you keep it in low light too long, too much space develops between tiers; slow growth is desirable to keep the size related to the location. Start with a good potting mix on a gravel base for drainage. Water thoroughly, then let the plant become almost dry before adding more. Repotting every two or three years is recommended with a top dressing each March.

A good cool-room plant, it likes 50° to 60° temperatures; ideal for a person away all day. It's a loner, too, and likes elbow room. It benefits from a summer outdoors under a shade tree. Leaf-drop happens when it is too wet or too dry; too much food will cause branches to turn brown, so withhold to twice a year. Sorry, if lower branches drop off, new ones will not appear.

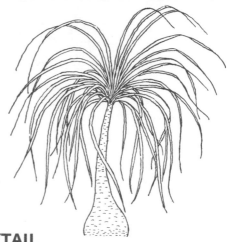

PIGGYBACK OR PICK-A-BACK

This is one of the most amusing "plants which do something." *Tolmiea menziesii,* which produces innumerable little plants in its growing process, also goes by the name of mother-of-thousands. It is a native and can still be found wild in the Oregon coastal forests where it is tagged youth-on-age.

Heart-shaped hairy leaves, light green in color, produce plantlets at the junction of the leaf stalk and its stem. By removing the entire leaf and inserting it in a pot of moist sand, roots will sprout and the new piggyback is ready for its two-inch pot. Or, you can leave the stem attached, move a tiny pot adjacent, and pin the mama leaf to the sand with a hairpin looped over the stem; it should root in ten days and then you can cut the umbilical.

The full-grown plant is woodsy, full and low-growing (the stems grow out horizontally). Watering is essential; a large plant can take one and one-half cups every second or third day, and plant food every two months. If left to dry too much, the pale stems will flop over. If they don't recover after a drink, pinch them off and don't worry because new action will come from the center once it gets on its wet feet again. Don't mist. Hairy leaves resent it. Furnish light from east or north windows and keep direct sun out of sight. Daytime temperature of 65° preferred.

PONYTAIL

Durable, distinctive, dramatic: good modifiers for the ponytail, *Beaucarnea recurvata.* It's for blithe spirits. Ponytail deserves a pedestal, with its fountain of slender leaves plummeting out of a giant swollen base. No top-of-the-refrigerator-ordinary (its other names are elephant's foot or bottle palm), ponytail is very elegant, very individual and comes in a complete range of sizes. The moisture reservoir in the base may be two inches across, or 10, and at times seems to fill the whole top of the pot. There are rare six-foot tall specimens in botanical gardens, more exotic than any neighboring contender, with huge pine-cone shaped blossoms.

Temperatures best suited would be a 72° day and no colder than 55° nights (its original home is the deserts of Texas, Mexico). Bright light, moderate sun suit best, as does thorough watering only after soil surface is dry or the base seems to be shrinking. Feed mildly, not more than every other month, and wipe leaves to keep them free of dust.

Repot only when it seems to have outgrown its home, in potting soil that has coarse sand added, four parts soil to one of sand.

29

ANYONE CAN GROW THEM

RUBBER PLANT

Probably one of the earliest greenhouse exotics to reach England in the 1700's from Malaysia, the India rubber plant has lived down the years either revered or ignored, depending on each generation. Right now, it is bouncing back to status. Much of this is due to the fact that it can withstand neglect, lack of light, and has the scale to match contemporary living.

This familiar variety of the fig family is labeled *Ficus elastica,* and it is related to the fiddle-leaf, the creeping fig and the elegant *F. benjamina. Decora* leaves are broader and glossier than the others; *rubra* are red initially, turning green with red edges. *Variegata* has long narrow leaves with patches of yellow mixed with green (difficult to grow).

If a leaf is removed, it bleeds with a thick, white, milky juice (keep it off floors and carpets). The leaves are broad, splendid and polished; they have dark-red underveining, and before the leaf opens, the cap stake and the new leaf are brilliant red.

Rubber plants grow better in good light but not sun, because the leaves will scorch and then should be cut off. Frequent watering is due in summer, also misting. Don't overlook good drainage: add a little sand or vermiculite to regular soil. Keep foliage shiny and don't let dust collect; cleanliness is insurance against scale and mealy bugs.

Propagation: by stem cuttings.

SWEDISH IVY

A funny thing happened on the way to naming this sturdy: it is not really Swedish, nor is it ivy. *Plectranthus* grows in abundance in Australia and very quickly found its way into the heart of America because it is a tough rookie. It has puckered leaves that overflow pots and baskets almost faster than you can pinch them back. Another common name-tag is creeping Charlie, but that is also hung on an unrelated vining type, *Pilea nummularifolia,* which has a rough hairy foliage. *Plectranthus* is a cousin of coleus and will stand a good share of the same kind of neglect before shouting "help!".

Bright, indirect light, or even modest, will suit its needs. Don't overwater because too much causes leaves to lose their crisp and turn dark. If they're small, or reddish, the pot has been allowed to dry out too much; humidity in the form of misting will revive natural energy. Bonus: tiny white flowers, faintly fragrant.

Propagation: Stems break or pinch off easily; start in a mixture with extra peat moss; cuttings also root well in charcoal-sweetened water.

ANYONE CAN GROW THEM

SPIDER PLANT

Like the piggyback, this is another cast-iron plant which grows its own reproductions in a simple process. You simply snip off the new plant, pot it and first thing you know—grandchildren!

The new plantlet at the end of a long swooping stem is a miniature edition of the parent, in this case, *Chlorophytum bichetii*, or perhaps a fuller variety, *Chlorophytum comosum*. The long thin leaves, with a white stripe in the middle, arch out of the pot in all directions, and the stems, which are weighted down with new little copies, need a shelf or hanging basket to show off best. Tiny white blossoms appear at the stem tips before the new plant pops out.

The spider plant likes warmth and lots of liquid at each watering; then, let it go through the wet-dry cycle before adding again. When the leaves go limp, rush in the watering can. To encourage longer leaves and more trailing stems, use a diluted fish emulsion once a month. Filtered sun is okay; it will do well in a north window, but more leisurely.

It is probably the most inexpensive plant you will buy because it is so easy to propagate. If it is not producing plantlets, change its time clock. Long-light days stimulate growth; eight- to 10-hour days seem to encourage runners, bloom and plantlets.

WANDERING JEW (Zebrina)

Zebrina pendula comes from Central America and Mexico. Its vibrant colors are easy on the eyes and a delightful change from ordinary greenstuff. Its textures and markings are nontypical, too. Although it has been considered a common plant without much social acceptance, it has an endearing way of giving new interest to a semi-shady spot. Or try hanging it near a painting or print which complements *Zebrina's* leaves with their rich maroon undersides and broad silver stripes on olive tops.

Tahitian bridal veil (*Tripogandra multiflora*) is the dainty lady of the wandering Jew tribe, with its olive-green leaves, an inch long, on multi-branching stems that form a vining thicket. In summer, there's a shower of delicate white flowers.

Wandering they are. Runners spurt like mad and you'll have to practice a firm pinching technique so it doesn't get leggy. If you wind the runners around they will root back at the center of the pot and give the plant a fuller look.

This is another water-baby; it can live for awhile in water only, but does best in a loose mix with the roots kept moist. It will appreciate a little feeding now and then. The more sun it gets, the darker the markings and color. It does well in almost any location except with too little light.

Propagation: cuttings root in water or damp soil.

31

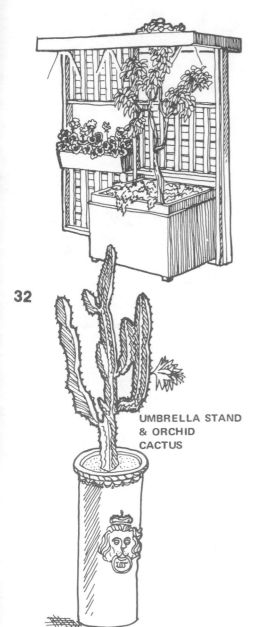

UMBRELLA STAND
& ORCHID
CACTUS

APARTMENT PLANTS

The word "apartment" is generic for any place you live in but *do not own*—a flat in Seattle, a houseboat in Sausalito, a commune in Arizona, a carriage house in Manhattan or a rented farmhouse in Idaho. These are places you move into and out of because of today's mobility.

The critical sociological turnovers in jobs, marriages, disposable relationships all contribute to expendable living. There are also the factors of owners and landlords who do not allow you to remodel, pound a nail or paint out drabness.

So, you move in your movables and hang a picture or three on nails left by an earlier tenant, but the real humanizing element for mobile living is greenstuff which you take with you—from house to apartment to room to shelf.

There have been many recent developments to help maintain a family of house plants. These include artificial lighting for keeping gardens alive in windowless rooms and halls, new and sturdier varieties in the plant world, mushrooming, one-stop plant shops with everything you want including packaged soil and additives, fertilizers and free advice to the leaf-lorn.

Take the doors off a kitchen cupboard, add two 40-watt fluorescent lights, and you have a charming lighted garden for fresh salads all winter. African violets bust out all over in an ordinarily dark hall with the addition of 18 hours of light daily. A simple room divider can be put together with a planter box on casters, a vertical trellis and a simple overhead shelf with a fluorescent unit attached. The planter will hold small trees and flowering plants.

Use plants in nontypical ways: lift them off the floor on painted lengths of sewer pipes, put them high on an old reed fernery, hang them on simple metal brackets from the window divider or the shower rod. By all means be bold with a tree in a tub or a giant cactus in a tall ceramic umbrella stand (they're movable on three-wheel roll-arounds).

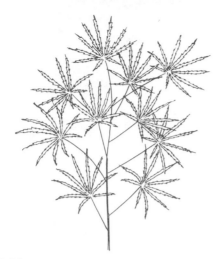

ARALIA

The lacy *Dizygotheca elegantissima* is a false aralia with very narrow notched leaves arranged fan-wise like a palm's, in a rich dark green, with rust-red undersides. The fans are attached to long, thin arching stems giving an interlaced linear look.

The true Chinese aralia is an outdoor tree of small scale which grows well in tubs. It has wider leaves which give filtered shade to a deck or terrace. The *Dizygotheca* inside a glass wall with the true aralia outside is a subtle arrangement if you want to play with look-alike plants.

The indoor plant can be found in supermarkets and on discount tables for a minimum investment. Buy several to make a group in the kindergarten stage; if one dies, it's no real loss. After a year of attention you will have some good-sized plants ready to repot into a single large container—a multi-stem specimen worth 10 to 50 times what you invested.

If the new plant outgrows its headroom or gets spindly, cut back the stems to force new growth from below the surgery. Dropping leaves is a fairly common problem that can be solved by keeping soil always barely moist and providing more light. The best source is north or east window. Feed *after* a good watering, once every three months.

Propagation: hardwood cuttings.

ARROWHEAD PLANT

Syngonium podophyllum is an evergreen dwarf climber often sold as *Nephthytis.* North light and medium temperatures will do, but warmth encourages bushy growth.

Arrowhead, or trileaf wonder, the commercial name, looks like a philodendron caught in the bleach bottle. It has ruffly arrowhead leaves about six inches long, some white, some green and some mighty mottled. There are other members of the family with dull-green leaves; some have emerald-green ones with silver rib and veins, and some are green, covered with whitish powder.

Syngonium as a small plant is a bedfellow candidate with other moisture seekers in small dish gardens or a hanging basket. But it becomes a personality on its own attached to a wire pyramid or a formal topiary shape. This is a flexible plant for fun; pinch it back for shaping. If grown in a long planter or a window box it will creep back and forth, rooting itself; arrowheads thrive in terrariums, too.

Protect the trileaf from drafts and sudden temperature changes. Watch for necessary watering.

Propagation: cuttings with attached aerial roots will start off rapidly in water (never cold, please).

AURORA BOREALIS PLANT

Also commonly known as kalanchoe, this succulent is perfect for enlivening a small space. When grown in full sunlight, the leaf edges fade to a pale pink but the plant sparkles with deep coral-pink or red flowers in January through spring. The blue-green foliage is small and difficult to distinguish from ordinary leaves, but *Kalanchoe fedtschenkoi marginata* becomes a visual magnet when four or more pots are massed on a coffee table. If you have limited space, make it bright with aurora borealis.

Spare the water so you don't spoil the nice balance of the succulent's nature. Let the sandy mix dry for three or four days before watering lightly. If the leaves seem a little limp, add more. If they turn yellow, hold back the faucet.

Propagation: cuttings at least four inches, and up to eight inches, in two or three inches of soil. Care needs to be taken that they don't get too much moisture or the cuttings will rot. Also keep in mind that the modest cost of the kalanchoe means you can go out and buy fresh stock each year; try *Kalanchoe blossfeldiana* for bright red-orange or yellow (Tom Thumb) bloom next time.

BROMELIADS: AECHMEA

The bromeliads are a large and diversified family from the tropics. Their stiff ornamental leaves are particularly suited to sophisticated apartment living.

Aechmea fasciata is a hardy glamor number with a vase-shape trunk. The big grey-green leaves have silver stripes and are shaped like a scoop; the watering is done into the leaf base, as well as into the soil. It bears one spectacular flower made up of modified leaf forms. During its life, the aechmea produces offsets at the base. Once the flower gives up, the foliage will follow, and the offsets become the new plantlets. They can also be removed to separate pots. Expect to wait two years for them to mature and produce their own offspring.

The pineapple, *Ananas nanus,* has narrow grey-green leaves which arch from the center into a 30-inch circle. Give it warmth, sun—and you may even end up with a flower *and* a miniature pineapple.

A recommended potting mix is half coarse sand and half peat moss, plus feeding at least once a month. Keep moisture at the roots and in the "vase."

34

BROMELIADS: BILLBERGIA

Bromeliads must have high moisture. On warm days they need at least one good misting; in scorching weather, mist twice; keep the plant out of bright sunlight when you do this. For good measure, add a scant teaspoon of fish emulsion to each quart of water when you do the spraying of leaves and soil; bromeliads eat with their leaves too.

The *Billbergia nutans* has dull spiny leaves, up to a foot and a half long. The leaves take on a bronze cast if the plant spends too much time in the sun—which it happens to love. The flowering shaft, which will stretch to two feet, is covered with rose-colored sheaths and has indigo flowers emerging during summer months.

There are several variations of Billbergia with similar life styles but different hues. They seem to do best in a good potting mix (minus lime) with sand added, plus a generous layer of gravel at the bottom for extra drainage. Fertilize every two weeks when flowering starts and keep the leaf cups watered.

Rescue a Billbergia from temperature extremes; it performs best at 65° nights, and 70° or higher days.

Propagation: from offsets.

CROTON

This is the plant to try for color accent. The croton isn't easy to grow, however, because it is fussy about drafts, dryness, full sun or a cold room. When it is unhappy, it signals by dropping a few leaves. If you can meet the requirements, however, it is spectacular enough with its exotic wild streaks, spots and rimmings of color to be worth extra attention.

The leaves are long and wavy, oval, lance-shape or narrow with straight or irregular edges. They start out deep green and take on a whole new rainbow pattern as they mature. Sunlight excites more intense coloring; but if you stick it too far away from sunlight, the color is subdued. The range is yellow, pink, red, bronze, purple—or any fusion of these.

Codiaeum variegatum is usually a single-stem plant, from six inches to two feet tall. It needs moist soil, but never let it get soggy. In summer, move the croton to an open windowsill (watch for drafts, though) or offer it a balcony airing. Spider mites are drawn to it; keep a wary eye for puckering leaves and grey webs. Douse in soapy water or spray with it.

Plant in a rich mix with assured drainage.

Propagation: cuttings taken during summer.

35

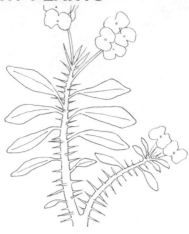

CROWN OF THORNS

Of all the 900 members of the *Euphorbia* family, *Euphorbia milii (splendens)* is top choice for a bay-window plant. I have had one for six years (in a gallon can hidden in a bronze pot) and the bright scarlet flowerlets have bloomed continuously the entire time. It gets modified west sunlight, the watering has been minimal, and it has been fed only once a year to reach its two-foot height.

Crown of thorns (also related to the poinsettia) is a spiny climbing plant which can be trained on a frame or on wires, or just lightly tied to a center stake (get out your heavy garden gloves because the thorns make it tough to tackle). It needs warmth; this is strictly a central-heating plant. Water sparingly, particularly during the resting months of November through January. Use lukewarm water; cold water makes the leaves drop off. A cold window can also give it a leaf-falling chill.

Euphorbias benefit from a half-and-half mixture of coarse sand and peat moss with a little old-brick-and-lime mortar. If you decide to cut out some old stems, do it in May. Be careful of the milky juice which leaks out as some gardeners are allergic to it.

Propagation: cuttings, well callused before rooting.

DUMB CANE

Dieffenbachia amoena has also been tagged the mother-in-law plant because it has a kind of stunning substance which silences anyone who chews a piece of the stem or leaf or puts it near the tongue. Actually, it is not harmful but should be kept out of the reach of little plant eaters (bugs do not like either).

Dumb cane is evergreen and grows vertically with a thick trunk and large marbled leaves which arch over gracefully. *Dieffenbachia amoena* will grow to six feet or higher, with leaves up to 18 inches in length. It will fit into the large-room scene with a nice helping of north light and warmer temperatures. *Dieffenbachia picta* is an impressive thing with huge leaves that have pale, translucent centers. *Dieffenbachia* is flexible and stem can be shaped or bent. Flowering comes to old plants at maturity; cut off when they fade.

This plant can take a couple of hours sun a day but will be more amenable to less light in a high-humid, 70° room. Use the wet-to-dry technique for watering. No special soil requirements.

Propagation: cuttings will root, even sections as short as six inches. Once they have rooted, transplant into soil.

36

FLOWERING MAPLE

This may not be an easy one to find, but *Abutilon hybridum* is worth searching out. It is pleasantly happy in a warm sunny apartment or mobile home. It will give you a small maple-like tree with Chinese-lantern flowers about two inches wide which hang around most of the year.

Abutilon grows actively and you may find pruning in order if space is limited; spring is the best time for this. Save any cutting over four inches and root it in moist sand for giveaways or more plants for yourself.

Some varieties tend to be trailers and are fine for hanging baskets. The bush varieties are better small-space brighteners; they include *Abutilon hybridum* (flowering in white, yellow, apricot, red-and-yellow and even purple) and *Abutilon pictum "Thompsonii,"* with pale orange bells and foliage painted with variegated creamy-yellow.

The newer hybrids are neat; they don't lose their leaves, particularly if kept in smaller pots. Water them well and add fertilizer once a month. They can be moved to a sunny balcony for an airing. Don't worry about night temperature unless it goes below 50°.

LEMON TREE

Stay away from the commercial or strictly outdoor varieties. *Citrus limonia "Ponderosa,"* American wonder, is the choice indoor plant. Its constant fragrance is pleasant and the huge fruit (up to two pounds) appears at the same time the little tree is blooming with fragrant, waxy, white flowers.

The glossy evergreen foliage won't get much above four feet tall and seems to do best in a redwood or cypress tub. Choose this lemon only if you have a generous space with high or bright light, like an enclosed balcony, an entrance foyer or a studio. If it is more than eight feet from a south-facing window, it will not flower or fruit. The thorny branches may need support when fruit matures. The lemons have a thick rind and mild flavor.

Plant in rich garden soil with organic fertilizer mixed in to give it a good start. Surprisingly, early growth is fast but once it starts setting bloom it will slow down. Putting it outdoors in the summer will give this tree a nice refresher. Water daily in hot weather; use a high-nitrogen feeding in late winter, June and August. Keep lemons cool at night and do your pruning in March and April.

Once you've experimented, look around for a kumquat, mandarin orange, Ranjpur lime or tangelo for new experiences.

Propagation: start from seeds.

37

APARTMENT PLANTS

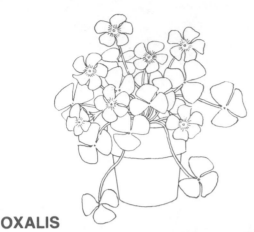

OXALIS

This is a small plant for window or table which can be moved easily when others have to be left behind. It is low-growing (in the eight- to 16-inch range), looks like an oversize clover and gives cheerful little flowers to brighten a glum day.

Oxalis regnellii is a compact, bright-green plant; its five-petal blossoms come in rosy pink, yellow or white through winter and spring. Larger *Oxalis hirta* grows 16 to 18 inches in a branching form; its leaves grow in clusters of three with rich-green tops and deep-red undersides, and its clusters of yellow blooms on stiff stems go on and on. *Oxalis variabilis* is a trailing variety with clover-shape leaves and pink or pale-violet flowers cascading over the pot rim.

Oxalis grows well under artificial light as well as medium-to-bright natural light. The flowers open on sunny days and usually close up like the leaves at night or on a very dark day. It does best with filtered light; bright sun may cause its collapse. Too much moisture causes the stems to rot at the base; let the plant be almost dry, then give smaller amounts of water. This plant will particularly benefit from the cooled water used to boil eggs.

Propagation: separate the small bulbs at the base in fall and plant in two-inch pots.

PALMS

Of the dramatic foliage palms, the easiest to adapt to apartment living is the miniature pigmy date, *Phoenix roebelenii,* which will stay within four to eight feet. Its delicate fronds, attached to a short stout trunk, are durable, resistant to invasion of insects and disease, and tolerant of high temperatures. The date palm rarely requires repotting, but when it does, don't disturb the roots. Best mix is a rich soil with leaf mold, humus and decomposed manure. Tamp the soil well around the edges once the palm is in place in the pot. It needs even moisture and good drainage; misting and sponging add extra humidity.

Chamaedorea elegans, recently renamed *Collinea elegans,* and commonly labeled *Neanthe bella,* starts small enough to be a terrarium highlight and probably won't get much taller than three feet. It likes north or east light and will stand neglect except when you forget to water it.

Cocos weddelliana (Syagrus) is a slender-stem dwarf which will reach six feet only under the most favorable conditions, and is slow getting there. Likes a deep tub, good drainage in a lime-containing soil; fertilizing will encourage new leaves.

Palms do best in damp air; if caught in drafts, the tips will brown off. Sponge the leaves regularly.

Give a palm a deep container with excellent drainage and a lime-type soil; overwater rather than underwater. Roots are easily damaged, so use care in repotting.

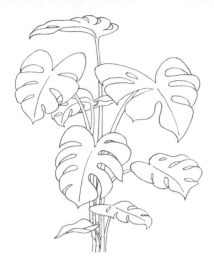

SPLIT-LEAF PHILODENDRON

These huge rain-forest climbers grow in places like Brazil and Hawaii as vining parasites on the trunks of defunct trees, but they have been tamed so that their presence in a household is no threat. If you are just starting to decorate, the split-leaf will furnish an empty room. It is impressively important and enriching. With a little attention the shiny "windowleaf," *Monstera deliciosa* (also sold as *Philodendron pertusum*) is an ever-changing sculpture for a low-budget art collector.

Pruning roots and top will keep the plant within acceptable size. Top leaves or first new ones after pruning revert to juvenile form without holes. Cuttings can be started by water-rooting or by setting them in separate pots. Water thoroughly on a wet-dry cycle; use your poking finger to test below-surface moisture. Don't let household grime accumulate on the foliage.

This is such a special house plant it calls attention to itself and should always look its best. Otherwise, care is fairly easy.

Provide a good stake to keep the vine lifted so that all the leaves show their best sides. Philodendrons can take full sun part-time, filtered sun or none. So that you can shift the heavy pot around, keep it mobile with a three-caster dolly. Some plants resist change; this one is cooperative and reliable.

UMBRELLA TREE

Brassaia actinophylla (Schefflera actinophylla) can be a mini-budget four-inch pot or a $100 multi-stem beauty over six feet tall in a great stone jar. The shiny umbrella leaves on long graceful green branches are made up of six to eight large, pointed oval leaf forms. A new variety, *Brassaia arboricola,* is a smaller plant with four-inch leaflets and much finer texture. It is especially adapted for low-light conditions.

This grand plant is about as beautiful an interior furnishing as you'll find, no matter what your budget. Multiple stems enhance what is already a winner. The umbrella's leaf can measure 16 to 18 inches across and so the plant needs elbow room to show off its small-tree characteristics. In the smaller edition, it may be half that size and ideally adapted to minimal apartment space.

Weak light alternating with good but not sunny keeps the schefflera in fit condition. The plant should face the light. It needs no staking because the trunks are strong and cane-like. Average soil and even moisture are all that are required. It does better in dryer air than most tropicals and is only occasionally bothered by bugs. Watering is soak-and-let-dry, then rewater.

Propagation: remove any suckers from the main base and pot in moist sand.

39

BEDFELLOWS

*Invite the whole family . . .
compose a family of kalanchoes
(at least 20 members to choose
from): Panda (K. tomentosa),
velvet or felt (4'-5' beharensis),
Christmas (blossfeldiana) air
plant (pinnata) . . . they're un-
troublesome house plants and
a joy for the beginner.*

There is no rule of thumb which says you have to accept a one-plant, one-pot thing. There *are* plants which have similar likes and dislikes, and can end up neighbors in the same bed.

For years, florists have offered the cliché of ceramic planters filled with three or more varieties of what they label "ornamentals." These are respectable groupings, but never very exciting, and after a few months of dust collecting are more problem than pleasure.

Indoor planters often get the philodendron-rubber plant blues, and you wonder why the builder put the darned thing there in the first place. However, add blooming pots of cyclamen, gloxinia or azalea and glum is replaced by gleam.

There are no plants listed under Bedfellows. If you want to try more than a single, look for family similarities in the case histories in the other sections about greenery. Each plant has its own needs, and maintenance is simplified when you deal with one set of demands. Putting several with similar needs in a big pot, tub or planter is a safe way to make a show, particularly if you're a timid starter. If one of the cast leaves, the rest will carry on and you can fill the empty hole with another stand-in. The results may give you courage to go out and blast the budget on one major plant which will be the star of the house.

When you put live-alikes together, study texture, leaf colorings and heights. One tall plant will disguise the shortcomings of a shorter neighbor. Two or more of a kind give a bold, lush effect which will back up a dramatic spiky neighbor. Accommodating trailing plants soften edges of the container; a creeper will fill the soil around tall canes of bamboo or palm and give pale-green, dark-green variables. Match plants which like light, foliages which dote on acid soil, blossoms which return the compliment of another.

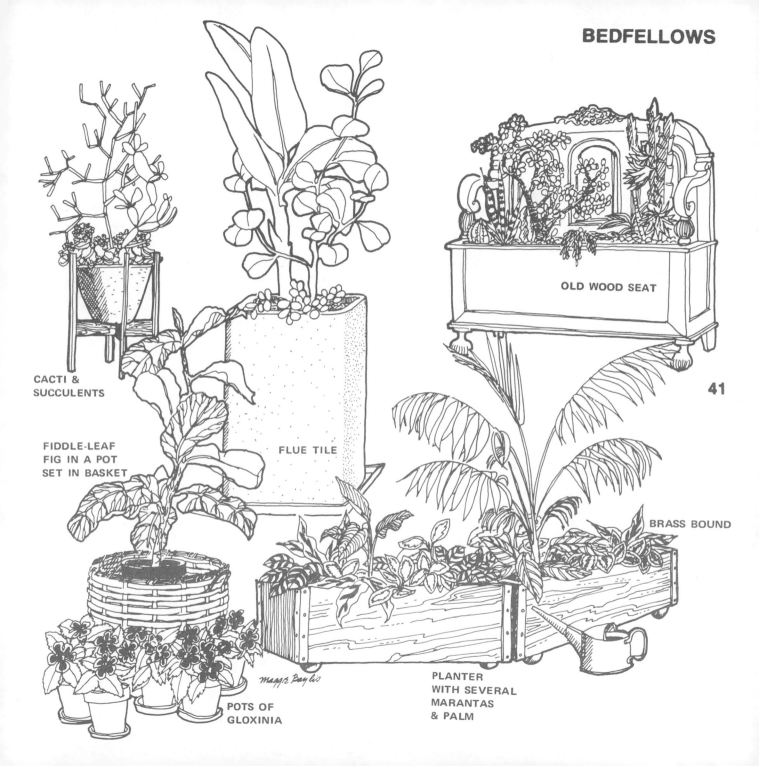

OLD WOOD SEAT

CACTI &
SUCCULENTS

FIDDLE-LEAF
FIG IN A POT
SET IN BASKET

FLUE TILE

BRASS BOUND

Maggie Baylis

POTS OF
GLOXINIA

PLANTER
WITH SEVERAL
MARANTAS
& PALM

ENGLISH
IRIS

42

TOBY JUG

BULBS

Those homely brown balls which look like onions produce a fantastic range of blossoms. From garlic with its dainty lavender sphere on top of a reedy stem to the giant breathtaking amaryllis with three to five huge pink or fiery red trumpets, these are the showpieces of spring. Daffodils, narcissus, clivia, crocus, scilla and chives give long-lasting loveliness and are worth the spoiled-child demands.

The first step is to buy large, top-quality bulbs for first-season satisfaction. Some bulbs are "precooled"—they've already gone through their wintering under controlled conditions and will flower sooner if you're in a hurry for results.

All bulbs need to go through a dark-side-of-the-moon period in order to form healthy roots before they start pushing out the green at the top. The garage or the basement, the darkened and ventilated lower cupboard where the temperature hovers around 50°—even under the bed if you have a cool sleeping room.

Bulbs require moisture, but never let one stand in water or be saturated: just enough moisture to make roots shoot. Very cold water is forbidden; rainwater is a help. Some bulbs, like narcissus and crocus, get starts by living on a two-inch pad of gravel in a deep bowl with only water just below the base of the bulb. The bowl must have darkness too. Hyacinths can go either the water or open-light soil route; they and daffodils like to start with their noses visible. The tulip and small bulbs prefer to cuddle under a blanket of soil.

Allow two to two and a half months before moving bulbs to moderate light to encourage the tops. Bring blooms to a bright spot but not full sun, and move them to a cool spot at night. After the blooming, let the leaves alone—if you cut them off immediately, it's the end. Put the bulbs outside to pasture next year and start with a fresh batch for new bloom.

AMAZON LILY

Eucharis grandiflora has few beauty rivals to match its dazzling white, three-inch blossoms which cluster on thick stems, brightening the scene at Christmas—or in June—as well as overflowing with sweet fragrance.

Most bulbs are programmed to bloom in late winter, but by the simple act of withholding water from the Amazon lily (except just enough to keep the foliage from expiring) you can set your own schedule.

The showy flowers are grouped three to six, each about two inches across, on stalks up to 24 inches tall. The leaves are handsome wide green strap shapes on the stubby side.

Amazon lily thrives on bright light and warmer-than-usual temperatures (65° to 70° at night and 75° during the day). Keep the potting medium very moist to match the warmth demands and fertilize at least once a month when the leaves appear. After the bloom has gone, retire the pot to a shadier spot and curtailed watering and feeding. The recommended potting mix is two parts peat moss, one part packaged mix and one part sharp sand or vermiculite.

Propagation: separate the small bulbs from the parent plant.

DAFFODILS

These great trumpets are the best spring investment because they are sure to bloom and increase in numbers over the years, if you plant them outdoors after the first bloom. *Narcissus* is the species name, and there are at least 30 good varieties to be found. Plant them 10 days apart and you will get a succession of bloom. Don't get hemmed in with just the old favorites; try some of the primrose-yellow and white-trumpet varieties. Jonquil varieties have clusters of trumpets on each tall stem, smaller than the singles.

Plant the bulbs, several to a pot depending on the size, in fall for winter bloom. Use a mix of equal parts of ready-mix soil, coarse sand, peat moss and ground bark. Set bulbs so that the tips are level with the soil surface and water thoroughly. Place the pots in a cold dark place and cover with peat moss or sawdust and layers of burlap; darkness is essential. (If it's only one pot, slip it in a plastic bag and hold it in the refrigerator for the rooting period.) Then after eight to 12 weeks, take a peek to see if the roots are coming through the drainage hole. Move them to daylight gradually, and when green shows, to bright light. Fertilize at least three times after leaves form, at two-week intervals. When blooming, daffodils do best in filtered or indirect light and like cool nights and average days. Keep watered until foliage turns yellow.

BULBS

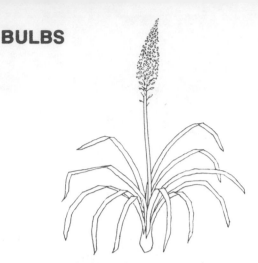

FALSE SEA ONION

This is a strictly-for-surprises bulb package which starts out as a huge sea-green onion form, and shoots forth on a great curved sheath a hundred delicate white starlets, each with an intricate green center.

Ornithogalum caudatum blooms in winter and early spring. To plant set the three- to four-inch bulb into a pot of good planter mix with a little sand and leaf mold added. The bulb must be exposed at least one-half or more. Water thoroughly and give full sunshine at least four hours a day, at temperatures of 68° to 72°, and above 50° at night. Let the soil get almost dry between waterings and give soluble plant food monthly during the growing season.

Sea onion is hardy and gets along with most people and places. The long green leaves emerge from the top in the beginning like an onion forgotten in the crisper. If you cut them short, they curl around the bulb; let them grow and they will trail over the pot at least two feet. Pot or repot in the fall.

Propagation: from the small bulbs which develop along the side of the main one, during dormancy.

Ants in your plants? Outdoor or in, water soil with a solution of insecticide like Sevin or Orthene. Follow directions on the label—don't overdo it.

HYACINTH

To force this bulb in water, you will need a hyacinth-bulb glass, water, a windowsill—and a big healthy *Hyacinthus* in any of the lovely pastels you favor: soft pink, yellow, Delft blue, carmine rose, pink pearl or dark blue.

The glass is cheap and easily available, so there's no need to try a makeshift arrangement. Fill it with water to the pinched-in line and set the bulb in the cup so that the water is just below the base of the bulb; add a few nubbins of charcoal to keep the water odorless. Now, carry the glass to a cool dark place where it can stay 10 to 12 weeks. Make a note on your weekly calendar to look in on the hyacinth, because once the roots start growing more water will have to be added. Temperature no higher than 50° is ideal. If you can't get complete darkness, make a paper cone over the bulb.

Once the bud starts pushing out, bring it to filtered light and a warmer room for 10 days. This gives the stem courage to put on length and bring the flower above foliage. Move it to a bright window.

The exquisite French Roman hyacinths are available precooled. They can be potted as well as treated like narcissus and brought to bloom over stones and water. Plant early October for Christmas bloom, and December for late January and February.

NARCISSUS

This is the easiest bulb to try if you're experimenting (see the section on Windowsill Water Gardening for other water-babies).

Narcissus hibrids offer two familiar types: daffodils and other large trumpet varieties, and the narcissus, which includes the most popular paper-white with a yellow cup in the center, and a relative, "solcil d'or," a golden yellow. These are winter bloomers, with blossoms lasting up to 10 days. Paper-white bulbs are normally discarded after one blooming.

The method of planting narcissus is different from the daffodils: narcissus do not need the precooling mentioned in the beginning of this section. Start with an attractive ceramic or glass container, four to five inches deep, and fill it half full of small, white or polished stones. Set the bulbs an inch apart and twist each one down slightly so that its pointed end is straight up. Add a thin layer of additional stones to anchor, but allow at least a half of the bulb to show. Add water until it reaches the base of bulbs. Then set the container in a dark spot—but not so far away that you forget to check for evaporation which has to be replaced. Once roots show a mass, bring your container out into the day world—but not bright sun. The light assures sturdy foliage to support the bloom.

SIBERIAN SQUILL

The other common as well as generic name is scilla, a woodsy little bulb often seen in rockeries, under pine or fir trees. In fact, it will grow almost anyplace, including inside your sunniest window. *Scilla siberica* has small, deep-blue bell flowers on stems about six inches long and stiff green leaves a little longer. The bloom should last at least a week and make endearing cut flowers.

As new bulbs, pot up half a dozen in each pot, at least two inches deep. Do this in the fall, using a good planting mix, and relegate them to a cool dark place for at least 10 weeks. Bring to full light gradually.

When they bloom, give them lots of sun, cool night temperatures of 40° to 45° and ordinary room warmth during the day. Keep the soil moist during the growing period. After flowers fade and foliage goes blah, save the bulbs for another year, and then plant outdoors to help them regain strength.

Propagation: buy new bulbs each year.

45

SMALL BULBS

JAPANESE HIBACHI TO HOLD POTS

46

AUTUMN CROCUS, *Crocus sativus* is the true flower of spring. It was called "naked lady" by the Victorians because it has no leaves. Plant half a dozen in a big seashell; layer the bottom with an inch of stone chips, anchor the bulbs and add water just to the base of the bulbs. You don't have to wait for roots—just give good light and they perform. Put the bulbs outside after the show.

CAPE COWSLIP, *Lachenalia,* is a small bulb from South Africa. It has stalks hung with orange-yellow or scarlet blooms which last six weeks. Plant at least three bulbs in a four-inch pot in October; water and place in a south window for December flowering.

GRAPE HYACINTH, *Muscari armeniacum,* has clear blue spikes which open slowly and is really quite different from true hyacinth. Force by planting a dozen close together in a shallow blue-and-white Chinese bowl; press them into the mix so only the tips show. Allow four weeks in the cool dark, then move to a sunny window and bloom in four weeks.

GUERNSEY LILY, *Nerine sarniensis,* is rare but look for it. The myriad individual blossoms in warm colors look like wild azalea. Plant six to a six-inch pot filled with rich soil, bulbs half out, like amaryllis; then water and put in filtered light. October planting gives late November results, with leaves arriving later. Water and fertilize until foliage turns yellow; then store dry until next year.

LILY OF THE VALLEY, *Convallaria,* is the most delightful of all the small bulbs. The forced blooms don't have garden fragrance, but they're dainty white and sweet. This bulb will flower in 28 days or less. Try them in a miniature strawberry jar, two to a pocket; or pack them in peat moss and vermiculite which must be kept moist but not soggy. Put them where you want them to bloom without resorting to a dark period.

CACTI AND SUCCULENTS

These are the self-satisfied members of the plant community. Many people write them off as oddities, but in the right container, properly placed where their peculiarities are exploited, cacti outperform their strictly green relatives.

The dry air which does in the general run of plants is ideal for aloes, sedums, crassulas, agaves and euphorbias, to list a few. They store large reservoirs of water in stems and leaves—that's why the forms take odd shapes and become like pieces of sculpture.

A sophisticated towering aloe which looks like the old Indian rope trick, set in a very tall, narrow container (pot within a pot) and top dressed with white marble chips, becomes the exclamation point by the front door. Try an oversize architectural planter with a spiny agave and a rose-like echeveria, some trailing burro tail and a needle rosette euphorbia interrupting a sunny glass wall. Or set an old iron kettle full of hen and chickens (there are about 25 species) on a block of driftwood underneath your doorbell.

The fleshy-leaved succulents are carefree about health. Some of them propagate like rabbits and need a disciplined pruner to keep them in line. And they have extravagant flowers, egged on by light. Being mostly desert oriented, keep them above the 50° mark, particularly in winter, and give them only enough water to prevent complete dryout. Drainage is critical: mulching with limestone chips to reflect heat and light is a bonus idea.

Christmas cactus needs exposure to cool nights (it is a native of the mountains of Brazil) to tempt out the buds. So experiment with exiling the pot to the garage—provided it doesn't freeze. Young succulent plants must be protected from direct sun and given some nourishment. Generally a good porous mix (now available in packages just for cacti), thoroughly moistened, is the best medium for successful starts.

Jade plant has a relatively small root system; can stay in same pot for years. Cut back lower branches, straggles, to encourage a tree form. Water after pruning with dilute feeding.

Getting the drop on Christmas cactus: When buds drop before opening, pot has probably dried out completely before watering— keep it always slightly moist. Also, a high night temperature, or a winter draft can upset nature's pattern.

Use tweezers to remove debris from a spiny cactus.

CACTI AND SUCCULENTS

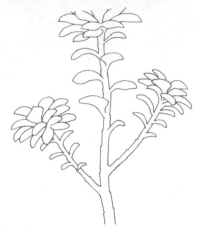

AEONIUM

Aeonium arboreum is a succulent, a slim, tree-branch form with rosettes at the end of each branch. It is daintier than most succulents and without spines. The leaves are bright green or dark purple, edged in red. Its characteristics are similar to the sempervivums, a cousin, but the stems are long and the rosettes open and flat. Small bright flowers in red, pink, white or yellow are clustered tightly, but it may take a couple of years before they appear. Once the blossoms die, the part of the plant to which they're attached dies.

Aeonium canariense carries flat rosettes up to two feet across and the flower clusters can be of similar size; so when you pot up this, allow plenty of room space around it. The dramatic size relates well with contemporary furnishings.

Mild waterings are in order, spaced far apart. Most civilized succulents require more moisture than their counterparts in the desert; *Aeonium* is more sensitive so you will do well to keep a water watch—withering leaves are a first sign of a problem. Succulents need repotting like other plants but not often; young plants can be potted up annually, older ones every three to five years.

Propagation: cuttings, which root rapidly.

BURRO TAIL

Sedum morganianum has light blue-green fleshy leaves on a droopy flexible stem (which stretches to three feet long). It belongs in a sturdy hanging basket or pot, because when the plant reaches its full growth it will be seriously overweight. Instead of an ordinary pot, search out a large, flat wok-shape which might hang from chains, or a Mexican jug to swing in a rope burro's muzzle, now available in most planteries for about two dollars.

Burro tail will put forth scarlet flowers at its tips after it decides to accept your house conditions. Most *Sedums* are grown outdoors in rockeries; they are succulents with predominant rosette form and are happiest in a gritty, sandy garden soil or in one of the cactus mixes available in packages.

Watering is minimal, just enough to prevent leaf shrivel. Give full sun. During the warm months you may hang the burro tail on a branch of a tree which will allow filtered sun, or on a heavy hanger outside an apartment window, or on a deck rail. When it comes in for winter, barber the long hair. Feed only two to three times a year with water soluble fertilizer.

Propagation: four-inch cuttings potted in barely moist sand to a depth of an inch or more.

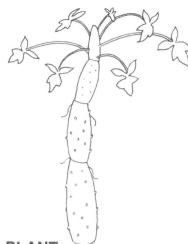

CANDLE PLANT

One of the most imaginative succulents, *Kleinia articulata* is a member of the thistle family and is a specialist's joy. The candle plant is long suffering and can be revived after indifferent attention. It also adds a touch of humor to any collection. This *Kleinia* looks like a tired burned-out candle; it has thick, fleshy, cylindrical stems, each balanced on top of the lower one, and for a short season it has ivy-like leaves. *Kleinia nerifolia* looks like a palm tree caught in a revolving door, with small clusters of lobed leaves spurting from the upper tips of the cylinders. It can grow to four feet and will have yellow winter flowers, ideal for an avant-garde apartment.

Give this particular peculiar lots of sun and stingy waterings. Put it in porous soil, add no fertilizer and remember that it needs rest in a shady spot after the blooms. If the leaves look bleached and the plant shows signs of losing its vigor get it back in full sun.

Propagation: young plants broken from the main one. Put them in sand and peat moss mixture, mildly moist, under glass (as in a terrarium) and add heat from an overhead light. It will root readily if you also add heat to the bottom.

CHRISTMAS CACTUS

The Chrismas cactus or crab's claw (formerly *Zygocactus*) is an old favorite. So is the Thanksgiving cactus—they're both *Schlumbergera*. Both flower with trailing blooms; Thanksgiving has a sawtooth leaf, blooms a month earlier than *Schlumbergera bridgesii* with rounded leaf edges.

The longevity of Christmas cactus is phenomenal; plants get passed on from parents to children to grandchildren. Today, when you buy one, it may also be labeled *Schlumbergera buckleyi,* a hybrid even more vigorous than its ancestors. The leaves are short and flat, and join one another in a chain, with translucent red to pink blossoms at the tip like exclamation points.

Care of both these cacti is similar to orchid cactus; give plenty of water when blooms appear and reassure the plant with rich, heavy, loamy soil. They are better off outdoors part of the year when not in bloom; enforce a dormant period in semidarkness, starting in late September until November except for a light sprinkle every 10 days to prevent dry roots. Then move the plant to more light, water and feed when new growth appears. After the flowers fade, reduce water gradually and stop feeding.

Rather than ordinary potting, keep these two cacti as hanging pots to encourage the trailing tendencies.

49

ECHEVERIA

Echeveria are members of the *Crassula* tribe of succulents. Like those other plants with rosette tendencies, aeonium, haworthia and gasteria, each has distinct variations in flowering which makes the whole group interesting.

Hen and chickens, the littlest of the rosettes is generally bought as a sempervivum, but others label them echeveria. Never mind the name; ask for the common name and you'll get something interesting.

Hens and chickens, *Echeveria elegans*, has rosettes in frosty blue-gray to white; blossoms vary, coral to rose. Mexican firecracker, *Echeveria setosa*, has red and yellow flowers with soft, felty leaves covered with white hair. *Echeveria pulvinata*, known as the chenille plant (not to be confused with another plant, also same name, in the section Flowering Plants), forms branched shrubs, with each branch having a loose rosette of narrow felted leaves vividly outlined in rich red.

Most echeveria flower in the summer; they may be crotchety and refuse to bloom indoors for the first year—be patient.

Propagation: take cuttings from any part of the plant except the flower; pot up in equal parts of potting soil and coarse sand.

HAWORTHIA AND GASTERIA

Haworthia leaves grow in the familiar rosette pattern but they are fat and almost translucent at the pointed ends. They are fleshy, with some plump leaves remaining low, some ascending, with long-stalked flowers in spike-like clusters. Haworthia flourish with the same conditions as the aloe (see Anyone Can Grow Them.) *Haworthia cymbiformis* has triangular pudgy leaves with "windows" in the flattened tips; rosettes appear in tight tufts.

Haworthia also is labeled the cushion aloe in the trade. Another popular variety is *Haworthia setata*, a three-inch rosette which tufts with many in one pot, and whose leaves have long slim teeth along the edge.

Gasteria, or ox-tongue, has white-spotted 14-inch leaves which alternate right and left on a flat growth; the upper leaves are each shorter than the ones below to form a squashed pyramid shape—at the top of which appears the showy flowers. Leaves are pale green or coppery. *Gasteria acinacifolia* has reddish flowers about two inches long. *Gasteria verrucosa* is much smaller and has white warts covering green-copper leaves. They are all tough and need little water.

Propagation: offsets from both.

50

INDIAN TREE SPURGE

Euphorbia tirucalli looks more like a drawing than an actual plant—that's why it is also called pencil cactus. It is a treelike form with slender cylindrical branches that spread outward, then upward, from a thicker cylindrical trunk. The entire plant is only one color, a soft grayed green. Branching is thick, with joints about four inches long and twigs one-eighth to one-quarter inch in diameter. This relative of the poinsettia and the crown of thorns will reach six feet in a pot.

Being a hardy succulent the Indian tree spurge is easy to take care of and may reach four to five feet in an eight-inch pot. The milky substance which flows when a branch is broken or cut can be irritating to the skin so wash it off if you've made contact.

Euphorbia caput-medusa, Medusa's head, is also a queer one to put on your list of oddities. It grows best in bright light, should be fed once a year in spring, and watered only when the top two inches of soil become dry. It has a globe-shaped stem and branches, similar to the spurge, which gives a snaky-hair profile straight out of Greek mythology. Branches may reach a foot in length. Give both good drainage, careful summer watering and strong light, and a winter resting period with no liquid.

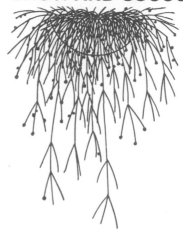

MISTLETOE CACTUS

Have you ever played with a magnet and a pile of nails? *Rhipsalis* is a member of the cactus family which looks just like those magnetized nails hanging together in a long series of stiff lines and grotesque angles—a titillating plant joke.

By itself, *Rhipsalis* is rather weak artistically, but when bedfellowed with agave and a globular cactus form, it becomes a handsome sculpture which requires very little from life but admiration. The stem branches can be flat or cylindrical, and are almost always angular. They have no spine as such and hanging is their thing. Mistletoe cactus is not the true Christmas mistletoe, sold to induce kissing, but a cactus from the tropics via Africa and India. The bonus white starry flowers—also sometimes pink, red or green—appear profusely in winter. The plant needs misting and warm humid conditions to put on a blooming show.

Potting mixture must be very rich peaty soil and porous. Strangely, it is one cactus which has to have shade. If you collect orchids, this mistletoe will make a cooperative neighbor.

Hold back watering in early winter to give a rest before the flowering period. Cactus does not get fertilizing—don't force it. If you push too much you're inviting intruders like the mealy bug.

51

CACTI AND SUCCULENTS

POINSETTIA

Thousands of words have been written by experts about this popular member of the *Euphorbias,* and rare is the person who hasn't had one hanging around to brighten Christmas—and into May on occasion.

For a pleasant diversion, consider the less familiar *Euphorbia pulcherrima var. alba*—harder to locate, but its delicate creamy-green-almost-white bracts are much more subtle than the familiar fire-engine red, and they last longer, giving their best in January through March. These blond poinsettias are available at most florists but cost more than the red. However, if you can get cuttings from a friend's plant, you can repay him with a newly propagated one—and have some left over.

Poinsettias can be exasperating and start shedding: their main complaints are fluctuation of temperature, dry air and insufficient light.

Propagation: start with a seven-inch pot, crock it, and fill with sharp, coarse, clean sand. Hopefully you can get at least five cuttings, each about six inches in length; dip the ends into hormone powder a couple of inches and plant around the edge of the pot, each halfway into the sand. Place the pot in a warm bright-light window, water carefully twice a week, keeping temperature above 60°day and night.

PRICKLY PEAR

Opuntia microdasys, the prickly pear, has a distinctive leaf form: flat round or oval pads with barbed bristles set in diagonal lines on the flat surface. This mad plant has earned a long list of common names: rabbit ears, angel wings, beaver tail.

One of Luther Burbank's major challenges was to remove the bristling spines of the *Opuntia* so that the plant could be developed commercially for its sweet edible fruit. Fruit-bearing plants rarely perform indoors, but if the plant structure intrigues you, don't worry about going into the fruit business and remember to wear heavy gloves around prickly pear.

Opuntia compressa is an acceptable test size to see whether you really want to look further into the *Opuntieae* family. Some have awl-shaped leaves which are on the plant for a short time and the stems are divided into flattened joints. Plant in porous high-lime soil; avoid too-wet wintering outside.

Propagation: from joints in pots.

Mealy-mouth bugs: Some plants can tolerate a light spray of rubbing alcohol, particularly thick leaves like jade. Test one small area before tackling whole plant in case it is allergic. Wash out mister before using with water again.

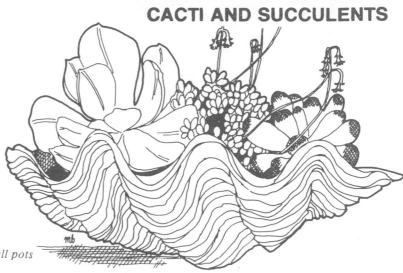

MULTIPLE PLANTINGS

Several in one large container or a grouping of small pots

HENS AND CHICKENS, *Sempervivum tectorum* (see also *Echeveria*, page 50), are tightly packed little stars, layer on layer, with copy cat offsets around the main rosette. The flowering is not showy, but it is a neat, compact plant and makes a ground cover for something more spectacular.

PIN CUSHION CACTUS, *Mammillaria*, is easy to grow, has spines and sometimes silky hair. The red, pink, yellow or white flowers are small and arranged in a circle near the round top of the plant.

CEREUS, *Harrisia (Eriocereus) jusberti*, dubbed moon cactus, is a summer-evening bloomer of such spectacular beauty and fragrance that you'll want to have a party to share it. The seven-inch flower, white with gold stamens, unfolds in late afternoon and opens petal by petal, giving out a sweet heavy perfume. The frame is a homely vertical cactus with myriads of infuriating spines to deal with (use heavy leather gloves or put soft thick folds of fabric around its waist to remove when repotting). Give full sun, sparse water. Hardy in winter if kept dry. To propagate from cuttings make a diagonal cut and dip cut end in charcoal, allowing to dry for several days. Plant in moist, porous rooting medium; keep fairly dry between waterings.

RAT TAIL CACTUS, *Aporocactus flagelliformis* has half-inch thick limp stems, covered with stiff hairs, which can dangle or be trained up a support, and once-a-year flowers which are firm and shiny and appear at random all over the long tails. Flowers give out an exotic fragrance and are longlasting. For a botanical switch, rat tail can be grafted to the top of a bare columnar cactus, to better accommodate its relaxed stems and show off the bloom.

PANDA PLANT, *Kalanchoe tomentosa*, is related to the aurora borealis (see Apartment Plants). It has thick, silvery, velvet leaves with scorched brown margins, grows to 18 inches and is attractive in a flower arrangement; leaves are spoon-shaped. Panda is a handsome succulent subject with rock specimens and beach driftwood.

SNAKE PLANT, *Sansevieria trifasciata*, is a great old cast-iron plant which may reach four feet tall. It has been sidetracked for years as too common (someone called it mother-in-law's tongue), but is making a comeback in modern environments. The twisting, mottled, sword-shape leaves will take sun but prefer shade. It is best joined with other succulents as the prime vertical element in arrangements. Avoid overwatering, its only affliction.

53

Don't repot an orcid cactus after the buds have set. Never let it dry out completely, even in winter; poor drainage, compacted soil are natural enemies.

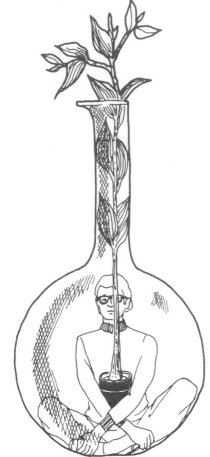

EXPERIMENTALS

There are plants and there are far-out plants. These are labeled "exotics" for want of a more descriptive word. Once you get the hang of house plants, you may find yourself hooked on trying the unusual—and end up supporting a harem of rare plant Mata Haris.

Where do you go to find the things you've heard about or seen over the back fence of an ardent botanist? Your nursery sources can't afford to "grow on" stock unless they are sure of sales; it simply costs too much to take chances with specialties.

There are fads in plants and what was great last year disappears this season. If the nurseries do not have an answer, try the yellow pages of your phone directory for plant societies. And if that doesn't work, check out the local horticultural society. Big cities like San Francisco have Park and Recreation Departments which hold once-a-year sales of excess plants from the arboretum.

If you're lucky, you can con a cutting from something you covet. Finally, you can grow what you want from seed. Several large mail-order seed and rare-plant houses have luscious catalogs to spend hours over; they also guide you to the proper methods of planting and the tricky raising of things you've probably never dreamed about.

Julius Roehrs Company, Rutherford, New Jersey 07070
("Exotic Plants Illustrated," by A. B. Graf,
available from them; 1300 pictures)

John Brudy Exotics, Rt. 1, Box 190, Dover, Florida
33527; offers a catalog for $1 to delight the soul;
refundable with order coupon in catalog.

George W. Park Seed Company, Inc., P.O. Box 31,
Greenwood, South Carolina 29647; features rare
flowers, herbs, foliage packets; 130-pg. catalog

White Flower Farm, Litchfield, Connecticut 06759;
$5 for the year's issue of catalogs; this sum
will apply to any order, $5 and over

BAT-WING CORAL TREE

The bat wing, *Erythrina vespertilio,* is a small tree which will make a handsome tub plant. It's leaves are like graceful little green bats flying at the ends of incredibly slim but strong stems. The leaves are three to four inches across, and they all move in any air motion like a mobile.

Branches are prickly, the leaves are not. Flowers and seeds, slow in developing, are red, but the shape and movement of leaves are what make the plant a prize. Propagation from seeds will be the only way you can grow the bat wing. Six of them, looking like dried orange and tan beans, are listed in a packet for $1.50, depending on current availability.

To start a seed, nick it with a small file on the side to a width of 1/16-inch to expose the endosperm (not near the hypocotyl which is where the seed sprouts). File on the opposite side and soak the seeds until they have swollen; plant in the soil mix recommended by the supplier of the seeds, with at least three inches of soil underneath, and the depth of two to three times the diameter of the seed on top of the seeds. Water by means of a mist spray; good drainage is imperative in any seed bed you use. Bottom heat improves germination—in this case it will take 15 to 25 days before there are signs of life. Keep the soil gently dampened; overhead light is an asset if you can can rig one. Once the plantlet is large enough to handle without damage, it can be potted in a two-inch pot; keep out of direct sunlight.

BLUE PLUMBAGO

Half vine, half shrub, this lovely sprawly character has azure-blue blossoms at the tips of each branch in phlox-like clusters from spring to fall. In a tub it will mound up to five or six feet and almost as wide, and its cool color is a refreshing antidote to summer heat.

Plumbago capensis has the makings of a great indoor vine. It is worthwhile to consider attaching the supple branches to a classic wood porch column which can be painted shiny white or dark blue. The flowering is lavish and foliage is nicely full, with one-to-two-inch leaves. Encourage the main stem by cutting back any suckers as they appear. The sheer informality is welcome in a stark contemporary setting; add flowering pots with magentas and pale greens at the base of the column.

If you can't find a plant at the largest nursery in your neighborhood, seed packets are available for the modest price of about $2.50 for 100 seeds. You start the seeds in a flat filled with a three-inch layer of recommended soil mixture (information furnished by the seed grower), a light sprinkling of soil to barely cover and the addition of water in a fine spray. Apply bottom warmth, keep out sunlight—and never let the soil dry out. Fifteen to 25 days germination time should bring first results.

Take cuttings in the fall; allow winter rest.

55

EXPERIMENTALS

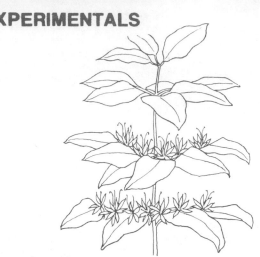

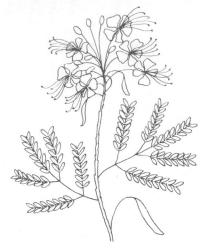

COFFEE PLANT

Even though you can't count on a crop for your own coffeepot, it is nice to casually mention you are growing a tree while everyone moans over the soaring price of a pound of coffee.

This has been a very popular house plant for many years, but is difficult to locate. *Coffea arabica* is a delightful sunny-window performer and will get big enough to claim a large stone or clay jar. Dense dark-green foliage and several blossomings over a period of months of tiny white starlike flowers with delicate fragrance are followed by red berries. Like most outdoor plants imported into the house, blossoms and seeds are not a sure thing, so if you achieve them, you can hang up your purple-thumb glove.

If no plants are available, start from seeds which come from good sturdy stock and are relatively easy to propagate. Use the same method as indicated for blue plumbago, and figure on at least 20 to 35 days waiting until you know how many "takes" you have.

As in all of the seed propagations of rare and unusual plants, the addition of a powdered fungicide is recommended for the plant mixture at the rate of one heaping tablespoon to each two gallons of mix. Be sure it is well integrated before adding the seeds.

DWARF POINCIANA

Another tree-form tub plant with a glorious color show, carries the likely nickname of bird-of-paradise bush. *Caesalpinia gilliesii* is an evergreen with delicate airy form, bright yellow flowers and protruding yellow stamens. These blooms grow in profusion the entire summer.

There are large-specimen poinciana in Florida and the Hawaiian Islands, but this smaller relative is just as colorful and will complement any sunny glass wall, indoors or just outside if the temperature is mild. It will need a large container—a heavy wicker basket or a Chinese water-chestnut jar—to house a smaller pot. (Be sure to provide trays to catch drain water from the plant.) The delicacy of the plant demands a handsome carrier. If the pot sets too low in the larger container, add a few bricks below to bring the two rims on the same plane.

Poinciana needs yearly trimming to look its best, usually right after the seedpods form. Fertilize generously in spring and early summer.

Seeds should be soaked in very hot water before planting in the seed bed. Once they are sown, cover with a thin layer of soil and spray-mist to water. Keep damp and watch for seedlings in 20 to 30 days.

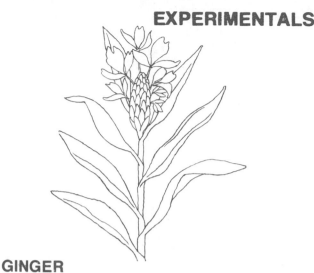

DWARF ROYAL PALM

Growing palms from seeds may seem a prodigal waste of time when there are so many varieties and sizes available as plants in nurseries and plant boutiques. But if you feel the magnetic pull of experimenting with seeds, the rare dwarf palm will be your supreme achievement. It is not usually on the market as a plant, but seeds are available.

Veitchia merrillii is daintier than the feathery queen palm. Although it is much smaller and more readily adaptable to tub growing, it still has the characteristics of a big palm. It takes much moisture to keep it happy, and a greenhouse is probably the ideal location. But for one dollar's worth of seeds you can have a lot of fun trying a remarkable plant under nontypical conditions.

Once seeds are planted you may have to wait two to six months for the first returns. They are planted one to a pot because they are big. Try covering the pot with a plastic tent to keep moisture in, and keep the pots in a warm place. The seeds, which may appear on the palm eventually, are brilliant red.

GINGER

For adventure, try a dazzling collection of gingers from root corms or plantlets—eight to a dozen will cause a sensation.

White ginger, *Hedychium coronarium,* has blossoms which resemble white moths and a heady fragrance. Yellow ginger, *Hedychium flavum,* is a pale lemon, petals are more slender and the perfume slightly different. Both white and yellow are started from root corms. Keep well lighted (not full sun) and moist.

Red ginger, *Alpinia purpurata,* has stalks of bright crimson flowers throughout the year and is excellent for color in shaded damp conditions. Shell ginger, *Alpinia zerumbet,* has drooping clusters of waxy pink flowers, like shells; it also grows in shade and is a knockout by an indoor pool and aided by artificial light. Propagation of these types is by plantlets which can be shipped by air from Hawaii.

Ginger needs a moist rich soil and a shallow pot as used for azaleas, with good drainage. The roots should be planted only a few inches below the soil level, and ample fertilizer will insure luxuriant growth. Tops die back in winter; trim them off neatly. The corms are treated like gladiolas and planted again next spring.

57

EXPERIMENTALS

HOLY BASIL

Organic buffs should be alerted to this sacred Hindu herb which is a member in good standing of the basil family. *Ocimum basilicum* is pleasingly aromatic, keeps its size a manageable two feet in both directions, and offers a profusion of rich-purple flowers on an elongated eight-inch axis.

The stems and leaves are fuzzy on all sides with minute purplish hairs, on a woody structure. It is virtually impossible to find this as a small plant, but try seeds. Once they have germinated, the basil will grow rapidly if it gets adequate sun. When it is in bloom, try cutting and drying the foliage; it will add a quixotic touch to salads and to cheese dishes.

Scatter the tiny seeds over a two-inch bed of soil mixture but do not cover; water with a spray mist and keep damp but not wet. Use bottom heat, and be prepared to wait for 15 to 25 days for the first green. If you can keep the planter in 72° to 78°, germination time is shortened.

To pot out, use sterilized two-inch pots. Make holes in the pot soil and using a small spatula as a spade, make a "plug" of the plantlet and slip it into the hole so that roots do not touch the sides; then firm the dirt around the top and water. Introduce a little liquid fertilizer at the end of the first week. Continuing growth under artificial light will give the basil a big boost.

PLUMERIA

No tourist returns to the mainland from Hawaii without extravagant words for the fragrance and exotic blossoms of the plumeria tree. The same fragrance fascinated the earliest visitors who sailed back to Europe and compounded a perfume to match: "Frangipani." Today, that name is almost as common as plumeria, and the attraction is still magnetic.

It's possible to buy 12-inch cuttings in Hawaii or to get them by mail. If they are planted in February or March, you should have your own bit of the islands and blossoms the following year, from April to November.

Plumeria acutifolia poiret has large, waxy, funnel-shape flowers in white, yellow and rose-purple which make the popular frangipani leis. Some of the clusters are nine inches across with more than 20 blossoms in each. The tree is bare of leaves for a short period but the silhouette of stout dark branches is dramatic because the clusters appear first and look like little bouquets tied all over the branches.

The young plant needs a somewhat dry location; hold back normal watering in the beginning. Good rich soil, well drained, is important. Once the young tree is successfully started, it can go outside for summer and be brought in about September. Water in winter only to keep the roots from drying out completely. Size can be kept to whatever space you have by judicious pruning.

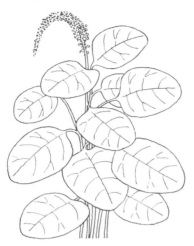

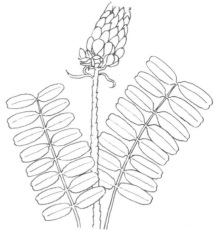

SEA GRAPE

When I was first introduced to house plants, a sea grape was the largest and most impressive of the lot. I identified it as an "unusual philodendron"—until the expert of the family unriddled its origin. But secretly it was always the philodendron to me. The moral of this statement is: if you have something green in a pot, don't worry about its name; make up your own.

Coccoloba uvifera grows by the sea in Florida, up to 20 feet tall, but comes indoors as a handsome potted specimen with a tall bamboolike trunk and big seven-inch, heart-shape leaves. The stylish leaves have wavy edges, a red midrib and heavy veins, rugged with a lot of flair. Grapes may never appear indoors, no matter how much sun you furnish; the fruit is edible but not intended for a wine press.

At the ocean's edge the sea grape grows in sand and broken shells without apparent nourishment, but for potting as an interior plant, use a rich sandy soil of light character.

Propagation: by seeds, similar to blue plumbago; 25 to 50 days to germinate.

Don't use insulation-grade vermiculite with soil—it's chemically treated and particles are too large. Use horticultural grade.

SHOWER TREES

Cassia is a dramatic Mexican tree (it produces the herb senna) with large yellow or pink blossoms, about an inch across. These are attached at the end of branches like blue plumbago, but cascade in a dripping shower.

Cassia alata, candle cassia, has flowers in golden yellow, large and upright when young, and is a fine tub plant if it is deliberately pruned. In the southern states it is a deck or terrace small tree which will have extravagant flowering when it is only three feet tall, but will grow to 20 feet in the ground.

Golden shower, *Cassia excelsa,* has large leaves and pendulous rich-yellow blossoms. Pink shower, *Cassia grandis,* is extremely dense with flower sprays; although it gets too big eventually for interior use, it can be enjoyed while still young on a balcony or deck.

Propagation: to start seeds, it is standard practice to nick them with a file, place them in a teacup of very hot water and then soak them for 72 hours before planting. The erratically long wait for germination lasts 20 to 60 days.

EXPERIMENTALS

TELEGRAPH PLANT

Desmodium gyrans is a funny little annual; in the sunlight its leaves never stop moving! They point in one way and then another, just like a semaphore.

The telegraph plant is an herb, grown for many years as a gardener's curiosity, and is rarely available now except when started from seed. It is addicted to a very warm room, up to 80°, and in the greenhouse it may act like a perennial. However, growing new pots each year will produce the most spectacular results—and give you enough plants to share with people who take to the kicky action. Maximum size is about two feet.

Telegraph plant's foliage is trileaf. The small flowers are not important and appear as if the plant had a second thought; they are violet and grow in racemes, or blossoms growing one above another on a stem. The seedpods are jointed, and sometimes the joints break apart and adhere to clothing or the fur of an animal by means of barely visible hooked hairs.

Plant seeds during February in a light sandy soil, in four-inch pots, to germinate; seedlings grow rapidly and can be repotted individually as soon as the roots are sturdy enough not to be damaged. Use a good plant mix and give the telegraph lots of sun and fertilizer to make it bushy.

WINDMILL PALM

Whereas the dwarf royal palm is a feathery exhibitionist, the windmill, by contrast, is a fan leaf with stout branches. The fans will grow to five feet across in warm tropic outdoor plantings, but are somewhat smaller indoors. The scale is magnificent and impressive, but growing such a palm from seeds will take patience and an adventurous soul.

Trachycarpus fortunei is also named fortune's palm or Chinese windmill, and is considered one of the most hardy of the species. I have one in my San Francisco garden which started in a soy tub and now lives in a low plant bed outdoors. The temperature dropped to 30° in the winter of 1972 and the palm was undaunted. Without benefit of fertilizing the fans measure two feet across and the plant is 14 feet tall.

Seeds are very slow to germinate, taking two to six months. You will have to soak them at least 48 hours before putting them in the soil; they are propagated with the same method as blue plumbago.

Soil condition and temperature for the young plant are not special—it's an ideal one for apartment starting. Once the plant has achieved several fans it can live outdoors in summer and move back inside in fall to protect the fans from tearing winds. This long-life palm will accept tub living for many years until you're tired of it—or find someone who's eager to play Don Quixote with the windmill.

FERNS

According to the prestigious Brooklyn Botanic Garden quarterly, there are about 6,000 different species of ferns that grow between the arctic and the equator—members of 150 different families! Most of them live in the wild, thriving on moist forest floors; others are vines which climb trees; some grow in tall trees (epiphytes); and some stand wet-feet in water. They have been around since dinosaur time when they were probably the dominant cave plant of prehistoric man.

During the Victorian heyday of heated greenhouses and Wardian cases, ferns became *ne plus ultra* with the swells. Then they began to disappear because they couldn't stand the fumes of gas and coal.

Ferns are not difficult to grow, provided unpolluted air and adequate moisture is at hand. A misting or two each day or a trip to the shower will remind them happily of their rain-forest heritage.

The epiphytic ferns can be planted on slabs of cork bark, cedar, cypress or redwood, or in hanging baskets filled with sphagnum moss—only don't forget the dampening.

Ferns are basically shade plants and will tolerate low light levels, but they benefit from a few hours of bright daylight. There are several accepted methods of generating more humidity: set the pots on trays of damp sand or pebbles, grouping them so they can indulge in joint transpiration; add a commercial humidifier; or turn down the thermostat. Lower temperatures give higher humidity; cold air absorbs less water than warm. Also, the cooler it is, the less bugs will bug the plants.

Don't overwater; never let the plant stand in water, but do not let it dry out either.

Growing soil should be loose, fairly inert and spongy. Osmunda fibre, sphagnum moss, peat or perlite, with some sand, should encourage a healthy fern. Feed sparingly.

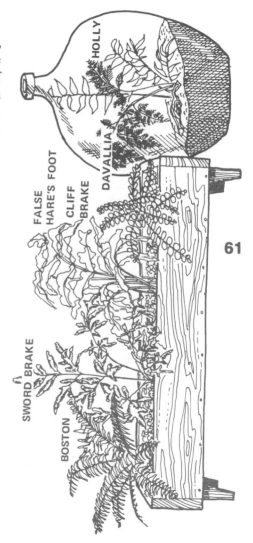

61

FERNS

BRAKE FERNS

Pteris (the "P" is silent) is made up of three species, all of which are easy to house train; each has several categories. Cretan brake, *Pteris cretica*, has fronds about a foot long; don't be discouraged if young plants don't have any glamour—they need time to become exquisite pale-green ribbon-like forking fronds which make them the real eye-catchers. Ribbon brake has a white line through each leaf segment. Riverton is ruffled and lobed. Some *Pteris* have tasseled tips to the leaves including Wilson brake, a compact one and most easy to find.

Sword brake, *Pteris ensiformis*, is a taller plant, and in the Victorian brake type is banded with a silver stripe. Siebold's brake is ruffled with both upright and dwarf spreading fronds.

Spider brake, *Pteris serrulata*, has narrower leaf divisions than *cretica*, with long brown stalks, and includes crested and variegated forms.

Brakes can stand low artificial lighting for long periods—that's why they're referred to as "table" ferns. If given too much moisture, they will turn black and rot off. They do well in a tight pot. If you think a brake needs repotting because the solid mass isn't taking in the water, remove the plant from the small pot, shorten some of the roots, repot with same mixture, and with a small stick press the potting medium around the rhizomes. For thrips or red spider, spray on a tobacco "tea."

DAVALLIA

Davallia is a delicate child of the tropics, usually found living on another plant or mossy cliffs, an epiphyte surviving on nutrients in the air and rain. It is a feathery light-green end-of-the-stem frond; furry rhizomes or ground roots creep along the planting medium. It does best in a hanging basket or hollow log filled with osmunda fibre or sphagnum moss (use wire to tie to the log).

Davallia bullata mariesii is the easiest to find and is quite at home in the humid atmosphere of an old bathroom where the mirror gets fogged after you've filled the tub. Modern heat lamps and fans make for dryness; however, if you give a fern a good misting each morning before leaving, it will thrive—keep a brass mist-spray can on the shelf next to the shave cream to remind yourself.

Davallia is a superior plant for tall terrariums. Or wind the rhizomes around a cone of osmunda, set in a small dish of water (moistening the top too). Put it in a north window for normal growth. It's deciduous— don't worry about dropping leaves.

Davallia canariensis, tree hare's foot, has fine, hardy foliage, with rootstocks covered in coarse brown-silver hair. These are dormant in winter.

Propagation: spores.

HARE'S FOOT FERN

Davallia pentaphylla is true hare's foot, and has deep green six- to 12-inch fronds, and creeping, brown, fur-like rhizomes which climb and roam far from the edge of the pot. It is a hardy plant with fronds thicker in texture than the Boston, maidenhair or brake ferns. Tough ones like hare's foot nevertheless need soil that is porous and has good drainage. Avoid overwatering, but do mist.

Polypodium aureum, false hare's foot, has beautiful blue-green fronds with clusters of spore cases underneath, and rusty-brown, hairy rhizomes which can reach four to five feet. It's spectacular in a hanging basket, or in an old serving bowl placed on top of a reclaimed porch column (if the house numbers are still attached, all the better). Leathery deep-cut fronds are durable. The variety *mandaianum* is crested in form, with interesting ruffled leaflets.

Repotting can be done at the beginning of the growing season in spring. Keep an eye out for insects and find out how to distinguish the spore cases from fern scale if you have several ferns in your collection.

Propagation: break off a "foot," pot separately.

Barber your Boston? Yes, also your maidenhair. These ferns will grow back new fronds for each one cut. Leave about two inches of stem above soil.

HAWAIIAN TREE FERN

"Hapu" is the Hawaiian name for this large tree fern. Give it plenty room and a high pedestal so you can see the fronds from underneath; its size is a happy one for a cool tall-ceiling room with white walls and lots of paintings.

Small trunks about eight inches long are usually sold with the fronds unformed. Plant it in a moistened, spongy and loose mixture of osmunda, shredded sphagnum, peat moss and perlite to retain the twice-daily watering you must give to keep the trunk always wet. Water drains through such material quickly and leaves space for the oxygen.

Cibotium chamissoi usually grows on shallow lava beds to 15 feet, but interior plants will manage about five to six feet with an equal spread. *Cibotium schiedei* is a smaller version, but more difficult to grow. At one time the Hawaiians used the long, silky brown hairs, which they call "pulu," to stuff pillows and mattresses.

Fertilizing makes the green greener but will not counteract poor conditions. Apply high nitrogen once a month after January through August. Obviously this is a big-tub plant, so moving it outdoors into shade takes some extra energy. If fronds turn yellow-green and feeding has been regular, try more shade.

63

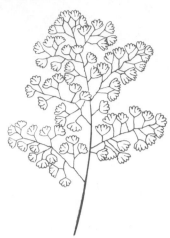

HOLLY FERN

Cyrtomium falcatum is a live-ringer for the holly which fills the house at Christmas, except that it *is* a fern. It spreads sideways in a graceful arch, has no berries and is one of the easiest year-round plants. Holly fern can stand less humidity and more warmth and cold than most, being adaptable to temperatures from 40° to 70°.

Fronds are about six inches wide and evergreen; individual leaves are varnished dark green, toothed like holly and need a dusting now and then as well as a tub bath once a week. The variety *rochefordianum* is recommended because it is shinier and neater than others, and can tolerate dark corners; never give it bright light.

Malathion and house-plant bombs should not be used on ferns to attack scale; it is the carrying agent, not the chemical, which will damage fronds. If the condition is acute, dip the fronds in a solution of nicotine sulphate with soap, then rinse thoroughly in clear water about three hours later. Controlling local ants will help keep scale from spreading.

Fern burn: Brown tips are probably the most annoying of fern blights. Tie it to too little humidity. Solution: Misting and a weekly shower.

MAIDENHAIR

The Latin name for maidenhair, *Adiantum*, is translated "unwetted," referring to the fact that rain flows off the fronds without seeming to wet them. This fern is not easy to maintain for long periods in its most beautiful state because the individual fronds start turning yellow in six to nine months. Keeping the temperature cool (less than 65°) and furnishing plenty of humidity as well as showing infinite patience and concern will still not guarantee a glorious plant, but the delicate fabric will be a special challenge—and worth it.

The variety *Adiantum cuneatum* is perhaps most cooperative. It has wiry black stems and fluffy ruffle fronds in every degree of growth, so if you constantly remove the old and weak, and cut back all the fronds in late winter to about six-inch lengths, it will all be glory-bound in three to four months. *Adiantum caudatum* has drooping fronds which root and produce plantlets at their tips; use in a hanging basket.

Maidenhair's prime enemies are dry air, artificial gas and undiluted sun. Misting is a requisite daily both for humidity and to discourage insect itinerants. Peaty or soilless mixes are best for repotting in spring.

Propagation: by division of roots—and carefully.

64

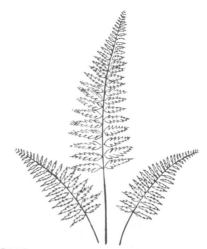

MOTHER SPLEENWORT

Asplenium bulbiferum is a fragile upward-growing fern with feathery bright-green leaves. Eventual size is about two feet. It develops almost-invisible new plants on its fronds. In the wilds of Malaya and New Zealand the little plantlets, or bulbils, fall off and take root. In your home they may be potted to produce new plants with the aid of a magnifying glass and a tweezer. Start with equal parts of leaf mold, sand, good soil and a little charcoal to keep the soil from getting sour.

Spleenwort can be cultivated in any temperature above 40°. Soak daily in the summer, being sure the drainage is active, and mist spray the foliage. Repot annually in fresh soil. This fern can be cultivated to best advantage in a spongy, fibrous mixture that will retain moisture but allow air circulation.

Asplenium has epiphitic, or tree-living, habits and likes medium shade. It forms a basket against the tree to which it attaches itself, and the space becomes a catchall for falling leaves and bugs that in turn decay and make the "soil" that the roots dote on.

TSUSIMA HOLLY FERN

This is quite different from the holly fern. *Polystichum tsus-simense* is tufted and small with dainty, finely divided, dark-green fronds, up to two feet long. It can be kept small enough to look well in a terrarium or as a dish centerpiece, but is best situated in a hanging basket.

Controlled moisture is a prime concern in the growing of a fern like this: roots rot quickly if the soil becomes water soaked. In their natural growth they always stand on mounds *above* water; they will not grow in wet conditions. Try placing a pot in an inverted saucer on a deep tray which has a layer of pebbles and a pad of peat moss, so that the daily watering will not threaten the pot's bottom.

Tsusima is classic in its form and will look great in an old wicker fern stand or a brass jardinière; shop the local Salvation Army or secondhand store. The Wardian case, forerunner of the terrarium, is an ideal fern house. In fact, that's what they were called by the Victorians, because they protected the delicate fronds from the fumes of gas, chills and such. Don't crowd several ferns in a small area—let their natural forms have elbow room.

Propagation: by divisions.

65

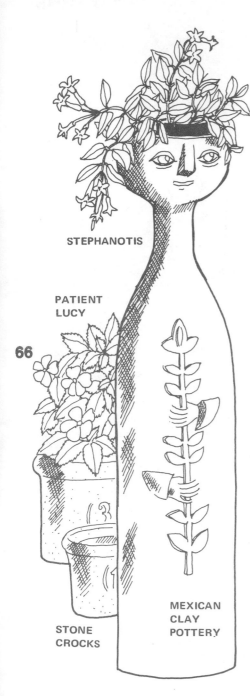

STEPHANOTIS

PATIENT
LUCY

66

STONE
CROCKS

MEXICAN
CLAY
POTTERY

FLOWERING PLANTS

Let's be practical: the ex-purple thumber makes it the easy way with green leaf plants for the first phase, from the standpoint of cost and care. The addition of pots in bloom brings up a whole new set of responsibilities; you may find they take more time than you can give.

Flowering plants need watching to be sure the light isn't scorching—or isn't bright enough. Many survive only with daily watering and regular feeding, and the color lasts for a limited period. Be prepared to pay through the nose for a pot of nosegay. However, the addition of color *can* be downright inspirational. As the French say, *"Au diable d'avarice"* (to hell with expense).

Add to a collection of existing greenery with a mass of pink geraniums (to complement other colors in the room); circle a small tubbed citrus with pots of yellow daffodils; put a glowing white marguerite on the hearth by the fireplace; spread a row of gloxinias on the kitchen sill; or line the entrance hall with clivia. Blossoms without color, like the white poinsettia, are winter sparklers worth the tender loving care needed.

Splashy blooming plants look greatest when you're above them; plants which seem all leaves and stems usually gather their best efforts on top. When you have several pots of color, display them on low tables or on the rug on a pebble-filled tray (with sheet plastic under). Grouping simplifies care; for extra greening, add small pots of foliage around the base to tie it all together.

When buying plants which bloom only short periods, look for leaf shape which will flatter the others in your collection after the blooms have faded. Keep the size compatible with your life style; don't get trapped into something which will outgrow its space and force you to hug the wall each time you walk by.

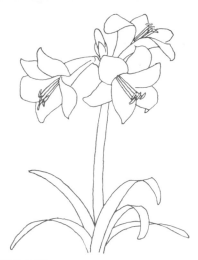

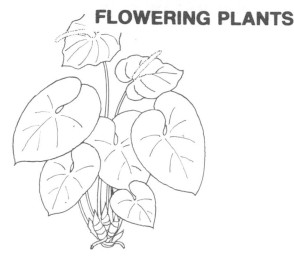

AMARYLLIS

Start by buying the biggest bulb with many live roots, if you want to try this brilliant holiday-time bloomer. Be sure it is the color which pleases. Amaryllis, *Hippeastrum*, comes in pink, red, apple blossom or candy-striped, with three to five great trumpets on a thick stalk and handsome, arching sword leaves. It is an expensive bulb (five dollars plus), but gives a better show than most Broadway productions.

Fill a fruit jar with water and set the bulb on top to let the roots get a wetting bonus for a week. Plant the bulb in a rich mixture, in a pot with a diameter not more than two inches greater than the bulb; the top half of the bulb should be exposed. Find a shady corner, add good helpings of moisture and move to sun after the leaves start pushing out—about four weeks. Give it a weak fertilizer once a week (to insure next year's blossoms); keep the moisture coming—and you can almost see it grow!

The trumpets will crowd the top of an 18- to 24-inch stem year after year if summered in the garden. Once blooms wither, razor the stalk at the base and sink the pot to its rim in a semishaded spot or store it in an east or west window until the leaves turn brown and loose. Bring the pot in to a cool spot and store on its side in dryness until you notice new green. Add new potting soil, start watering and the cycle repeats. Don't repot.

ANTHURIUM

A difficult child to keep happy and worth the effort only if you are mad for the flowers. First, you must furnish constantly moist conditions above 70°, partial shade and soft water. Central heating is okay, as long as you keep the pot wrapped in moist sphagnum and double-potted. Setting the plant on a tray filled with pebbles which you keep moist will maintain needed humidity.

Anthurium andraeanum, of several species, seems to do best indoors. Its exotic, heart-shaped bracts, or leaf form, may appear in white, orange, salmon or deep coral. They last for months, and one follows another throughout the year. Anthurium plants demand space, more than average watering (they resist both cold and hard water), filtered sun and frequent feeding—twice monthly. Spray the foliage daily, if the atmosphere is dry.

When the plant refuses to bloom and new leaves keep coming, move it to a cool corner for six weeks to two months, then return to warmth. Like most tropicals, it needs winter rest and less water. Keep the leaves free of dust. Soil requirements include a rich mix with charcoal, leaf mold and fragmented sphagnum moss. They need to be potbound and do well with a once-a-month water-soluble feeding, one-quarter strength of a 15-30-15 fertilizer.

Propagation: division of roots when repotting.

AZALEA

Both rhododendron and azalea are members of the' same tribe and are treasured for their showers of color in the woods. The ones related to house-plant living are the showy hybrids *Azalea indica,* or Indian azalea which usually arrive as gifts via the florist.

If your plant comes this way, keep it moist, cool—and away from radiators. Setting the pot on pebbles in a water tray, plus misting, will help keep the leaves on longer; if your living area stays warm at night, move the azalea to soothing coolness, 40° to 55°, out of drafts.

The azalea will need a couple of years to recover from the florist's forced blooming. If you remove dead flowers and cut down the watering, it will winter in a cool place until spring when the pot can be sunk into an outdoor bed. Come September and the addition of a top dressing of acid-peat, and it may flower again. (See the section Gift Plants.)

Azaleas raised under nursery conditions grow to two feet tall and give masses of white, mixed and red-pink blooms in late winter. They do well with four hours filtered sun and cool sleeping if potted in two parts acid-peat, one part soil and one part perlite or vermiculite. Fertilize with iron sulphate according to the package label. Watch for red spider.

Propagation: stem cuttings.

BEGONIAS

Begonias come in three flavors: tubers, rhizomes and fibrous. *Begonia semperflorens "Fiesta"* is a hardy, fibrous, indoor showpiece with dark, bronze-red leaves and one-inch flowers—brilliant little ones in limitless hues of red, salmon and yellows. From Europe comes a brand new hybrid, the single-flower *Rieger elator* which will bloom its head off indoors winter and summer; it is easy-care, happy in bright light.

The tuberous group, including *Begonia tuberhybrida,* with three- to four-inch camellia-like blossoms, is usually grown in window boxes and hanging baskets. The rhizome variety, the fancy-leaf *Begonia rex* is leafless and dormant in winter; reduce water and feedings. It has a smallish pink or white flower, but is most prized for huge, often hairy leaves in reds, bronzes and greens.

Begonias are shallow-root plants, preferring flatter containers than usual. Use a soil mix of one-third loam, one-third perlite and one-third peat moss, with bonemeal and charcoal added to bring out leaf and blossom color. Be certain the crocking is good to assure moisture movement. The plants get stronger at temperatures of 68° to 75° with slightly lower at night. Some, like the iron cross, can do with 75°. Furnish humidity and feed liberally every four weeks with a high-phosphorous food. Use Malathion spray on mealy bugs and mites; powdery mildew appears during a cold, damp spell and calls for a fungicide.

Propagation: seeds, stem cuttings and leaf wedges.

68

BOUGAINVILLEA

It's nice to discover you can do something most people think can't be done. Gather your courage and bring that grand ol' Southern belle, bougainvillea indoors—in a pot or tub. This vivid vine *can* be housebroken, and in fact will stay obligingly pretty with blooms from July into winter. If your interior color scheme can stand a dash of the red spectrum, this is what you can get—from magenta to orange.

Bougainvillea sanderiana has magenta bracts; variety Crimson Lake matches its name—both are especially good choices for house living. Barbara Karst is another crimson and variety Laterita is a rich brick red.

Stems can be tied to a stake to give vertical poise. The bougainvillea isn't fussy about warmth, but if you keep the thermometer around 70°, it blooms better. Hold back watering in between the soak-dry stage and also during winter rest until February. Put the pot where it will get plenty of sun. A spot near a reflecting warm white wall on a plant stand or pedestal will furnish fascinating shadow patterns. If its profile needs plastic surgery, do your pruning heavily after flowering, and save the cuttings for propagation.

Bougainvillea does right well in rich soil plus extra helpings of food.

CHENILLE PLANT

Also sold under the name of red-hot cattail, *Acalypha hispida* is a good bathroom-window candidate if there is lots of sun and high humidity part of each day.

The plant shouldn't get too big, even for a small bath. The sight of the long red tassels trailing down will certainly be worth the space to give your morning a boost. The blossoms last long and profusely in the latter half of the year. The plant itself is upright with coarse, long, dark-green leaves.

Set the pot on a tray which has a layer of pebbles you can keep wet; don't let the water reach the pot bottom for the chenille can't stand soggy roots. In fact, you will need to repot it once a year and do some serious root pruning. The top also should be barbered back to eight to 12 inches of growth to keep it from outgrowing its favorite location. Keep a misting spray handy and give the leaves a shot of moisture daily. Pot in a mixture, half-and-half, of sandy mix and humus; be sure the drainage is efficient and keep a watchful eye on possible spider-mite invasion.

CHRYSANTHEMUMS

70

Mums are discussed early in this book, particularly the forced ones which are found in supermarkets and on the discount table. Chrysanthemums which are grown in normal processes for outdoor planting in tubs can be invited indoors. Their pretty yellow and white blooms are cheerful the year round and their natural habits rewarding.

Chrysanthemum frutescens, or Boston daisy, is a single yellow with less coarse foliage than most. Marguerites are the white-blossoming ones; look for a new strain with one and a quarter-inch faces—they make neat bouquets, too. *Felicia amelloides* is a soft blue with bright yellow center, also a dainty face, which mounds into a great sea of blue.

These mums look their best in larger tubs and containers because they tend to get leggy in a small pot. If the plant gets larger than you want by spring, divide the clump into several pots and by fall they come back indoors to brighten several spots.

Daily watering and a good soaking will keep blossoms coming; any wilt calls for water reviving. Sun is important; avoid excess heat and add fertilizer only occasionally. Never hesitate pinching back; keep dead blossoms removed.

Propagation: cuttings. As soon as the cutting is established, pinching back to two or three leaves and stem pinching is in order to assure bushy character.

CLIVIA

Kaffir lily, showy relative of the amaryllis, has a tall stalk with a topknot of fragrant, orange, trumpet-shaped flowers with yellow heart. A late-winter brightener, *Clivia miniata* may have as many as 15 trumpets in the period between January and March. The long strap-like green leaves do not get cut back like those of the amaryllis but continue yearly.

By October, relax on watering but don't let the plant get dry. Rest in 55° until Christmas, then bring it to warmth and start feeding weekly with soluable plant food, every two weeks from April to August. When the new stalk is six inches tall, start watering; if you can get rainwater use it at room temperature.

Clivia can be a temperamental bloomer, particularly if you disturb the large fleshy roots. Repotting is required every three to five years, right after blossoming, and must be handled with care. Potting soil needs to be rich in humus and organic fertilizer. Good light is important—keep it out of hot sun. Transfer the pot outdoors to partial shade in summer.

Propagation: seeds. Remove flowers in late summer before seeds set to keep plant strong; if you do want to experiment let the hips dry in the sun for a month, then squeeze to free the seed which may take 10 months to ripen. Recommend propagating from offsets.

FIRECRACKER VINE

Manettia inflata is also named the Brazilian fire-cracker, which locates the origin. It is a low-trailing little number who likes the sun, which in turn encourages it to bloom and bloom. Firecracker will have an inclination to get leggy and needs firm pinching action to keep it pleasantly full.

The tubular, two-inch blossoms that appear at each leaf axil are red (what else?) with a gay yellow tip. Rather than accepting this as just another hanging basket filler, attach it to a trellis or to a wire form; tie the spidery branches with raffia or an inconspicuous green twistem to form a screen in a sunny window which has an otherwise blah view. It will grow to four feet or more and rapidly.

Keep a firecracker moist (but never soggy) all of the time and give frequent feedings, perhaps once every two weeks; it will grow like Jack's beanstalk. This is not a traveling plant and it doesn't like wind so don't move it outside. Soil requirements are modest; warmth and light are a must.

Propagation: stem cuttings at any time.

> *Gardenia bud drop: Nights are too warm. Mist every morning and feed with acid-type food twice monthly. Citrus will drop its buds if overfed.*

FLAME-OF-THE-WOODS

Also amusingly called "jungle geranium," the ever-green Ixoras have been rediscovered thanks to a hybridizer in Florida. *Ixora coccinea* was a popular greenhouse plant in Europe a hundred years ago, and in contemporary times it is used as a hedge in the southern United States. There are new colors and a new tolerance for shade in the hybrids available.

Ixora "Frances Perry" is a brilliant yellow, compact as a potted flowering plant. "Super king" is a winter-flowering red, and "Trinidad red" has blossoms up to seven and a half inches across, of deep, deep red. *Ixora colei* is a pure-white, dwarf type; "Helen Dunaway" is intense orange.

Flame-of-the-woods is an apartment natural for it has to stay in warmth above 65° and should get all the sun possible in winter. Fertilize only in periods of bright sunlight because overfeeding stimulates the gardenia-shaped leaves instead of the starry blossom heads. Leaves are bronze tone when young and become dark and shiny green as they mature. Plant size can be held to less than two feet in both directions by pruning. About soil: a mixture of two parts peat, one part packaged mix and one part vermiculite is desirable; add no lime.

Propagation: from cuttings in spring.

71

FLOWERING PLANTS

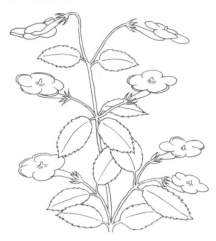

JERUSALEM CHERRY

A smallish plant in the beginning, the Jerusalem cherry will brighten a side table or counter with its bright red-to-orange fruit. (Keep out of reach of little hands; this fruit is poisonous.) However, it will get to be four feet tall and command a large-bush space unless you persist and pinch back the stem tips. After fruits shrivel, remove and let grow normally. Prune back in spring and place outdoors for summer. It should rebloom and set fruit.

Solanum pseudocapsicum is usually grown as an annual for the Christmas season, but the plants can be kept for the following year if cut back and repotted in spring. Continue to pinch back the tips until early summer to encourage bushiness. Tiny star-shaped white blossoms appear then and the fruit gets going in November.

Jerusalem cherry, or Christmas cherry, has narrow, pointed leaves about two inches long; the fruit is good-sized and will stay around until the end of December or into January. It does best in 68° to 72° temperatures, with nights about 50° to 55°. Find at least four hours sunlight and constant moisture in both soil and on the leaves. Package mix seems to furnish ideal soil.

Propagation: seeds.

MAGIC FLOWER

Achimenes is one of those it-can't-be-grown-elsewhere greenhouse specialties which has finally achieved house-plant status. By the simple formula of maintaining a 60° night temperature, giving the magic flower a little sun in spring and bright shade in summer—and never letting the soil dry out—you can add *Achimenes* to your success record.

This plant starts from rhizomes, unusual-looking horizontal root-like stems which in this case have scales like long pine cones. They are so productive that a single separated scale will put forth a new plant. (Propagation by cuttings in spring in moist sphagnum is possible too.) Between February and May activate rhizomes in moist sphagnum or vermiculite, and transfer to pots of two parts peat moss, one part each of package soil mix and sharp clean sand. Several plants in a single large pot hung in a sling will give showers of pink, red, orange, white and blue-purple blossoms.

During the blooming period, give *Achimenes* a feeding twice a month; and never let it dry out or it will retire into dormancy immediately. However, as the blooming tapers off in late October, hold back on water and let the plants cool down naturally. When they are ready for winter rest, take the rhizomes out of the pot, clean and store them in dry sand or vermiculite at 50° until time to replant.

ORCHID CACTUS

Epiphyllum hybrids are sophisticated cactus fingers whose coarseness would cause African violet lovers to shudder, but you may just get caught up in a new beat. This is a jungle plant, not desert. Its homely character goes through a transformation in March or April when great blooms pop out of the sides in a fireworks burst of glory—maroon, pink, copper, red, orange, pastels, up to a foot across.

These Cinderella flowers appear on the notched edges of the fingers, satiny and sensuous, and they make magnificent cut flowers. Blooming will extend into June, and will repeat year after year, if the plant got its start in rich humus soil and plenty of moisture, with good feeding once a month during the show.

To insure long life remove the top inch of soil once a year and replace with more humus and leaf mold stuff. Orchid cactus will do well in strong light as well as direct sun; it accepts fresh air, too. If the bloomless plant is less than attractive to you, store it in the garden, protected from winter cold, or indoors, where you don't have to look at it every day.

Propagation: cuttings from the long stems, at least six to 12 inches, carefully callused.

PELARGONIUM

Confusion has always raised its voice when pelargoniums and geraniums are mentioned. What's the difference? Well, they're both *Pelargoniums*, botanically, but the fancy show specimens drew the name, *Pelargonium domesticum*, and common garden varieties are referred to as geraniums, or *Pelargonium hortorum*. (To confuse things more, there *is* a genus *Geranium*, occasionally grown in the garden.)

Pelargoniums are also called Martha Washington or Lady Washington. There are at least 75 varieties: the ivy-leaf types, scented or rose, show or fancy. Some have silver-edged leaves, some are vine-like for hangers and window boxes, and the scented ones in riotous flowering choices are a mad collection of lemon, balsam, rose, apple, nutmeg, peppermint or pennyroyal—you get the fragrance by crushing a leaf.

Pelargoniums need sun, heat and dry air. Watering should be done as soon as the surface soil becomes fairly dry. It's better to have a pot too small, rather than too large, for the water to get through the root mass. Dunk the pot, then let it almost dry. Pinch back to keep a good shape.

Propagation: stem cuttings, four to six inches long with lower leaves removed and ends dipped in powdered hormone. Too much moisture will hasten decay; keep the bottom of the propagation container warm, about 70°.

73

FLOWERING PLANTS

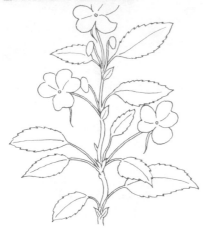

PATIENT LUCY

Impatiens sultanii (I. wallerana), also implausibly named Patience, and Busy Lizzie, is another old-time favorite that blooms all year with only modest attention. The built-in sunset colors—red, pink, orange, coral, gold and even white—give a charming bouquet mood. Look for the sun-loving New Guinea hybrids—large flowers, unusual depths of color in both bloom and foliage.

Seedpods have a far-out explosion mechanism that catapults the ripened seeds on touch.

Impatiens is not a large plant, rarely getting taller than a foot, and benefits in importance if you mass four or six in a single location. The flat flowers are one to two inches across; the leaves are about the same size, in maroon and variegated green-and-white as well as green. Pruning is the accepted method to keep a nicely rounded or pyramidal plant.

Pot in two parts peat moss, one part packaged mix and one part sharp sand, and cater to the moisture demands. Fertilize every two weeks. Try bright non-sunlight, filtered light or shade and warm days.

Propagation: stem cuttings, or seeds. Cuttings should be at least six inches long, started in sand but not kept too damp as the cutting is susceptible to rot.

SHRIMP PLANT

When you set out to enjoy offbeat indoor plants, put the shrimp plant on your list for an amusing Mexican contribution. *Justicia brandegeana (Beloperone guttata)* has arching red-brown-to-pink scales, prawnlike, and will remain in bloom from November to March or April.

The shrimp grows rapidly and will need constant pinching back to keep it full and within your space allotment. And make that space a very sunny south window. Keep the plant moist; check for especially good drainage because it needs more water than average and has to be able to handle it. Don't let it dry out completely (try the soak-and-almost-dry method) and stand it on a pebble-tray so the moisture will build up humidity. Too much or too little water and the leaves tend to turn yellow and droop. Cutting back in September is a must to keep it bushy.

This is one plant you can remove from the pot, plant in your summer garden and dig up to repot in the autumn. Radical pruning is in order to keep the shrimp about 20 inches tall; it will start flowering as a mature plant at 10 inches—you don't have to wait for it to grow up.

Propagation: cuttings from the pruning.

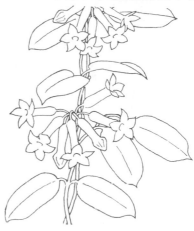

SPATHE FLOWER

A look-alike to a miniature white anthurium, *Spathiphyllum clevelandii* has been a cool choice for house growing for many years, and is less fussy than its cousin, the anthurium. Delicate snowy-white, jack-in-the-pulpit blossoms will get to be four inches same length. *Spathiphyllum cannaefolium* has narrow lance-shape leaves with center ribs twisted and bent, set on long wiry stems; the pale-green sheath turns white as it opens to show the lovely blossom. A new hybrid has flowers large as the anthurium and is rewardingly scented.

Spathe flowers bloom in January and February and each will last for weeks. When the flowers are gone, it is still a knockout of a medium plant, up to 18 inches tall, and the many individual vertical leaf stems form a linear thicket.

Give it filtered sun, east or west light, but good light—no cheating. Temperatures of 65° to 70° and high humidity plus daily watering and misting are on the schedule; and keep the leaves wiped off. Repot each fall in two parts peat moss, one part packaged soil mix and one part sharp sand or perlite. Fertilize every other month.

Propagation: divide the plant when you repot.

STEPHANOTIS

Madagascar jasmine or *Stephanotis floribunda* is a superb evergreen climber with heavenly fragrance. The waxy tubular white blossoms in clusters of dark-green foliage are the bride's favorite.

Stephanotis is usually considered a greenhouse plant, the florist's exclusive, but it can be grown indoors with success provided you control a couple of **75** important things. Keep the pot cool in winter, no warmer than 50° to 55°, and water only moderately; it is susceptible to insect invasions if the temperature rises. During the summer when it is growing and blooming, add more water, give four hours of bright filtered sunlight daily and fertilize March to October.

This jasmine follows a trellis or wires with the help of a few inconspicuous ties. It can also be encouraged to bush-up by pinching off tips of new stems.

Slow-growing cousin *Trachelospermum jasminoides,* star jasmine, is also a ranging plant (doubles as a ground cover, too) with small, creamy, fragrant blossoms which reflect light like tiny mirrors. Its night fragrance is romantically enveloping. *Jasminum officinale,* poet's jasmine, is also a fragrant choice; it grows in warm conditions, likes to climb.

Propagation: stem cuttings.

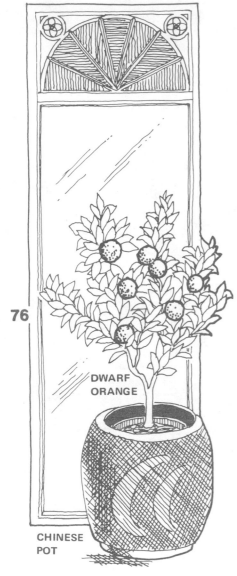

DWARF ORANGE

CHINESE POT

FOLIAGE WITH A BONUS

The label "green" attaches itself to "thumb" because it is our mental computer's first reaction when one says leaf, tree, vegetable, grass—and the work it takes to keep that green *green*.

But, if everything in plant families were color-me-green, it could be a colossal bore. Fortunately Mama Nature stirred up some variety, and a lot of it has spilled over into the house-plant section. There are variegated greens, leaves which have vivid or pale reds, orange, cream, silver, purple—in stripes, speckles, edgings.

These are the plants which contrast and enhance greenery when you don't want to deal with the trickier aspects of flowering ones. And their color is permanent, provided you remember that the color is dependent on daily sunlight to keep from fading. Some, like the crotons, need higher temperatures and may not do so well in ordinary environments. But the coleus, some geraniums and begonias are easies.

Color appears in the fruits of some house plants. They are not edible, however, except for citrus, pineapple, banana, natal plum, kumquats and strawberries. "Decorative" is a better name tag: the fruits add cheerful notes during fall and winter and the plants require minimal care, a soaking once a week and direct light. They are usually slow growing but tree forms eventually will outgrow pots and move up to big deep tubs, so be prepared to give space—or find another home.

Herbs and spices (see the section on these) are worth propagating for the nice smells they furnish. Pleasant also to have around are lemon verbena and lemon balm. Geraniums come in fragrances like rose, nutmeg, French lace (lemon) and peppermint; crumble a leaf and your hand will carry the afterglow for an hour or more. A small bay tree in a tub will carry faint memories of marvelous stews (winter this tree in the house, put outside for summer).

CALADIUM

The leaf size—12 to 18 inches from tip to tip—is impressive, but the colorful masses of foliage of the caladium are what really steal the show—reds to vie with a sunset, shocking pink, creamy whites and exquisite pale greens. There are dozens of varieties and each is a spectrum of color, variegated, splotched, veined, streaked and even a potpourri of all markings. Some of the translucent leaves are heart shaped, some arrowhead, some straplike. Caladium was " elephant's ear" to old-timers; now there are several dwarf varieties with which to experiment.

Caladiums are not tall but spread sideways and need stage center to dramatize their extravagant color. They thrive in partial shade or filtered sunlight in warm rooms, 70° to 80°; leaves will scorch and bushy plants dry up in direct sun. Warm summer days are perfect for an outing in the shade, the leaves bending gracefully in a pleasant breeze.

Propagation: start tubers in April, one to a pot in moist sphagnum, in very warm temperatures of 75° to 85°. When established, repot in a mixture of coarse clean sand and packaged potting mixture plus a little horticultural charcoal and a tablespoon of bonemeal in each pot. The soil should be acid for the deepest color. Provide good drainage for the quantity of water they like. When foliage dies back, keep the tubers bone dry for two months.

CYCLAMEN

Cyclamen is also briefly listed under the Gift Plant section, but important enough to include here as foliage with a bonus because the thick leaves with silvery markings and red translucent stems and veins label it decorative even without the bonus of delicate butterfly blossoms.

Cyclamen persicum usually comes into the house collection as a florist's plant. Plants can be propagated from seeds in early spring but it will take 15 to 18 months for blooms to show, and for a one-time display (plants are difficult to make bloom a second time) it isn't worth the lengthy care unless you have a greenhouse to tuck it in.

If you really want to try for a repeat of the delicate pink, red or white blooms, start holding back watering in the spring to about twice a month (cyclamen is a December show-off) until the leaves come loose from the corm. Put the pot on its side in a cool, shaded spot outdoors. By late summer, at the appearance of new leaves, repot with a rich soil mixture into a slightly larger pot and sink the new pot into the garden up to its rim. Water frequently. Before the first frost, lift the pot, wash it and bring it inside.

Never wet the foliage of a blooming cyclamen. Soak from the bottom in a bucket or in the sink; root rot from too much moisture is a common blight. Keep a cyclamen in a cool room, about 50° at night and not more than 60° during the day.

77

FOLIAGE WITH A BONUS

DWARF ORANGE

Citrus trees up to four feet tall will produce just as fragrant blossoms when grown as tub plants as when commercially grown in the great groves of California and Florida. The fruit of the dwarf varieties is insipid however, and the juice tart in the small orange. But *Citrus taitensis,* otaheite orange, is still a terrific bonus plant and makes a charmed Christmas gift with little bows tied to each fruit (the plum-size oranges hang on for months).

Pink-tinged blooms and fruit are on the dwarf orange at the same time and often when the plant is less than a foot tall. The orange should have four hours of sun, but given too much warmth without ventilation in a room, it may lose leaves.

Citrus mitis, calamondin orange, stays less than two feet tall indoors and has fruit the size of ping-pong balls after the tree starts bearing. Actually, it will have fragrant flowers, green fruit and ripened small oranges almost all year. Calamondin is happy when it is heavily pruned to hold its shape; use sharp woodcutting shears so outer bark is not hurt. Purchased plants are usually grafted, and are available in a flowering condition.

Potting soil loaded with good humus and loam, and well-decomposed manure will do the job best. Water on a soak-and-dry basis. Add iron if leaves turn yellow. To get a fruit crop, hand pollinate with a small brush: take from the pollen of one blossom and add to the stigma of another, when it is moist.

DWARF POMEGRANATE

A splendid house decoration, *Punica granatum nana* has shiny green leaves year round, unless it gets caught in a chill or draft; then the leaves drop. The bell-shape flowers are neat, small and scarlet, opening in summer, but the burnt-orange to red fruit is the real attraction, ripening in early fall through winter. Chico, a new variety, has flowers like little red carnations, opening in summer later than the other types.

Pomegranate was known to the Romans as the apple of Carthage, and still charms strangers to its juicy many-seeded fruit. The dwarf form has small branches which are inclined to be spiny. It is hardy, moves out of doors in summer, and grows only 12 to 15 inches tall.

Try *Punica granatum nana* in at least four hours direct sunlight each day, night temperatures of 55° to 60° and ordinary house warmth daily. Keep the soil moist and fertilize only once in three or four months. The dwarf pomegranate isn't fussy about soil or exposure to humidity, but it must have sun. Prune in late winter or early spring while dormant; flowers form on new wood.

Propagation: stem cuttings in summer.

GARDENIA

Gardenia jasminoides is a demanding beauty; don't tackle it unless your time is your own. Repotting must take place once a year, in the spring, with fresh acid soil. Use a mix of two parts peat moss, one part packaged potting mix, one part sharp sand or vermiculite. Don't hesitate to cut back severely; plants like gardenia and fuchsia need discipline.

Plan to summer the pot outdoors, sunk into a plant bed up to the rim. Pinch off buds as they first appear so that the plant is encouraged to bloom in winter months.

Ideally, gardenias like winter sun and bright shade in summer. Day readings of 72° and nighttime about 60°, plus humidity and a well-drained acid soil are required. Leaves should be misted every day; when buds drop off, offer water. Food should be high in aluminum sulphate and administered from March to November. If leaves turn yellow, try applications of a chelated iron solution.

JESSAMINE

The night-blooming *Cestrum parqui*, the willow-leaf jessamine, has powerfully fragrant green-white flowers in midwinter and black berries. Leaves are long and thin, like the willow's. All jessamines are inclined to be rangy and can be cut back to advantage, particularly after flowering. Give it a warm shady spot with generous amounts of water, humidity and feeding. Most of their lives they enjoy a 70° temperature, but as with most tropicals when resting, do better with 50° to 55° in winter. They require a short day to set buds (like poinsettia, etc.) and that means no TV light, no street light.

Cestrum diurnum is a day-bloomer. Its fragrant inch-long blossoms appear intermittently throughout the year and are also followed by black berries. Glossy three- to four-inch long leaves seem to respond to direct sun half a day. To encourage branching, prune old growth after flowers fade.

Cestrum nocturnum is another night bloomer but its scented flowers appear off and on during the year. It has thin eight-inch oval leaves and white berries.

Carolina jessamine, or jasmine, *Gelsemium sempervirens*, is more likely to be successful on a deck or terrace in a container with support, more truly a vine than the others; it also will do well in a hanging basket, given full sun but cooler nights than the *Cestrum* varieties. Prune after flowering in spring.

Propagation: cuttings, *Cestrum* and *Gelsemium*.

FOLIAGE WITH A BONUS

KUMQUAT

Fortunella margarita, the Nagami kumquat or oval kumquat, bears a small fruit similar in form to the dwarf orange. Its small, fragrant, star-type blossoms in spring precede the inch-and-a-half-long oval orange fruit which appears most of the year, but particularly October through January. Growing only three feet tall indoors, the kumquat is decorative with glossy small dark leaves. *Fortunella hindsii* is an even smaller variety, about a foot in height, with cherry-size, red-orange fruit.

The tiny fruit appears in abundance and can be eaten, skin and all. If there's a sufficient crop for a batch, try putting together a kumquat marmalade. The hardiness of this dwarf form makes it a good choice for minimal care; also, it will stand lower temperatures than the orange or lemon.

Another offbeat hybrid is *Eustis limequat,* a cross of kumquat and Mexican lime; the fruit resembles the kumquat, flavor favors the lime. It has a small leaf, is fast growing, open in form but hardy.

Give all the kumquats four hours of sun daily and allow the plant to dry slightly between soakings. Fertilize in very early spring, early and late summer.

Propagation: stem cuttings or seeds anytime.

MYRTLE

For sheer symmetry and elegance in a small tree, choose the classic myrtle of ancient Greece, *Myrtus communis microphylla.* Use it in a formal entrance, in a chaste grouping by a grand piano or in a row in front of a great expanse of glass. Each compact form is covered with very small aromatic green leaves and starred with exquisite, deeply scented white flowers in summer and fall. Once the flowers fade, deep indigo berries follow into winter. The myrtle takes to shaping into any form you desire, as a neat hedge might be trimmed.

Ugni molinae (formerly *Myrtus ugni),* Chilean Guava, is evergreen, widely used on patios and terraces in the west. It is a tidy, restrained plant with half-inch leaves, dark green above and whitish underneath. The fruit is slightly larger than *Myrtus communis* and edible; flavor is a mixture of guava and strawberry. It likes sun in the coastal area and filtered shade inland.

Give the myrtle a slightly acid soil, one made up of peat moss, well-decomposed manure and sharp, clean sand. Temperature range is 55° to 60°. Permit to dry between waterings.

Propagation: four- to six-inch cuttings in spring.

NATAL PLUM

Carissa grandiflora is cherished for its compact glossy, oval leaves and its snowy-white, two-inch flowers with the scent of a lily. The rich-red fruit which follows is about the same size and for fruit taste, considered even better than true plum—more tart and distinctive like cranberry.

The natal plum is bushy and spreading but rarely reaches over two feet in the house. The most popular dwarf varieties, "boxwood beauty" and *Carissa macrocarpa nana compacta* can be kept even smaller for apartment dwelling.

Blossoms appear any time of the year and their fragrance is particularly appealing. Give this tree fresh air in a window or on a balcony, at least four hours sun daily in summer and a temperature range above 50° nights and usual house-range daytimes. Keep it evenly moist with efficient drainage and add a misting often to encourage bud formation.

For potting use one-third loam, one-third well-decomposed manure and one-third peat moss or humus. Fertilize every three months except in the winter when the plant is resting; then reduce water.

Propagation: from stem cuttings anytime.

PAINTED NETTLE

Perhaps the name coleus *(Coleus hybridus)* is more familiar, but whatever you call it, you probably either love it and have a collection of a dozen different types, or you hate it! There is no middle ground.

With its splattering of velvety many-hued leaves, few plants can match it for a spreading palette of color. It grows rapidly and sometimes has a tendency to look weedy, however. The common variety, *Coleus pumila* has red-brown leaves with pale-green borders; these need to be pinched back weekly or the plant will look tacky. Put the coleus on a shelf or in a hanging basket where it can cascade. Coleus must have a warm, light place; lack of light minimizes color and causes leaf drop. Watering is all important, too. Keep it slightly moist all the time, particularly if the sun hits it; the leaves will suddenly start drooping if the plant is dry.

By no stretch of the imagination can this be called an "elegant" plant; the colors are raucous and its habits can be annoying—particularly its weakness for attracting mealy bugs. If there's a bad infestation, better junk the plant; however, first try salvaging a few cuttings and picking off the individual mealy bugs, so that you can make new plants. (Painted nettle is sensitive to insecticide bombs which will kill the pest, but hurt the plant.)

Propagation: cuttings, each year, to replace the parent plant.

81

FOLIAGE WITH A BONUS

SUGARCANE

Sugarcane? Yes, in your own sunny window this bold, tall grass will actually produce up to six stalks on one cane section.

Saccharum officinarum is the same plant which supplies the world with sugar and its by-products. The name is unimportant, however, because it is almost impossible to find either seeds or plants. The simplest propagation method starts in a visit to a greengrocer of exotic food, Mexican, Spanish, South American; look for a stalk or two of real sugarcane, ones with green tops and red bamboolike cane.

Each stalk is divided into segments, and on each side of a joint you will find a kind of shield; just below are two rows of tiny dots of a light-colored ring. Using a pruning saw or a carpenter's backsaw, cut an internode section which will have an enclosed joint at both ends, and the ring of dots at the lower end. (That's where the roots emerge, if you're lucky.)

Place the lower end of the section in a pot containing two-thirds planting mix and one-third humus, well moistened. Seal off the top of the cane with candle drippings to hold in moisture. Within a week there should be signs of action by the shields—a bud. If you have a large pot, you can place the cane on its side and bury it about an inch deep. This furnishes a good anchor for the heavy plants which hopefully will appear. The fresher the cane, the better the chance for sprouting.

SWEET OLIVE

Looking for a tall slim tree for a cool spot on a porch or a balcony? *Osmanthus fragrans*, the "sweet olive," is your friend. It is a great background plant for more insistent show-offs. The vertical form of sweet olive is treelike, growing at least five feet high with foliage light enough to allow the structure of the plant to create a sculptural excitement. The almost-hidden little greenish-white star flowers nestling in the dramatic dark foliage are wildly fragrant, reminiscent of orange blossoms.

Osmanthus is a cool-room plant, needing 50° nights, sunny winter days and filtered shade in summer with maximum 68°. Potting soil recommended is loam with well-decomposed manure and peat moss. Keep the mixture on the moist side but never soaked; fertilize monthly in spring and summer. It suffers in alkaline soils, so give food with high phosphoric-acid additive. Also watch for signs of legginess and be prepared to prune back in sweet olive's youth to keep the slim look.

You can move it outdoors in summer, but protect it from wind as leaves are sensitive and flowers will brown off. Wherever it lands, be sure it's where the fragrance is appreciated.

Propagation: by cuttings, early summer.

GIFT PLANTS

These are the staples of the quick-turnover growers' market—poinsettias grown for Christmas, precooled lily of the valley pips promising to bloom for dear little old ladies; primroses and cinerarias pushed to overloads of blossoms for the fast ride to the hospital's appendix-elimination department.

Gift plants hold people together in trying times and in celebrations. Little matter that they have a speeded-up life cycle and will spin off in orbit into the trash. Enjoy their marvelous momentary show—and if you can, coax them into staying a little longer with the help of guidelines on the next couple of pages, or the informative florist's tag which tells you what time the two o'clock feeding occurs.

Realize that special hothouse lighting makes chrysanthemums bloom in April as well as October and shamrock pots flagrant with green for St. Patrick while they still sleep in the old sod over there. Growers' skill works magic, and the plants arrive on stage like stars in foil robes despite the shock of being taken from ideal conditions of the greenhouse plus two trips in cold delivery trucks.

Gift plants need to be watered; but to repeat, don't let the pot sit in a saucer of water. A deeper dish with a layer of pebbles added and water just below the pot increases the humidity circulation. Plants with spongy roots, like hydrangeas, azaleas and poinsettias, appreciate dampness. Strong sun is out; blossoms and opened buds respond to draft-free strong light and temperatures above 70° in the daytime (60° for Christmas plants).

For the adventurous who have caught the green ring on the merry-go-round, forget the above circumspect gift list! Give a friend a dwarf banana tree, several pots of Jerusalem cherries, a Norfolk Island pine decorated with miniature lights for Christmas, a dwarf lemon or orange tree, tiny pots of Alpine strawberries or a grapefruit tree in a soy tub, grown from the seed of the fruit you ate!

Columbus brought back pineapples to Isabella in 1493, so they say.

Aloe is the chef's best friend: For minor burns, break off part of a leaf and use the jellylike substance that oozes out. This pulp soothes the burn, promotes quick healing.

GIFT PLANTS

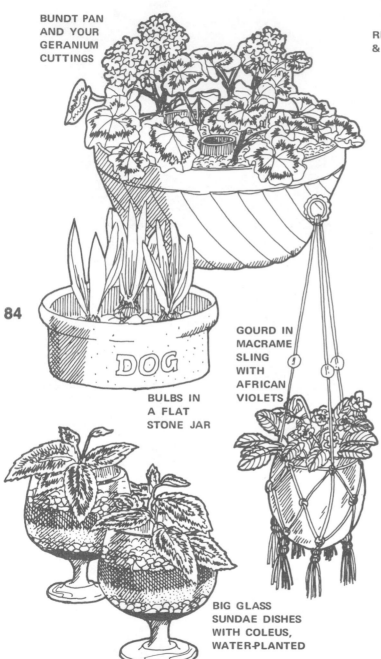

BUNDT PAN AND YOUR GERANIUM CUTTINGS

DOG

BULBS IN A FLAT STONE JAR

GOURD IN MACRAME SLING WITH AFRICAN VIOLETS

BIG GLASS SUNDAE DISHES WITH COLEUS, WATER-PLANTED

84

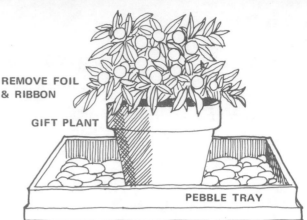

REMOVE FOIL & RIBBON

GIFT PLANT

PEBBLE TRAY

AFRICAN VIOLETS: Place one 60-watt incandescent bulb over a violet 18 hours a day, and it will grow a foot in diameter, and continue blossoming; keep light at least 24 inches above bloom; grow best at 68° to 70°, wilt down at 50° (see Flowering Plants).

AZALEAS: Want at least four hours direct or bright indirect sunlight at 65°; night temps 40° to 55°. Keep medium-moist; add acid-type fertilizer every two weeks from time flowers fade until fall, after the first year's bloom, then monthly; none while in bloom.

CALCEOLARIA: Annuals with red and yellow pouches; discard when through flowering.

CALADIUM: Leaves are many-colored. Likes partial shade, 70° to 80°, foliage begins to die back in spring. Keep tubers dry for two months; repot in August with fresh soil, add water again.

CHRISTMAS CACTUS: See Cacti and Succulents. Pink, reddish three-inch bracts. Leave plants outdoors until frost starts, then try 60° to 70° indoor night temperature; do not fertilize when plants are resting.

CHRYSANTHEMUMS: Bloom for two to three weeks; keep out of direct sun. Plant in the garden or give away when flowers go.

CINERARIA: Enjoy and toss out.

CYCLAMEN: Plants blossom well for long periods in curtain-filtered light, cool nights, moderate days. Feed every two weeks during growing season. Difficult to salvage; better to replace each year.

EASTER LILY: May last for years outside, but rarely with peak blooms again. Water until leaves mature; remove from pot and plant in shade and you may get fall blooms.

FUCHSIA: Like gardenia, should spend the whole summer in the garden. Prune and allow to rest in fall. Keep away from sunny window; keep moist and cool (50° in dormant period).

GERANIUMS: Give them full sun; keep soil on dry side, but spray foliage once or twice weekly and keep faded flowers picked off. Must be potbound to show heavy color. Look for plants with scented leaves: lemon, mint, rose, apple.

GLOXINIA: Distant relative of the African violet; (see page 95).

HYDRANGEA: Does best in bright indirect light, with cool nights. Keep soil very wet with no fertilizing. Difficult to keep flowering as a house plant; put it outside but be prepared for loss at lower than 55°.

HYACINTH: Needs four hours sunlight a day except when flowering, then partial shade. Moisten soil while blooming, then dry out after foliage matures, allow bulb to rest in a paper bag and plant outdoors in fall.

JERUSALEM CHERRY: Bright red or orange berries last for weeks. (They're poisonous.) Likes full sun, outdoors in the summer. Never allow to dry.

KALANCHOE: Another red blossomer likes full sun or part shade—hot and dry. Needs more water during bud-flower stage. Prune back well after flowers fade, put in shade. By September bring to sunny window and water regularly.

LILY OF THE VALLEY: Give them a sunny window and check daily to keep moist while in bloom. Relegate to the garden and buy fresh pips each year.

MARGUERITES: Treat like chrysanthemum.

ORCHIDS: Check the section on orchids, African violets. Cattleya, the most common variety of orchid, blooms November to February, needs at least four hours direct light—but not hot sun, at night temperatures of 55° to 65° and 68° or higher daytime. Keep pot on a humidifying tray and keep medium dry between waterings. Fertilize with high nitrogen.

PEPPER: Ornamental pepper plants with bright green, white, red fruit, which is definitely not edible. Need sun at least four hours daily, and warmer temperatures. Discard after bloom because they are considered annuals.

POINSETTIA: True Christmas plant, keeps its red bracts for at least three months with care. Likes winter sun, no drafts; allow soil to almost dry between thorough waterings. Cut back in spring, repot and fertilize twice a month in spring and summer. To insure more flowers, put in closet or dark corner 16 to 18 hours a day during October.

MINIATURE ROSES: Grow well indoors and may bloom most of the year. Keep moist, fertilize occasionally. Watch for red spider mites. Like bright light.

TUBEROUS BEGONIAS: Wax begonias are very rewarding—like four hours sun a day; rex begonias must be protected from sun. Let wax variety dry slightly between moistening, but others barely damp. When plants are dormant, withhold water. Fertilize during growing season.

Don't feed any newly purchased plant for at least six months. That's because the grower usually forces pots for quick sale, or may have dosed it with a time-release fertilizer that will be good for months. Don't put extra strain on your plant when it has to face so many new conditions.

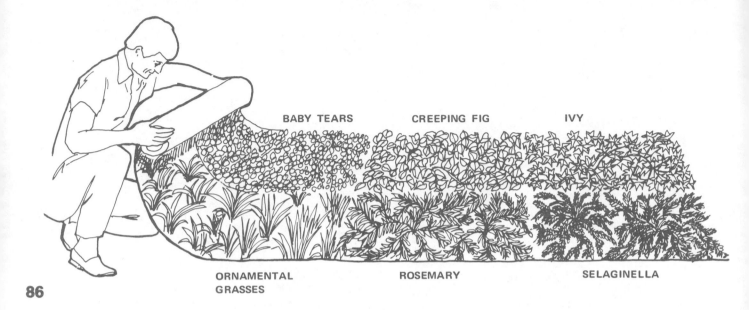

BABY TEARS   CREEPING FIG   IVY

ORNAMENTAL
GRASSES   ROSEMARY   SELAGINELLA

GROUND COVERS

This is a small section on bedding fellows for large pots and tubs, the oversize containers.

Big plants, tall specimens like the monstera, the citrus trees and the philodendrons whose leaves start part way up the trunks, have a naked dirt complex around the base of the plant. A blanket of spreading clubmoss or baby tears, or small-leaf ivy like Hahn's to spill over the edge softens the scene.

Choice of a ground cover should relate to the requirements of the major plant. If the big one gets infrequent waterings, try kangaroo treebine—keeping in mind it needs the discipline of a firm hand to pinch out overvining. Its curly tendrils and dark handsome leaves provide a cool foil for the large bare spaces.

In the section Getting Potted, there are some further suggestions for covering, and the merits of toppers and mulches are discussed.

Fish emulsion fertilizer seems to cut down on the nematode population in the garden.

BABY TEARS, *Soleirolia* (Helxine), also called Japanese or Irish moss, has tiny leaves on slender stems. Horizontal shoots must have contact with the soil, so it won't grow very far over the edge of a container. It is a beautiful clear-pale-green creeper, very effective for covering the area under shade-loving plants; it has to have moisture, however, and so should be used with large specimens which crave water. It is sensitive to cooking or heating gas and dry air and its leaves resent wetting; otherwise it is hardy. Propagation: by division.

CREEPING FIG, *Ficus pumila* or *Ficus repens,* is a woody, sturdy climber with aerial roots, but also covers the soil and becomes a good trailing-over-the-edge plant. Suitable for bottle terrariums, too. Give liberal watering, feeding and shade; the pot's soil should be peaty, with sand. Small heart-shape leaves rarely bothered by insects. Propagation: cuttings.

IVY, *Hedera,* takes many forms, the small varieties most successful as creepers over the soil. English ivy, *Hedera helix,* the most suitable as a ground cover, will do well in a relatively cool interior (subject to spider mites if it lives in a warm room too long). Hahn's ivy is a compact, free-branching type, which falls gracefully over tub edges; this same variety is used as a climber but has to be tied to wires to stay in place. There are miniature variegated ivies, some with mark-ings, others with heart-shape uncut foliage. All do best in cooler rooms; keep roots moist and protect foliage from direct sun. Propagation: by cuttings.

ORNAMENTAL GRASSES, *Acorus gramineus* is a eight- to 10-inch fleshy root plant which looks like a miniature iris without bloom. It will take low or artificial light as well as filtered sun—an ideal soil covering under big specimens which have few lower leaves, like fiddle-leaf fig and philodendron. A variegated type has white markings on the slender dark-green stalks. Also, *Acorus* adapts to planting in a large bottle garden. *Sisyrinchium bellum,* "blue-eyed grass," and *Lagurus ovatus,* "hare's tail," take brighter light and grow in undistinguished soil, as does the *Acorus.* All require plenty of water. Propagation: by division.

ROSEMARY, *Rosmarinus officinalis prostratus,* the creeping herb, has dark-green narrow leaves and light-blue flowers in spring. Plant at the base of a big tub plant which will get full sun. Likes good drainage. Propagation: by cuttings.

SPREADING CLUBMOSS, *Selaginella kraussiana,* a small trailing plant, usually associated with terrarium planting, is also a good ground cover when conditions are shady and moist. It is halfway between a fern and moss in looks, is bright green when healthy and has closely branched stems about six inches long. It's unhappy around gas fumes—give plenty of ventilation. Purchase plants in small pots as starters.

*Rooting hormones have a long
shelf life; don't worry if the
container has stood around
a long time.*

87

HERBED VINEGARS

DRIED LEAVES

HERBS

Most of these are hardy and come through year after year. The list is endowed with an indisputable magic. Each culture in history has its classics, fragrant with stories of herbing in alchemy and medicine.

Today, no self-respecting chef will whip up an appetite teaser without thumbing through the herb index. No fish is festive without its lacing of tarragon or lemon balm; an ordinary hearty soup depends on that bag of bay leaf, garlic, peppercorns, a smidgen of marjoram and some thyme to swim with the onions and carrots.

Herbs for your own experimenting can start with a basic few—a bought rack or a shelf in front of the kitchen window (not bright sun). Four, six or eight are enough to tackle in the beginning. Start with basil, chive, tarragon, mint, marjoram, sage, thyme and rosemary.

If you find heady success, consider lovage (it tastes of celery); peppermint (there's a whole raft of mints which dry well when snipped off, to add to tea); catnip, if you have a feline friend; chervil for the béarnaise sauce; dill to infuse wine vinegar; garlic, oregano and parsley (an ideal plant for a child to grow from seed).

Then there are the herb fanciers' fancies to spice up the doldrums: nasturtiums and dandelions for salads, watercress for a peppery accent, sweet cicely to chop into cold dishes and lavender (try burning a little in the fireplace for old nostalgia's sake).

If your local sources can't come up with a healthy assortment, you can turn to the mail-order firms. One sure supplier is the White Flower Farm, Litchfield, Connecticut 06759; their catalogs are full of much besides herbs, including friendly growing advice on old favorites and new hybrids (see page 54).

Preserving herbs is an ancient and important ritual. Dry them by hanging loose bunches in a warm shaded airy place; strip the dried leaves into glass jars with tight lids. Make herb vinegars by stuffing a bottle and covering with either wine or cider variety.

BASIL, SWEET *(Ocimum basilicum)* Small bushy plant with golden-green leaves, sometimes shiny as if they had been sprayed with a fragrant oil. Leaves grow up to two inches long, but are best used when they are young (be sure to leave at least two on the stem of plant to encourage new growth). Give partial shade, well-drained planting mixture with a little sand added, and weak, liquid fish emulsion once or twice a month. Plant remains bushy if buds are pinched back and seed not allowed to set. Wash the basil once a week under sink spray to keep it insect free. Likes a sunny window.

CHIVE *(Allium schoenoprasum)* Long, thin, hollow, green leaves constantly grow from tiny bulbs planted many to a pot. Plan to buy a growing pot at your supermarket; when it's home, remove and repot the chives into a four-inch clay pot, adding rich loam and never letting it dry out. To keep up growing action, trim chives often whether you use them or not (try quick-freezing cuttings in a small sandwich bag); too-tall leaves start going over the edge literally and the plant looks unkempt. A blooming chive produces lavender pom-poms, giving you a supply of cut flowers from your own kitchen. Keep chives away from cats; they'll nibble the greens down to the root.

MARJORAM, SWEET *(Organum majorana)* Oval leaves in soft gray-green on woody stems. Small white flowers are followed by tiny brown seeds (that you can propagate for gifts). Leaves, soft and velvety, may be gathered whenever you need, but for drying take them in the summer. Marjoram is a perennial which does well in slightly alkaline soil; plants can be started from cuttings or seeds. To prevent from getting too big or too heavy, keep blossoms cut off and plant trimmed. Grow in full sun and keep moist.

MINT *(Mentha)* A hardy perennial that has many variables, including orange, or bergamot (slightly like oranges) with lavender bloom; golden apple, variegated yellow-green; peppermint, strong-scented, three-inch toothed leaves and purple spike flowers; spearmint, dark-green and crinkly, used in jelly and with lamb. Pennyroyal, downy oval leaves and rosy flowers, said to repel bugs; Corsican mint, very tiny and creeping like a moss, with purple bloom and sagelike fragrance. Mint likes rich soil, shade and moisture. Propagate with cuttings, division.

OREGANO (*Origanum vulgare,* also called wild marjoram.) A perennial with dark coarse leaves, it is shrubby and has many little stems that cause a thicket. Grow oregano in full sun in well-drained garden soil or packaged soil mix. Give routine watering and remember to cut it back to encourage a nice roundness and thick foliage. Replace about every three years when it gets woody, by dividing or grow new plants from seeds.

PARSLEY *(Petroselinum crispum)* Grows six to 10 inches in a pot and with leaves tightly curled and ruffled; an Italian variety is more like a young fern. Although parsley is often used as a garnish, it has high vitamin value: more A and C than oranges, also lots of iron. Grow from seeds (at least three weeks to germinate) or buy a small pot and replace it once a year. Will grow in sun or shade; prefers coolness and fresh air. Evenly moisten with warm water. Chinese or Spanish parsley (cilantro) is a different plant altogether and may be grown from coriander seeds.

HANGER OF WOOD WITH HOLES CUT FOR POTS

ROSEMARY *(Rosmarinus officinalis)* Grey-green needle foliage, grows to a rugged 15-inch shrub with soft blue flowers in spring. Plant in ordinary well-drained soil and feed biweekly. Partial shade or full kitchen-window sun; add a little lime once a month on the surface—wood ashes a nice treat also. Makes a nice ground cover for larger plants.

SAGE *(Salvia officinalis)* Grows larger than a good window herb should, unless you cut it back firmly. Grey-green oval leaves, one to two inches long, with blue-violet flowers. Also interesting: pineapple sage, a tender perennial with fragrant leaves and blossoms. Sage is satisfied with ordinary soil, well drained, and full sun (overwatering may cause mildew). Cut back stems after blooming, and fertilize if you cut often. Propagate from stem cuttings, seeds.

TARRAGON *(Artemisia dracunculus)* French tarragon is a horizontal plant, woody; it creeps along on rhizomes. Slender, dark, shiny leaves, very aromatic, with green-white flowerlets rarely appearing. Prefers moderately rich soil, good drainage, and full or partial sun. Propagate from cuttings, divisions—not seeds.

THYME *(Thymus vulgaris)* Low growing and often used as a ground cover, thyme is semi-woody, shrubby and a perennial which grows six to 12 inches and has oval greyish leaves, only a quarter-inch long, and flower spikes. Grow in well-drained soil, without too much watering. Cut back growing tips to keep bushy. Propagate from cuttings taken in the summer or from seeds. Look for other varieties: lemon thyme and wild thyme.

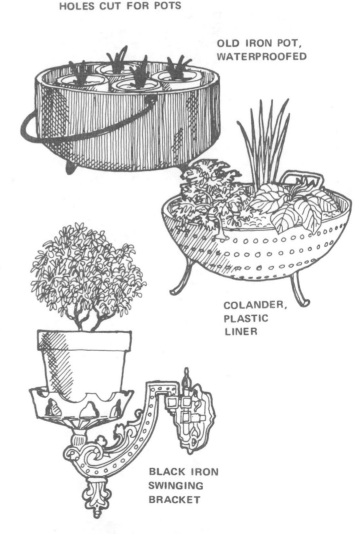

OLD IRON POT, WATERPROOFED

COLANDER, PLASTIC LINER

BLACK IRON SWINGING BRACKET

INDOOR/OUTDOOR PLANTS

The rotation theory works like a charm for many house plants; at flowering time, for example, bring in the bulb family, the fuchsias, hydrangeas and azaleas. In fact, most of the hardy types perform nobly when brought in, bright with blossom, for show-and-tell.

Also, there are plants of tropic origin which should be protected in winter. If they require dark periods, they may hibernate in the basement or be stored in the pool house with a polyethylene covering to ward off freezing.

There is another group which, although they're commonly put into the ground outside, *will* make handsome indoor plants. The only drawback is that they grow more slowly inside—an asset, actually, if you don't have much space. You can pamper them by sending them to summer camp in your garden or in a window box or on a sunny stoop. Plants in pots of moderate size do best in the garden when the pot is incorporated right into the plant bed up to its rim; come fall and they're returned to the house, you simply clean the dirt off (or repot, if it seems necessary) and reinstate in honor.

Bring the big plants in from the terrace, under the overhang or near the entry during the holidays or when they show signs of feeling the cold. If the container needs dressing up, double-pot it into a larger tub or basket with a liner rather than repotting; the larger container will also catch excess water and protect floors. Add a top dressing of peat moss, beach rocks or bark to cover the soil. Massing several plants of a kind where they will reflect in mirrors or windows or a waxed floor will give you double for your effort. To help them live in this temporary environment, give them a cool location and add artificial light.

Don't be afraid to experiment. Enjoy *big* plants. The surprise of having the indoor company of large-scale plants (move out a chair or a chest and try the foliage as a piece of new furniture) is enhanced by a new awareness of the plant itself. Add a strand of tiny white Christmas tree lights or a concealed spotlight—and you've created *theatre.*

Sow bugs sometimes set up housekeeping in summered pots. Try a drench of Diazinon (half the amount recommended on label) a week before bringing plants indoors.

91

Pineapple: If you started a plant from the top of a commercial fruit, remember that it is a giant plant, not likely to give out bloom in a small pot. Instead, look for Ananas nanus, *a smaller species that will flower.*

When plants are outside in summer, near a swimming pool, don't be tempted to add water from the pool. The chlorine will do them in.

92

BAMBOO, *Phyllostachys aurea,* is the most popular outdoor bamboo grown in the west, but will do fine indoors if given good light, a once-a-week soaking and good drainage. Bamboos should be double-potted in an outside container of ceramic or wood. It grows slowly in the house or apartment to about five feet. The stalks, or culms, are gold-yellow; long, thin, pale-green leaves move in the slightest breeze. Bamboo like being potbound—the more crowded, the faster the growth. Cut back older culms to allow the new growth. For filtered sun and privacy, plant bamboo in a long floor plant box, placed either inside or outside a big window. Propagation: by division, rhizomes.

FATSIA, *Aralia japonica* or *Aralia sieboldi,* usually a patio tub plant, is equally dynamic wintering inside. It looks most impressive as a loner with no competition, because it is never a commonplace plant. The fatsia, or aralia, commands attention in a big tub or jar. It is possible to train the young plant by pinching if you want it bushy; otherwise it develops long, graceful curving trunks. Small white flowers are followed by shiny black fruit. Will grow in full shade or filtered light (too much sunlight causes lackluster yellowish leaves). Propagation: by cuttings.

FERN PINE, *Podocarpus elongata,* is a tall, thin evergreen, a tree form of slightly irregular growth habit with ferny foliage. Versatile, like the bamboo, it can give any room a vertical greening, live indoors or be moved out and be kept to the height you want by pinching back or pruning. Combine it in a tub or container with large ferns and shade-loving ornamentals. Keep out of hot sun, away from sea air, frosts. Young plant needs staking and a good mulching over the roots, but when mature is quite tough. Seedlings start in terrariums. Propagation: by cuttings.

GOLD DUST PLANT, *Aucuba japonica,* is a hardy shrub two to three feet tall, ideal for a tub on a balcony or a cool hallway. The gold dust is named for the yellowish specks on its oval or oblong evergreen leaves, which are toothed above the middle. Being informal and irregular, it fits interiors with wood paneling or brick and combines well with hardy ferns. It is considered a rough diamond among gardeners, but its good behavior inside and out makes it worth including on this list. It winters well indoors in a north window; put in full shade outdoors in spring after the frost and protect from sunburn. Plant in well-drained acid soil. Propagation: by cuttings.

HYDRANGEA, more likely to reach you from a florist than a nursery, is a bold shrub with huge blossoms which show off best indoors; it then moves out to the garden until the next buds appear. Blossoms of the French hybrids are brilliant hues of reds, blues and violets. My favorite is a green-white which I accidentally grew from one blossom and stem left too long in water. It rooted and now fills a 10-inch pot in less than 18 months later. Hydrangeas grow in rich porous soil and respond to fertilizing and generous watering. Aluminum sulphate added during bloom will turn colors deeper. Shade from the sun. Propagation: by cuttings.

LILY OF THE NILE, *Agapanthus orientalis,* has clusters of superb blue or white blossoms on regal two-foot stems rising out of a fountain-shape whirl of leaves—impressive with or without bloom. Good for large rooms or decks because the foliage requires space; two or three banked make a beautiful display for a party. It is sold at nurseries as an accent plant for the garden, but will pot up for indoor blooming. Plants flower faster if the pot is filled with roots; keep them moist and fertilize every two weeks when color shows. Give at least four hours sun, 68° to 72°. The dried flower stalk is used in arrangements with dried weeds and baby breath. Propagation: by divisions, February or March.

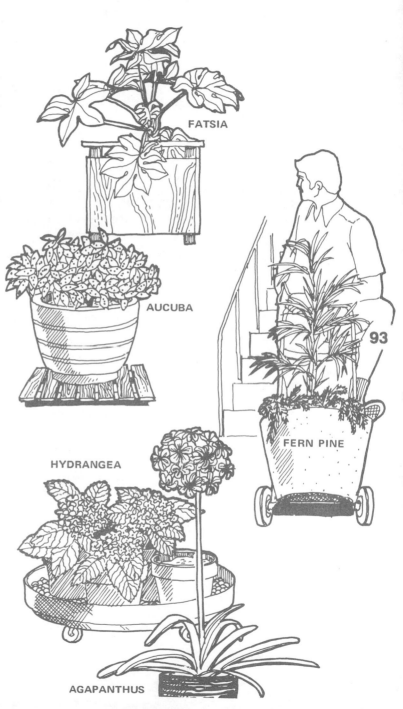

FATSIA

AUCUBA

93

FERN PINE

HYDRANGEA

AGAPANTHUS

ORCHIDS AND GESNERIADS

These are members of the two most exclusive plant clubs you can join. Orchid one-upmanship includes boarding out plants to specialists when one can't be around to personally tend and love. For pure snob appeal, ownership of some of the exotics represents achievement—not money, but mastering the wily ways of growing them. They are difficult to coax into flower, but they have iron constitutions, and with the aid of humidifiers and plant lights you can wade your way through the 20,000 or more species, with success.

Gesneriads, which include gloxinia, African violets (not *true* violets, incidentally), columneas, achimenes, streptocarpus and a hundred more tropicals, are the blooming beauties whose owners are hooked once they specialize. Gesneriads like moist higher temperature, at least 60° and up to 70° at night.

Ventilation is important to orchids because they are children of air and light; some, like the phalaenopsis, have no mechanism for taking in nutrients yet they rarely stop growing. They demand higher-daytime, lower-nighttime temperatures. In the case of orchids with stems, like the cattleyas, dendrobium, odontoglossum and the calanthe, the plant takes in organic compounds during daylight which it breaks down later. If you fall in love with orchids, be prepared to give love in exchange for lavish bloom.

Fresh air is beneficial if it does not change the temperature but beware of drafts. Orchids absorb water through leaf surfaces as well as roots. Once the plant shows growth and new roots appear, more watering and misting is in order. Some orchids take to terrarium living, and with added light live long and happy lives.

Gesneriads' clan appeals to housewives, shut-ins, businessmen and diffident individuals who prefer the Bentley to the Rolls Royce, but with the same fierce loyalty. The varieties are endless, and the results testify to their popularity.

ORCHID

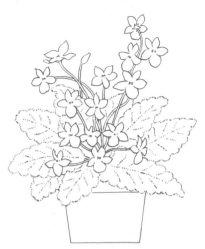

AFRICAN VIOLETS (Gesneriads)

A temperamental little plant, *Saintpaulia ionantha* has probably challenged more lovers of small house plants than any other variety. Listening to an African violet connoisseur enumerate his problems and his conquests completely turns off most of us.

However, the current breakthrough of successful growth of plants like *Saintpaulia* under artificial light puts a whole new perspective on one's consciousness of its charm. Plant physiologists have proved that three 40-watt incandescent bulbs placed above a group of pots will double the number of blossoms. Commercial fluorescent phosphor lights (see section Keep it Light) like Gro-Lux, Plant-Light and Plant-Gro have become bywords with amateurs; 600 foot-candles or more will perform the miracle. A dark hall, given two fluorescent tubes and incandescent lights shielded by translucent glass will take care of a whole collection—not to mention plants like cyclamen, flowering maple and bougainvillea.

Saintpaulia likes warm nights and day temperatures of 70° or higher. If your pots are wick-watered (violets should be warm-watered from the bottom), let wick become dry before refilling the saucer. Plant in a commercial African-violet mixture and buy special violet food (tiny amounts at each watering).

Propagation: by leaf or plantlets.

GLOXINIA (Gesneriads)

Sinningia speciosa is also known as the "florist gloxinia" and next to African violet is the most popular member of the gesneriad family. Large, inverted bell-shape flowers rising out of a rosette of velvety leaves are white or purple, and rarely in the red spectrum. These flowers may reach five inches across; some are ruffled, frilled or striped. The plant is considered a flat one, usually growing not more than a foot above the pot.

Sinningia eumorpha is most easily found in nurseries and plant boutiques; its white-tinged-in-purple blooms which appear in profusion above glossy green leaves most of the summer, earn its popularity. *Sinningia discolor* has flowers in a broad tube shape, mostly bluish-purple. *Gloxinera* (the result of hybridizing *Sinningia* and *Rechsteineria*) is a closely related genus whose flowers are tubular scarlet, orange or yellow; it makes a rather special house decoration.

Gloxinia lives well in an east or west window, with 70° temperature and ample humidity. Water by soaking, then let almost dry before repeating; keep water away from leaves. Potting medium of loam with a handful of peat and one of sand will take care of the annual repotting.

Propagation: tubers, potted in January, one to a six-inch pot with a fourth of the tuber above soil; buds in a month, to late spring. Rest in semi-shade until September, water and watch for October bloom.

95

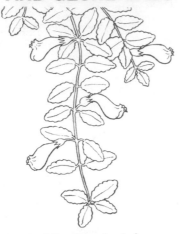

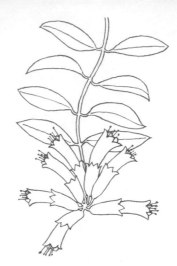

HYPOCYRTA (Gesneriads)

A friendly little plant whose name has been changed recently to *Nematanthus;* requires 75° days and light feeding at each watering while blooming. It has trailing strands, glossy thick leaves and unusual pouched red and orange flowers that look like tiny helmets. Most easily located would be the goldfish plant *(Alloplectus nummularia),* sometimes deciduous in fall, with red blossoms having a black and yellow line around a narrow throat. Nodules like tubers form on stems.

Hypocyrta makes a cheery basket in spring with its clear hues and shiny foliage. A massing of several plants, hung at different levels, will deliver a blaze of color. It needs constant warmth 24 hours a day, and a minimum of 60°; any drop in temperature or a draft will slow growth. With minimum watering and some sun, there's little to do but wait for the blossoms. Humidity is essential and the higher the temperature, the more spray-misting is called for. It is difficult to water these trailing plants without wetting leaves; if you can't take down a basket, use a watering can with very thin nose so you can reach right in to the soil.

Propagation: by seed sown in fall. Or a leaf cutting, its stem shortened to one inch and dipped in rooting hormone and a fungicide, is set in a moist sterile mix in a two-inch pot and all enclosed in plastic bag for three days; open bag, wait for roots to form in two weeks and repot in rich soil mix.

LIPSTICK PLANT (Gesneriads)

Aeschynanthus does best in a greenhouse because it loves warm humid living, but if you place it in a bath or dressing room where there may be moisture part of the day, it will bend over backward, literally, to please. Amusing four-inch blossoms open slowly from purple to red. It is an epiphytic, a tree-growing plant of the tropics, with waxy leaves on trailing stems.

Aeschynanthus lobbianus is considered more desirable than *Aeschynanthus pulcher* which has larger leaves and vermilion blossoms with yellow throat; *Aeschynanthus grandiflora* has a larger bloom of orange-yellow.

Besides asking for plenty of moisture, lipstick responds to moderate-to-warm, draft-free room space. Like others of the gesnariads, bright light but no sun is in order. Water carefully to keep droplets off leaves; it does best with a good soaking (room temperature), then holding off until the soil is almost dry. Small pots take more attention. Growth slows down in winter, but by March a series of monthly feedings will bring it right up to trim.

All gesnariads can be demanding and are worth devoting yourself to only if you recognize their remarkable blooming pattern and velvety character.

Propagation: leaf cuttings.

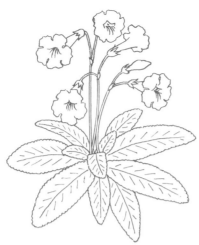

STREPTOCARPUS (Gesneriads)

A South African visitor, only recently adapted to house planting, *Streptocarpus* is the fun member of the gesneriad tribe. It may have tiny leaves, rosettes of medium size or a single great leaf up to 24 inches in length and a foot wide, covered with a deep velvet and blossoms popping right out of the leaf! Flowers are stemmed or stemless in different varieties, but mostly they are long graceful tubes with flaring mouth, in brick-red, white with purple hairs, mauve, pale green with violet, and pale blue to purple.

Streptocarpus saxorum (also called "Cape Primrose") grows to 20 inches tall and has delicate lavender four-petal flowers whose long buds are horizontal at the ends of long slim stems. The bloom may last six months starting in fall. *Streptocarpus rexii* has 10-inch-long velvety leaves in a rosette with large mauve blossoms, also on long dark stems.

Temperatures of 65° to 80°, in a moist atmosphere, are most appreciated. These are humus-demanding herbs with a shallow root system; they are for the most part perennials but should be repotted annually. A good mix consists of two parts loam, two parts coarse sand and one-and-one-half parts peat moss. Tolerates not-too-hot sun, constant moisture but never saturation and a heavy hand on the mist spray.

Propagation: divisions, seeds, leaf cuttings.

ORCHIDS

To deal properly with orchids would take a whole book. Frankly, if you're just coming out of the purple-thumb haze, hold off until you feel you're ready for the Mercedes-Benz of the plant families—and ready to spend money and attention.

Plants can be found for a nominal five dollars and up; rare ones are real purse-busters. The pansy orchid, *Miltonia*, grows lovely blossoms on a "spray" (the trade name is spray orchid); it is exotic enough to please a beginner. *Oncidium*, butterfly orchid, and *Epidendrum* are pleasurable miniature blooms dancing on long curving stems. *Cypripedium* will flower in average comfortable temperature while *Cymbidium* and *Odontoglossum* require a cool room; *Vanda* (those small lavender beauties so ever present in Hawaii), *Dendrobium* and *Phalaenopsis* want a higher temperature. *Cymbidium* and *Cypripedium* grow in porous soil; the others are air plants and must be potted up in osmunda fibre or a similar material.

When you start acquiring, try for plants which will bloom at different times of the year. Most commercial orchid growers give directions for growth, cultivation and temperature extremes. And to repeat, orchids must have ventilation, even on winter days; watering, spray-misting and humidity are critical items. One unexpected bonus: orchids have fragrance —something not recognizable in a florist's blossom because the smell has been chilled out.

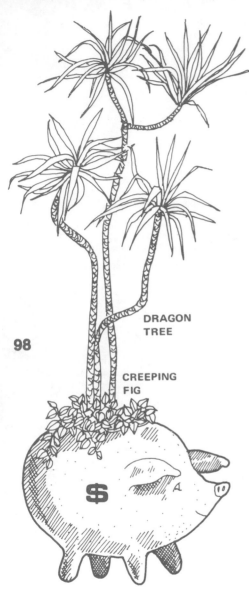

DRAGON
TREE

CREEPING
FIG

STATUS PLANTS

There will always be one group of earlier-than-thou enthusiasts in every crowd—people whose noses can spot a trend, an *in* idea developing. Indoor planting is not immune from this group. In fact, it is a hotbed of one-upping because there are so many thousands of choices. The status plant appears to be of more interest to men. Over half the expensive specimens bought in New York plant sources are owned by men. Plant élitists have special permits to hunt orchids or rarities halfway around the globe, bringing 'em back alive.

Decorators invest in private nurseries, the better to status the green scene for a wealthy lady in Texas or a social leader in Pebble Beach. The list of *in* plants changes weekly, and what one group likes now may be discarded tomorrow because it is too copied. For instance, West Coast suppliers are hard put to cope with the demand for giant prickly pear whose tortured form is the lastest symbol of chic—while just around the corner in the wings, the aspidistra may suddenly emerge once again as the love object of status people.

The tremendous growth of specialized plant boutiques and the rental circuit has given new excitement to the chase. Tall plants for contemporary two-story rooms, or the high-ceilinged brownstones and Victorians, are very much sought after. (One can cheat by buying a cheaper specimen and giving it platform soles with a pedestal.)

What happens if the plant goes out of fashion? Move it to the bath or a bedroom. Or, a severe pruning like a sharp haircut can transform an old plant to tree form, barely recognizable and newly acceptable.

The plant case histories in this section are offered without any social Neilsen ratings. Set your own trend by acquiring what *you* like—that's superstatus.

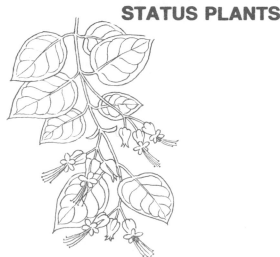

APHELANDRA

Zebra plant is a show-off, a rare and unusual union of white-veined, shiny, dark foliage and awesome, square, terminal flower spikes, up to eight inches of brilliant yellow with red-painted edges; each petal grows at exactly 90 degrees to the next one. Its formal elegance made it a favorite of Victorian conservatories, and the seventies have furnished precisely the climate for its return.

Aphelandra squarrosa louisae and hybrids like Brockfeld, Dania and Fritz Prinsler are the most popular yellow blossoming; *Aphelandra aurantiaca* is a scarlet beauty and *Aphelandra aurantiaca roezlii* an orange-scarlet. All bear flowers for about six weeks in fall, occasionally in summer. Feed twice a year.

After flowering, keep the plant growing until late winter, then take four-inch cuttings from the tips to start a new plant. This is a prima donna which charms for one season, but will rarely live to give more. Filtered light and high humidity are a must. Potting soil should be two parts peat, one part package mix and one part sharp sand or perlite. Fertilize every two weeks when in flower. Keep evenly moist (never let them dry out) from March through October because they wilt easily. Use a humidifying tray to boost the moisture level.

Propagation: tip cuttings.

CLERODENDRON

Clerodendrum thomsoniae is a twining vine of remarkable determination; in one season it will rise up from the pot to the ceiling unless you exercise your prerogatives and pinch it back in line. It carries winter-white flowers like balloons at the bottom and flaring red tips. Clerodendron is fairly large, stays best at three feet and will rivet the attention in a plump Japanese pot; if you have space, you may let it have its head, but give it plant supports. This particular variety will also transform into a hanging basket synonymous with its other name, glory bower. If given enough warmth (65° day and night), it will bloom for weeks in late winter; otherwise blossoms appear intermittently, on old wood, during spring and summer.

Clerodendrum bungei blooms red in summer, and *Clerodendrum fragrans pleniflorum,* which has the fragrance of hyacinth, blooms with blue-white flowers on and off during the year.

Clerodendron likes warmth, four hours of sun. It should be potted in rich loam and fertilized monthly with well-decomposed manure. Soil should be moist during growing season when new leaves are showing and buds forming, and dryer when the plant is resting.

Propagation: from stem cuttings in spring.

99

DRAGON TREE

Dracaena marginata is the renegade of the dracaenas: its trunks grow vertically for awhile, then veer out as if they want a new direction in life—and later return to a normal tree pattern. This tree can be a grotesque structure when there are several trunks, each doing its own thing at different times.

The huge tufts of very long flat leaves at the upper reaches of each sparsely branched trunk are burnished fountains of green. This sophisticated large-tub plant is ideal for studio, an office reception area or an indoor balcony. It is ornamental and woody. Each tub should contain at least three, preferably at different stages, to stagger leaf tops.

The dragon tree is rugged, but care must be taken to protect the stubby tap root. The tree will grow under almost any condition but does best in a rich well-drained soil. Leaf edges will brown-spot if they get too much sun; keep them shiny clean with a damp sponge and soapy water. If tips brown, look for water without fluorides.

This branch of the dracaenas is closely related to the ti plant, *Cordyline terminalis,* in appearance and habit, but the latter has a creeping rootstock and broad leaves more like the palm's. Look for *Cordyline australis* and *Cordyline indivisa* as dynamic hardy substitutes if you can't find or afford *D. marginata.*

Progapation: pieces of stems with a bud or top cutting of an old plant.

DWARF BANANA

Finding a banana takes perseverance and getting it to fruit indoors healthily requires patience—and a minor miracle. Don't be drawn by extravagant ads that promise a boatload in a jiffy. Rather, seeds of the *Musa* variety can be bought from reputable suppliers, and you can grow the tree just to prove your prowess. Germination is erratic, anywhere from a week to four months. They need bottom heat, about 85° under the seed pan; to maintain this, keep a thermometer handy and put layers of insulation between pan and heat source.

One offbeat problem: if you *do* get a crop of bananas, they will give off ethylene gases which won't hurt you but will upset other nearby plants, particularly a papaya. Nothing is easy.

Even if your plantation has no crops, raising a banana, like raising coffee trees is status insurance.

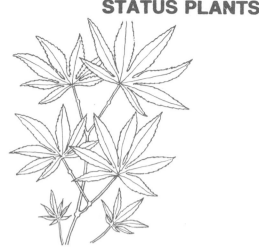

FLOWERING TOBACCO

True tobacco is a large coarse plant, but the dwarf types are refined and add an exotic profusion when used as a grouping of several pots. For instance, put together six or eight of the dwarf *Nicotiana alata grandiflora,* perennials with large tubular blossoms which rise above the relatively small 10-inch plants on dark-green stick stems. Blossoms may be pink or white, wine-red or lime-green, chocolate-brown or chartreuse. Leaves are hairy and sticky ovals like petunia foliage, four to six inches long.

The flowers nearly close on sunny days and open at dusk. A variety called orange blossom will grow to 18 inches, has dainty scented white flowers and grows happily in pots. If the blossoms are cut for a table centerpiece, they stay open.

Unlike most foliage plants, flowering tobacco likes a short day—at least 14 hours of darkness is needed to encourage the blooms. Give filtered sun, enriched soil and plenty of moisture. Watch for white flies; apply a soapy solution of nicotine insecticide if plants are invaded.

Propagation: by seeds in flats, or seedlings started outdoors and potted when they are six inches tall.

JAPANESE MAPLE

It's a tossup whether the Japanese maple or the weeping Java fig is the more romantic tree for indoors. The fig *(Ficus benjamina)* is easier to grow, but both have style and decorative charm rarely found in tree form. (Maple trunks are fairly straight and architectural, the fig's go in several directions in the course of growing.)

The delicate airy foliage of the maple, *Acer palmatum,* gives all-year interest next to a floor-to-ceiling window; inside the house leaves may not defoliate as they do in the garden. Young growth is glowing red, summer leaves are a soft green and in fall they show red again. The new branchlets are a warm red-brown and the saw-toothed leaves backlighted are magical.

Japanese maple takes to filtered sunlight and not too much warmth. It can stand a good weekly watering and feeding about every two months except when it is resting. One trunk in a 15-inch box will look lonely, so put two one-gallon cans and one five-gallon can together to add interest.

Lean soil keeps the tree slow-growing. Prune branches to develop planes of foliage for the best silhouette and so you can see through the window to the garden or view beyond.

 101

KENTIA PALM

A specimen *Howeia Forsteriana* or *Howeia belmoreana,* all grandeur and tropical magnificence, is just what the doctor (or lawyer or merchant or thief) orders when the chips are up. This is the standby palm for concert stage, weddings and white-tie-and-tails entertaining. Rental florists bundle up tubs of kentias in layers of newspapers and cart them to and from great events in good and bad weather; the palms survive over and over again.

Most large containers are made up of several plants, with a large palm surrounded by smaller ones to fill in the base. Another spectacular is the *Rhapis flabelliformis,* lady palm, which can reach 18 feet indoors, and the *Chamaedorea erumpens,* bamboo palm, for areas of limited light, but with a steady 75° temperature. These are expensive; if you develop a yearning for a big palm start putting larger denominations in the piggybank.

The most active growing time for the kentia is during the warmest weather. In May and June remove old fronds and give a dose of liquid well-decomposed manure. Plant a palm in a deep tub or box for root room. Spray-mist occasionally, and keep leaves clean by washing to avoid scale and mealy bug. In summer move the plant to a warm porch or patio in a shaded windless spot. Use yearly top-dressing technique to renew the soil surface, and repot only if rootbound so water doesn't soak through.

NILE GRASS OR UMBRELLA PLANT

Cyperus alternifolius is related to the ancient Egyptian papyrus, the plant from which paper was made. A waterborn, bushy plant whose natural habitat is marshy ground, it was first introduced into the hothouse tradition 200 years ago from Madagascar. In order to live well, Nile grass should be planted in soil, but the pot must be set in a deep container of water with liquid fertilizer added. Its umbrella-like leaves welcome a frequent misting (add a little granular charcoal to the water to keep it from souring).

Nile grass is a clump of stiff stems with narrow palm-form leaves radiating from the top of the stem like the ribs of an umbrella (the name umbrella is also given to the schefflera, mentioned in the section on Apartment Plants). There are flowers, too, which bloom from June to October, and they are also umbrellas; don't let them run to seed because it will weaken the parent plant.

Its free-growth habits and massing are a fine decorative shape worth cultivating. Count on a height of about four feet. Prefers semishade, cool temperatures of 60°, and all-important moisture; it will be fair game for bugs if it dries out. Plant in rich soil, in smaller pots than usual for a plant this size. Trim off brown leaf tips without harming rest of the plant.

Propagation: by division; leaf rosettes will root in soil or water.

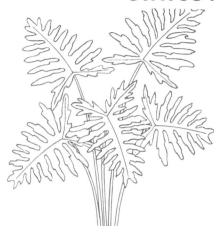

SCREW PINE

Pandanus veitchii is another look-down-on decorative accent which the Victorians described as a "stately, fine-looking stove plant." The sword-shape leaves are very long and narrow, dark green banded with white, and edged with short spines; they spiral out from a short stem, each new leaf moving around the stem like the threads of a screw.

Pandanus will grow at least two feet tall and the same across, and may eventually outgrow those dimensions; a small pot will hold back root development. It doesn't seem to mind poor soil (but that's no reason to deprive it) and moderate temperature. However it is particular about constant warmth in the winter resting period, and is fussy about water standing in the axils of the leaves which will invite rot (just the opposite of bromeliads). Keep soil very moist in summer, a warm 75° and add misting to the list. A little sun goes a long way and don't overdo it, particularly on hot days.

The screw pine has exposed "prop" roots from the stem, a family characteristic. If the plant becomes so rootbound that the root cap starts coming out of the top of the pot, shift to a larger container.

Propagation: by offshoots which look like rosettes, in warm weather; pot up in compost-type soil with added peat moss.

PHILODENDRON SELLOUM

The *Philodendron* is the largest, most popular and easiest-to-grow family of house plants, but many are so common they have little magnetism. Two large-leaf forms are the darlings of decorators.

The *Philodendron selloum,* usually specified by landscape architects for oversize containers in paved terraces and courts of contemporary buildings, is also radiantly at home in the company of antiques or stainless-steel furniture. The polished deeply indented leaves, rising up from a central crown at soil level, grow up to two feet long and 18 inches wide.

Philodendron hastatum rubrum is a climbing giant with arrowhead leaves up to 18 inches long of a soft maroon cast, red undersides and sometimes reddish stems. One which we had in the studio blossomed on rare occasion with such overwhelming fragrance you could tell in another part of the building the instant it happened.

Philodendrons want good light, without too much sun, and ample watering. Pot in a mixture of packaged soil, peat and sand; feed only lightly. Keep a philodendron's leaves dust-free and polished to attract admiring glances. As the lower leaves finally drop on older plants, cut off the top, leaving a short stub; the top can be rooted and replanted. The stub will start leafing again. Air-layering is also used to root the top before it is separated from its old stem; do this in spring or summer.

103

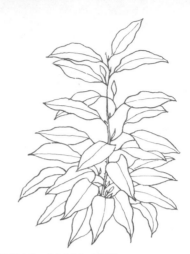

SILK OAK

If there's a really "cool" status plant, it must be the willowy *Grevillea robusta,* a lacy tree with silver-green ferny leaves, on curving branches. The silk oak is an excellent transition plant at an entrance, in a summer room or on a protected balcony, provided the temperature doesn't soar. It likes cool, fairly light conditions and ample waterings. The leaves will drop off if it's allowed to dry out and the only answer then is to cut the top off the tree, root it as a cutting.

It can be propagated from seeds available from mail-order houses (see page 54), and will attain a nice size within a year. Under ideal conditions, you can hope eventually to grow a 10-foot tree, but be pleased when it reaches six. Give it space, a special container with rich garden loam (sterilized to remove any foreign agents) and an important location. Remember to turn the plant each week so it grows straight and doesn't lean toward the light. To encourage branching, pinch out center growing point when it is several inches tall.

Never apply so much water it is soaking wet. Just play it on the moist side, misting as needed. Filtered sun, from either east or west window, is acceptable. Silk oaks do blossom, rarely indoors.

Propagation: by seeds, during July and August.

WEEPING JAVA FIG

Most prestigious of the *Ficus* family is the *benjamina,* a lovely pendulous tree with bark similar to the birch. It branches gracefully and carries long, glossy, willowlike leaves with thin wisps at the end that turn backward; new leaves are a pale, delicate apple-green.

Benjamina is not an easy addition to a household and must be treated gently when introduced to new surroundings. It likes to stay in one place, once the conditions are right. So, if your new baby starts to shed, do not be unduly disturbed: it will calm down eventually and proceed to live right and delight.

This tree likes a moderately high humidity and soil moist to the touch. Grow it in medium light, never bright sun, and it will reach eight feet, so mark off a large space for its exclusive use.

Plant in ordinary garden loam or packaged mix. Practice the water-let-dry-water method. You may discover it will need a stake to assist the narrow woody stem and branches. Keep the leaves dusted. If it shows signs of unhappiness, it will start shedding; try another location.

Ficus nitida, a small-leaf cousin usually chosen as a compact street tree in moderate climates, grows well in tub, preferably rootbound to keep the size in hand; use in pairs for formal decor.

TERRARIUMS AND BOTTLE GARDENS

The terrarium is a miniature greenhouse which sets up a complete environment, a handsome theatre for plants and a dust-free, care-free space. You look through the glass at arrangements which would ordinarily be lost in a forest of small pots.

The principle of the mini-greenhouse is that of a covered jar: the glass lets in the light and moisture evaporates from the soil and transpires from the leaves. This water condenses on the sides and the top of the glass, runs back down to the soil and is used over and over by the plant in a perpetual-motion cycle.

Terrariums and bottle gardens are primarily for collections of small plants. Large glass cases with special microclimates for larger specimens have been produced commercially, costing over $800. Coffee tables made of upturned half-domes of plexiglas and covered with thick circles of glass measure a yard across. The container size depends on *your* space and what *you* want to plant.

The tiny pill bottle may house one precious fern; kids make terrariums out of discarded aquariums, adding turtles, salamanders or snakes to the planted scene. Kits come complete with glass or plastic container, special soil mix, charcoal and instructions on how to plant. But, if you have an old battery jar, candy glass, brandy snifter, coffee-maker—in fact any glass which you can roof over partially or entirely with glass, you can put together your own mini-arboretum.

Bottles have become popular because they can be corked, or left with a little air space. Tools which help you thread plants through the bottle neck simplify installing a bottle garden. The earth is removed from the roots and the leaves folded around and carefully lowered; the trick is to keep the soil off the bottle so the glass is clean. Wine jugs, demijohns and tall liqueur bottles are starters.

Rather than chance harsh deterrents, do your planting in special ready-mix soil substitutes available everywhere. They insure drainage and the proper organic ingredients to provide healthy growth.

ALTERNANTHERA, *Alternanthera amoena,* less well known as "Joseph's coat," is a happy dwarf with varicolored small pointed leaves in a compact mass; responds to pruning to keep size reasonable, about eight to 12 inches tall; colors are mixtures of cream, rose, red, purple and green. Give average to bright sun; plant in standard potting mixture and keep moist. Propagation: stem cuttings.

ALUMINUM PLANT, *Pilea cadierei,* is neat and bushy —well covered with striped or spotted silvery-marked leaves, a good contrast plant with leafy greens. Grows to nine inches, takes warmth, humidity, ample watering; package soil mixture best medium. Propagation: root cuttings.

ARTILLERY PLANT, *Pilea microphylla,* grows close to the soil, to about 10 inches tall; mini-foliage is light green and fernlike. Small clusters of blossoms appear at leaf joints, exploding little clouds of pollen when touched. Keep soil moist, not soaked; in restricted light it will live for months without changing size. Propagation: root cuttings.

CALATHEA, *Calathea roseo-picta,* is a close cousin of maranta, or arrowroot, and is most at home in a terrarium. Botanically it is a dwarf variety but will grow to a showy eight inches, admired for its distinctively-marked oval leaves with pointed ends. Give moist conditions, partial shade, rich loam with proven drainage. Propagation: by division.

CRYPTANTHUS, *Cryptanthus zonatus zebrinus,* zebra-marked member of the bromeliads, has crinkly leaves marked with bands of white, green and brown. *Cryptanthus bivittas minor* has similar structure, but striping is the length of the leaf with a lighter-colored middle strip. This stemless, small-to-medium plant is used to cover area under taller selections. Does well in sunny window or shade. Propagation: offshoots.

FITTONIA, *Fittonia verschaffelti,* is a creeper, wide spreading and low growing. Shiny dark leaves have innumerable veins which are white, making a pattern not unlike cracked unbreakable glass. Give it shade, warmth and not too much water; takes to general-purpose soil. Propagation: cuttings.

PEPEROMIA, *Peperomia obtusifolia,* is low growing and bushy, with rather fleshy, patterned leaves on pink or red stems. The silver stripe marking recalls the watermelon; in fact one variety is called "watermelon" and another "emerald ripple." A third variety, *Peperomia magnoliaefolia,* is easy to find and grow, has variegated cream and pale-green, heart-shaped foliage which contrasts nicely with dark-green neighbors. Peperomia also resembles the begonia, but all this masking only hides its true identity which is to yield black pepper. Give medium-bright light, warmth, high humidity. Repot seldom, feed occasionally, pinch back. Propagation: leaf or stem cuttings.

POTHOS, *Scindapsus pictus,* a middle-size terrarium plant with heart-shape marbled leaves streaked unevenly with lemon yellow. "Marble queen" is creamy-variegated, and "silver queen" is almost white. These are vigorous climbers, need pinching back, moist soil and filtered light. Leaves get larger as they grow along the stem. Use packaged soil mix; give more water in summer, and sparingly in winter. Propagation: cuttings. (Ask for devil's ivy.)

SPREADING CLUBMOSS, *Selaginella kraussiana,* and SWEAT PLANT, *Selaginella emmeliana,* are not true ferns but only an expert can penetrate their disguises. Sweat plant has close-branching stems, usually six inches long, with tiny leaves. Creeping moss is bright green and like a pincushion in growth. Give moderate light (leaves turn yellow if too much, or if plant needs feeding). Both selaginellas are suited to bottle gardens; pot in packaged soil with heavy addition of peat moss. Propagation: division or cuttings in warm temperatures.

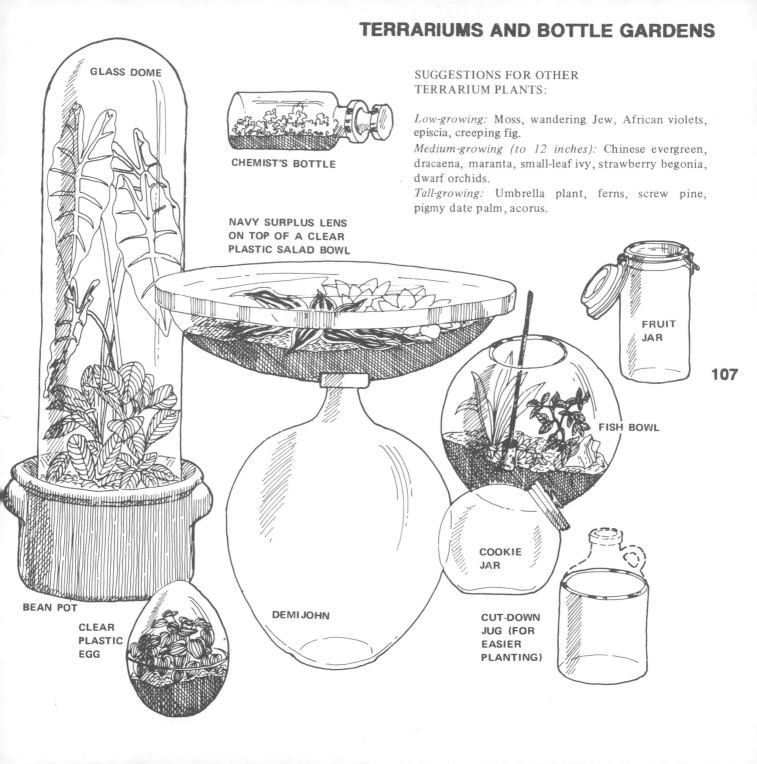

TERRARIUMS AND BOTTLE GARDENS

GLASS DOME

CHEMIST'S BOTTLE

NAVY SURPLUS LENS ON TOP OF A CLEAR PLASTIC SALAD BOWL

SUGGESTIONS FOR OTHER
TERRARIUM PLANTS:

Low-growing: Moss, wandering Jew, African violets, episcia, creeping fig.

Medium-growing (to 12 inches): Chinese evergreen, dracaena, maranta, small-leaf ivy, strawberry begonia, dwarf orchids.

Tall-growing: Umbrella plant, ferns, screw pine, pigmy date palm, acorus.

FRUIT JAR

FISH BOWL

BEAN POT

CLEAR PLASTIC EGG

DEMIJOHN

COOKIE JAR

CUT-DOWN JUG (FOR EASIER PLANTING)

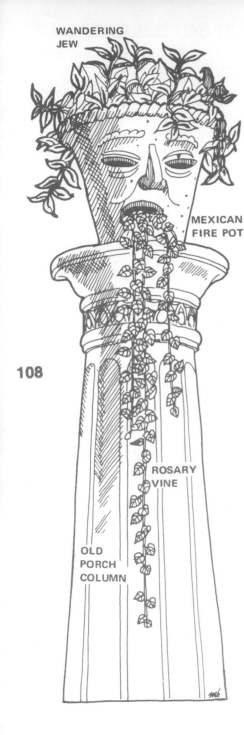

WANDERING JEW

MEXICAN FIRE POT

ROSARY VINE

OLD PORCH COLUMN

TRAILERS AND CLIMBERS

These are the plants which go places: they clamber up room dividers, they hide an ugly window view, they spill over the edges of hanging gardens and they send out new shoots which go up or go down, depending on your whim. They can be long hair and outgoing or they can be pinched back to be elegantly formal.

These climbers can be foils behind glamorous plants in pots; they can be portable screens when several are held at different levels; they can be safety factors in front of big glass areas; or a warning to watch one's step on steps or one's head in any partially obstructed area like the lower end of a spiral stair.

Hanging plants are difficult to water and often suffer because the water may not get to the center of the pot. Complete immersing is the best method, but if the plant is too high or too heavy, you'll need a saucer as part of the hanging contraption or a large tray on the floor—both iffy answers.

The hanging basket is a special planting procedure (see Getting Potted). Your choice of ways to get pleasant hang-ups has widened a lot in the past year. Besides the standard wire units available from the nursery, there are leather slings; rope baskets which started out as donkey muzzles in Mexico; pottery, metal or glass pots with cord or leather straps already integrated; and the irresistible and varied macrame put-togethers which you buy or make yourself.

There are purchasable pole units with brackets attached to hold several pots. Pedestals and shelves afford vertical space for cascades. Wrought-iron tables with glass tops have accommodation under the top for plant-watcher plants.

In addition to vines, the list of plants which give free fall or can be trained to jump through the wire hoop is large: fuchsia, orchids, ferns, ivy-leaf geraniums, succulents (including the donkey-tail sedum and crown of thorns), Christmas cactus, columneas, spider plants, the color-leaf wandering Jew, begonias which take north light and lantana.

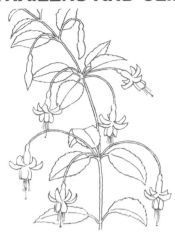

FLAME VIOLET

Episcia, a relative of African violet and gloxinia, is a charming, small hanging plant. It has fibrous roots instead of the tubers and rhizomes of other gesneriad family members.

The dainty blossoms that appear continuously from early spring to September are not necessarily flame violet in color. *Episcia dianthiflora* has downy green leaves and white blossoms; *Episcia punctata* has purple-marked flowers; and *Episcia lilacina* has rich bronze foliage and lavender bloom. Leaves of all may be partially marked with bright color. Other varieties have flowers ranging from white to red and including yellow.

It is important to keep the soil moist at all times, and to add extra humidity if the temperature climbs. Bright light or filtered sun is ideal, with night temperatures above 65° and days of 75° or higher. Keep the *Episcia* cooler in nonblooming periods; the rest periods are erratic diminish watering during a noticeable slowdown. Cut back to encourage new growth and fertilize monthly.

Flame violet's natural enemy is the nematode found in ordinary soil; a packaged soil mixture with humus added, or a mix of shredded peat moss, sifted sphagnum and sand with fertilizer offer the best growing conditions.

Propagation: runners or stem cuttings, anytime.

FUCHSIA

Fuchsias are summer-blooming shrubs which need cool conditions and shade from the sun, but plenty of light. Some grow upright and arching; the cascading ones, mostly hybrids like *Fuchsia magellanica gracilis*, make the most beautiful display and give purple and red winter bloom. (There are over 2,000 named varieties, and the American Fuchsia Society is the place to locate specialists or to join if you decide to put all your energy in one clan.)

Fuchsia is also called "lady's eardrop" for the delicate, drooping, hoopskirt-shape blossoms, up to three inches long. Some blossoms are double, like "abundance" with light pink; "cascade" is single, pink and red. Other winter bloomers sport blossoms in rose-lilac and red, or salmon with orange-scarlet.

At least four hours sunlight a day is recommended (but avoid the hottest noonday sun in summer), and night temperatures above 50° to 55°. Keep soil moist and fertilize twice monthly when flowering; reduce both water and food for plants when they are resting; and avoid overwatering until the new growth is established. Pinch out shoot tips during early stages to develop a bushy plant. Prune summer-flowering fuchsias to about six inches from the soil level in late fall.

Propagation: from stem cuttings of new growth.

TRAILERS AND CLIMBERS

IVY

True ivies are usually low cost and require minimum care (except for insect nuisance—red spider mites and scale). The English variety, *Hedera helix,* already indicated as a good ground cover, also carries names like Irish ivy. *Hedera h. hibernica* is exceptionally vigorous and parent of a dwarf-branching type, Pittsburgh, which in turn gave new descendants like Hahn's Miniature, Long Point, Manda's Crested, Maple Queen and Sylvanian—all good for trailing pots. Most ivies produce long single trails; some are self-branching.

Hedera h. cordata has slow-growing heart-shaped unlobed leaves; *Hedera h. minor,* baby ivy, has heavy grey veins; *Hedera h. marginata* grows three-lobed leaves edged in white.

Keep ivy cool. Normally, roots should be moist but not waterlogged, drier in winter. The shower washing once a week, with spray hitting both sides of the leaves, will discourage any infestation of pests. Large-leaf ivies can live in warmer rooms than the English. *Hedera canariensis,* Algerian ivy, can stand more light, and the variegated form is a handsomely marked six- to eight-inch leaf. You just have to decide what texture your setting needs.

Propagation: cuttings will root in water, can be kept for several months. Use general-purpose soil mix.

ROSARY VINE

If you're looking for a small vine which will grow under trying conditions, the rosary may be your green friend. *Ceropegia woodii* is a fragile-looking mass of thread stems which may trail six feet from a three-inch pot; the tiny heart-shaped leaves are fastened in pairs spaced wide apart. Easy to grow, the rosary vine can survive several days without water, almost totally dry and will accept little light in an area lit by a north window. So don't be fooled by the deceptively delicate look.

The tiny lanternlike flowers in purples and pink are often overlooked when they show in late summer, but you may be intrigued by the tubers which also form on the stringy stems in older plants, and on the soil. These tubers are ready-made starters for new plants: just remove one or several and pot up in rich garden loam with extra sand and humus mixed in; the tuber should be half in and half out of the soil.

Ceropegia sandersonii is a climber instead of a trailer, with the same paired leaves, widely spaced. It will grow on a small trellis or several bamboo stakes. The flowers are a rich cream and pale green, imitating parachutes descending. This *Ceropegia* prefers less water than the trailing variety.

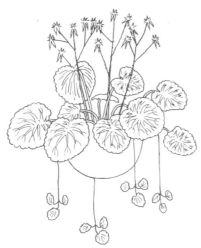

STRAWBERRY GERANIUM

Saxifraga sarmentosa or *Saxifraga stolonifera*, also less commonly called "strawberry begonia," is a happy, positive kind of hanging plant and particularly welcome in a bedroom or sunny dressing room because it has a feminine delicacy not common to most cascading hanging plants.

Strawberry geranium, neither a geranium nor a begonia, has reddish runners, similar to those of a strawberry plant, which produce little plantlets in the air. If you pin them down to soil, they will anchor and start growing roots. You can also cut them off, root them in water a few days, and then pot them up.

Flower stalks will grow to 12 inches, and have delicate little white blossoms at the ends. Leaves are green, bordered in white with a thin red outline, and violet under-leaf coloring. *Saxifraga stolonifera tricolor*, also called "magic carpet," is a smaller type, its green and white leaves edged in a pretty pink with rose underneath.

Give light shade, cool nights and relatively cool days; let soil dry slightly between waterings. Fertilize only three times a year for more colorful foliage.

Propagation: by runners and plantlets.

TRAILING LANTANA

Common lantana grown in the garden *(Lantana camara)* is a shrubby vine (or viney shrub) of great vigor, with small, dense, flat clusters of flowers in yellow and orange, later red-scarlet.

Lantana sellowiana and *Lantana delicatissima*, "trailing lantana," are the basket-hanging specialties. They bloom with rosy lilac flowers, mostly in summer and grow trailers up to four feet long, creating a fountain of pinkness.

Full sun four hours a day is necessary for lush complexion. Lantana seems to perform best with little watering and feeding only once a month. Be prepared, however, for mildew if the setting is too shady. Prune back once a year and thin out the trailing stems in early spring when budding and branching starts, since lantana flowers on new growth. However, don't be afraid to pinch back any time of the year to keep it in line. Feel free to experiment with its form—make it into a little shrub, a hanging basket, an espalier. Lantana grows in good potting soil in a temperature range of 55° to 68°—even higher. Allow soil to dry slightly between watering. Give it a summer airing in the garden.

Propagation: six-inch cuttings in spring. Use half sand, half peat moss, and put in semishade in a window or outside until fall. Pinch off buds which form to give leaves more chance to shape up. Bring indoors for winter show of flowers.

TRAILERS AND CLIMBERS

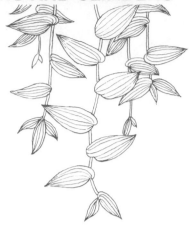

WANDERING JEW (Tradescantia)

Tradescantia fluminensis is often mistaken for the *Zebrina* wandering Jew (see the Anyone-Can-Grow-Them section) but they are not really related except in general form. The mature tradescantia is a hanging plant with naturally glossy pale green leaves showing cream or white stripes of different widths; some are almost all green, others strikingly albino. These are often called "inch plants" because they inch across or down any surface—creepers. A variegated type, *T. blossfeldiana variegata*, quick silver, has leaves one and one-half inches long with pale olive-green stripes and a purple midrib, as well as purple undersides, and constantly blooms with white to purple flowers.

Tradescantia stems are fleshy and jointed, with a leaf at each joint. All varieties root easily at these joints when they make contact with soil; they can also be rooted in water. Dry air will cause lower leaves to shrivel, but the plant needs warmth, so give filtered sun and a misting now and then. It will grow in shade, but coloring deepens the more light it gets. To keep a tradescantia from getting rangy, pinch back stems, or double them back to the pot's soil and pin them down with a hairpin or opened paper clip so they'll take root.

Allow the soil to become almost dry between waterings. This plant does well in a windowsill water garden also. And be sure, when you locate a wandering Jew, to give elbow room for it will spread horizontally as well as take off with vertical trailers.

WAX VINE

Hoya is a natural for training on a trellis; it's a twining plant with leathery succulent and waxlike leaves which have a red tinge when young, turning green later. The variety *Hoya carnosa* is most easily obtained. Its very fragrant flowers form two-inch bouquets of tight waxy shapes which open to a creamy-colored velvet in a perfect five-point star with dark pink center. *Hoya australis* has blue-white flowers with red centers in fall. Hoyas do not take well to moving or dryness when in bud stage.

The plant has small aerial rootlets, but must be assisted to climb in the direction you want by tying to the trellis. It is not necessary to have a bulky structure; a series of U-shape nails put where ties can be attached (in a post, a window frame, a piece of bark or driftwood) will give the wax vine a lift.

This vine grows best with four hours of bright light or filtered sun. In shade, it will live for years—and do nothing. It wants warm nights and days, with liberal watering during bloom and almost dry otherwise. Feed once a month in spring with a high potash formula, during the growing season. Extra rich soil and sand with leaf mold is the best mixture. For more bloom, keep potbound. Warning: *never* remove stubs where flowers appear; new blossoms return here year after year and if cut off, no bloom.

Propagation: stem cuttings (slow to root).

VEGETABLES AND FRUIT

Want to try a kooky idea? Grow salad greens in the winter, *inside!* Imagine picking bibb or Boston lettuce grown under lights when the snow swirls outside your window. The June flavor is there. It's simply a matter of where you have space to make a garden, and an outlet to connect the lights.

Tiny sweet carrots, radishes, beets, parsley and even watercress respond to winter growing. If there is a basement, a spare room or a sun porch, simply add a planting box with sheet plastic under to protect the area, and two 40-watt fluorescent tubes in a standard fixture placed six to 18 inches above the plants. Now you're in business.

Use the top of the washer or a freezer, or a counter in a storeroom (the temperature has to range between 60° and 70° in the daytime) for two months. Attach an automatic timer to the lights so the seedlings get 16 to 18 hours of light daily. Then come spring, try the light system for propagating outdoor bedding plants, for growing cuttings.

Then, there are the vegetables grown for decoration. A simple overblown Chinese cabbage in a can sells for three dollars at a local boutique—and you furnish the fancy pot to camouflage the tin. Take less than 10 cents worth of seeds and you can grow your own. Or try the lovely red cabbage with its huge bouquets of unheaded leaves (trim up the leaves from the bottom to give a trunk and greater height). Lettuce allowed to grow without cutting becomes a tall green pyramid. Asparagus foliage develops into an ethereal linear mass, four feet tall. Zucchini and eggplant started outside in wood tubs can be lifted inside for blossom time; they have huge hairy stems and leaves, and only a gardener can guess what they are.

Don't overlook the eat-now-plant-later department. Oranges, lemons, grapefruit, date and avocado seeds rescued from the kitchen disposal are challenging.

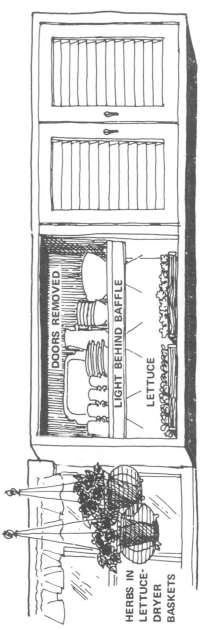

DOORS REMOVED

LIGHT BEHIND BAFFLE

LETTUCE

HERBS IN LETTUCE-DRYER BASKETS

VEGETABLES AND FRUIT

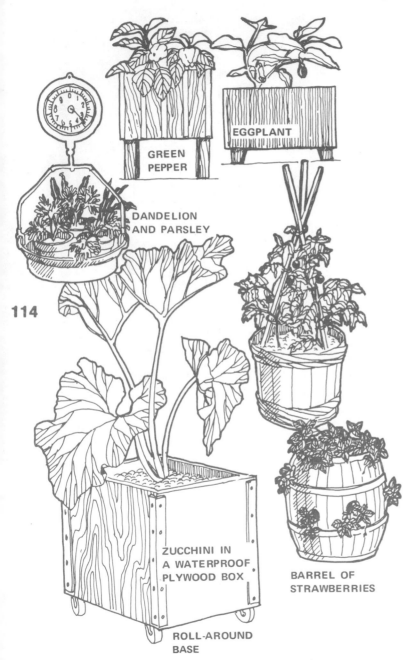

GREEN PEPPER

EGGPLANT

DANDELION AND PARSLEY

ZUCCHINI IN A WATERPROOF PLYWOOD BOX

ROLL-AROUND BASE

BARREL OF STRAWBERRIES

AVOCADO, *Persea americana,* is also sold commercially as the "alligator pear." Start by picking the ripest one on the greengrocer's stand, because the pit inside has already started to sprout. Carefully cut avocado in half without injuring pit's skin and rinse away any of the fruit remaining. Let it sit in a warm spot overnight, and the skin of the pit will peel away.

You can start the rooting process by piercing the lower part of the seed with three toothpicks spaced around the fattest part, and then rest the picks on the edge of a glass filled so water just barely covers the bottom where roots will appear. Or you can plant the pit directly in a six-inch pot filled with two-thirds loam and one-third humus, plus a handful of vermiculite. Before planting slice a dime-thin sliver off the top and bottom of the pit with a razor blade to speed germination. Place it flat end down, buried two-thirds into the soil, and water well. Germination time: one to three months, away from direct sun.

When roots have formed on the toothpicked pit, plant a pot as above. When the shoot is about six inches high, cut back to two leaves to force branching; repeat when plant is two to three feet tall. Don't repot until plant is taller than six diameters of the pot. Avocados dote on sun, moisture.

CABBAGE. Grow in pots for the attractive foliage and delicate color. Start seeds in July to November; they like cool periods after sprouting to develop rich deep pinks, lavender and purple hues as well as white or cream markings. Grow flowering kale as well as cabbage in full sun once it's on its way. Furnish deep pots filled with rich loam, steady abundant daily supply of moisture, and complete liquid fertilizer every three weeks as well as a weak solution 10 days after repotting seedlings. One head will fill an eight-inch pot, or put three in an 18-inch fern pot. Cut cabbage heads make long-lasting arrangements; cut off rosette and rest in container of water or combine with poinsettias at Christmas.

CUCUMBER. Try a miniature variety, "Cherokee," a hybrid which will give a crop on three-foot vines in 60 days. Plant two or three seedlings in a tub, or make a little "hill" in a tub and plant six or eight seeds (later to be thinned out to three or four); add a stake or trellis so the vine can be trained before the cucumbers begin to form. Start in spring and allow 55 to 70 days to mature; you can possibly start harvesting small ones in 40 days. Leaves like sun; young cucumbers prefer shade. For a fresh experience, try a hanging basket with trailers to the floor.

EGGPLANT. An early variety, "Morden midget" with soft grey-green foliage, is a sturdy pot plant, bearing medium-size fruits (each enough for one serving) of high flavor. Select at least a 12-inch clay pot, transplant three or four seedlings from two-inch pots, using rich loam; supply large doses of sun, soluble plant food (they're heavy feeders) and watering. The growing season, two-and-a-half to three months, will be followed by blossoms and fruit through the summer. Pick the less-than-full-grown eggplant while it is still shiny; old fruit can be tough and bitter.

GRAPES, *Vitis var.*, are welcome house plants which can be moved in or out without complaint. From seeds to six-foot vines in 18 months is a pleasant prospect. Select the seedy grape of the variety you want to enjoy and eat the fruit tenderly so you don't bruise the seeds; then wash and dry overnight on a paper towel. Propagate in two parts potting soil and one of humus; lay seeds on top of mixture (up to 20 in a 10-inch pot because not all will germinate) and cover with a quarter-inch layer of humus. Mature grapes do best with much sun, but never give young plants more than a couple of hours daily; watch for wilt if too warm.

Give a six-inch plant support, so stems take off vertically—they die back if left horizontal. A criss-crossing of macrame cord makes a jungle gym for several vines. Kept indoors, a vine may keep its leaves all year, but growth is slow, so give it summer in the fresh air. Cut back three-fourths of growth the second winter (first year is unpruned to encourage more leaf and root growth).

GREEN PEPPER. One of the prettier plants, symmetrical and lustrous dark green with peppers turning red if you don't pick them. Plant seeds or seedlings and administer same conditions as eggplant. If the pepper lives in a big container with indoor-outdoor growing choice, wheel it indoors when blossoming starts. First peppers will appear eight weeks after transplanting. Picking before peppers reach full size encourages more harvest. Try pruning back for second-year action. New variety "canape" bears two- to three-inch peppers, sweet and mild, and will grow 20 to 25 inches tall. Just for foliage, try three pots in a sunny corner, one with peppers, one with eggplant and one with cherry tomatoes.

LETTUCE. Farming your own salad is instant joy. Leaf lettuce needs no transplanting; sow seeds in rows in a flat wood box, or a container like a foil baking pan with a half-inch layer of mini-gravel and an inch-and-a-half of good potting soil; moisten the soil and apply the seeds according to the packet directions. Cover with a sheet of kitchen plastic to provide humid air after final mist-spraying; keep in a warm location (65° to 75°), not in sun or near direct heat. When the first green is in earnest, remove the plastic and bring to more light or artificial light. Lettuce can't take heat, but it does want moisture. Thin out as necessary. When it's lettuce-picking time, start with the outer leaves. Plants two months old start to get tough; discard them or let the plant go to seed. Varieties like "salad bowl" have curly leaves, long stems and grow tall; "oakleaf" is more heat resistant and a rosette form; buy "black seeded Simpson" in preplanted kits; "Burpee bibb" is for gourmets.

VEGETABLES AND FRUIT

LITCHI, *Litchi chinensis,* which bears those sweet nuts served at the end of a Chinese dinner, is really a fruit and can be tapped for seeds to raise a tree in your own Oriental hideaway. Seeds in the chewy dried "nuts" are dead; you'll have to try locating fresh litchi in July or August, or secure them through a seed catalog. It may take 10 years for the tree to bear this fragrant strawberry-flavor fruit, so accept it for the challenge, the conversation and the beauty. Small multiple leaves are first translucent red, then pink, then white and finally deep green.

Plant seeds right after removing from the fruit; use the terrarium method of propagating with closed top, high humidity and good drainage. Away from heat and direct light, germination should take place in a week or two (seed should be placed horizontally under one-half inch light soil; roots spread laterally). Gang up several in one pot to make a stunted-growth forest.

Crocking the pot with a residue of litchi shells gives good drainage; more shells on top as a mulch will encourage growth. Avoid sunlight; only an hour a day until plants are three months old. Water mildly every day, but don't let soil get muddy. Use mist spray daily. Acid-type plant food recommended.

MANGO, *Mangifera,* is a member of the same family as pistachio, cashew and poison ivy! When removing the pit, handle the peel carefully and wear rubber gloves if you are allergic. Remove the pit from the fruit, getting as much flesh off it as possible and scrub pit with an old toothbrush and lukewarm water; there will be hairs left on. Soak for five days in a warm place, changing water daily. Plant, eye up, one-half inch below the surface of loose soil mixture. Add mildly warm water until soil is almost muddy, after planting. It may take four months to germinate; keep it on a wet-dry cycle. The dark red leaves which eventually appear will promise a superb status plant once it's on its way.

ONIONS AND LEEKS, planted in January or February, grow nicely under artificial light and make amusing and tasty friends. Plant five or six to a pot, starting with "sets." Encouragement from 1000-foot-candles of light 10 to 12 hours a day will produce an impressive show of tall vertical stalks. Spanish sweet onions, the "white globe," are overproducers in size.

PAPAYA, *Carica,* is somewhat like a palm tree in build, but botanically labeled an "arborescent herb." Halve the fruit and remove the mass of seeds from the cavity; slip the outer covering off each seed by squeezing it between thumb and forefinger and popping the "aril" (outside covering) off to free the seed. Dry seeds overnight and pot in soil with a quarter-inch covering. After five weeks' germination, at least, some will show signs of life; once all are up to two inches, remove the weak ones. Allow no sun until they are twice that tall, increasing amounts as the plants grow; keep moist, not wet—in fact, be careful not to overwater. Papaya is affected by pollution from autos, may even keel over. Keep humidity high all day and spray with a mister to refresh.

STRAWBERRIES. Try the "everbearing" varieties like "ogallala," prodigy of the wild strawberry, which is hardy and sweet. Plant indoors, in a strawberry pot, or on a deck in a wood barrel (with one-inch holes drilled in the sides). In either case strawberries are to be found and eaten with utter pleasure minutes after plucking from your high-rise patch.

Fill the container to the openings, insert the plantlet in the hole so it is poking forth on the outside; then add more soil, more plants and a gathering on the top. Two important factors: proper plant depth is just to the level of the crown where the roots and stems meet and be sure of the drainage. Add soluble fertilizer once plants are established. Pick off flowers which appear until July; then let the first crop work its way to an August orgy. Four to six hours sun daily is essential to a big crop.

TOMATOES. Start with bedding plants from your nursery, seed store or supermarket. Or grow from seeds or from preplanted tomato kits, which are cubes of artificial soil and ready-to-go seeds.

Tomatoes need warm temperature, sun and staking to grow successfully. Fertilize when you transplant the little ones, then in three weeks and then weekly (more phosphorus to set the fruit). You have to pretend you're a bee and pollinate, otherwise no tomatoes; each day, when plants are in bloom, give them a shake or take a soft brush and move the pollen from blossom to blossom. Keep temperatures above 55° at night—but never above 68°—and be warned plants can't stand hotter than 95° days without expiring. Prune young plants, particularly of suckers which appear between the main stem and the leaves; if plants are in full sun and get glass reflection, don't prune after the first two or three suckers. However, if the sun isn't direct, prune to a single stem to open plant to light.

First crop of tomatoes should start in 10 weeks, continuing right through fall. Look for "small fry," cherry type, to 30 inches; "Tiny Tim," to 15 inches high and wide, very ornamental; or "hybrid patio," bred for tubs and containers, to 30 inches.

ZUCCHINI. Bedding plants from a local nursery or seedlings started in two-inch peat pots but plan for a big container eventually and a sunny location which will take this wild vegetable. Once the new starts are under way and ready for transplanting, fill the container with a good garden loam and watch them spring out of the ground. Hopefully, your container will be near a window where you can watch the great leaves. This is an especially decorative plant for an indoor party, particularly when it is covered with the soft yellow bloom which precedes the squash. Harvest when they are young for tenderness and flavor.

TWIST OFF TOP, PULL OFF ALL LOWER LEAVES EXCEPT TOP 8 OR 10; ROOT IN WATER

OR CUT OFF TOP AND REST FOR 48 HOURS: PLANT TO BASE OF LEAVES

1"

PINEAPPLE START

SPRAY DILUTE FERTILIZER INTO CROWN

117

CUT OFF BROWN TIPS

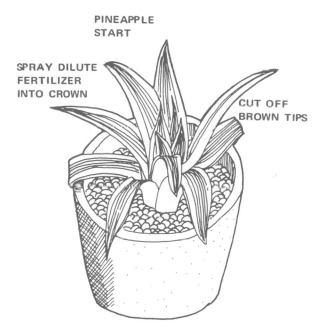

POT IN HALF SAND, HALF PEAT AND ADD A HANDFUL OF WASHED-AND-DRIED COFFEE GROUNDS (FOR ACID); COMMERCIAL IRON IN DILUTE FORM HELPS "TIRED BLOOD"

WINDOWSILL WATER GARDEN

Now, because someone refused to believe it couldn't be done (great ideas always start this way!) charming foliage water gardens can be put together with small effort, familiar materials.

Buy plants in small two- to three-inch pots. Cuttings from plants usually potted in soil will grow more slowly and are less desirable for this experiment. Locate a glass or plastic container to hold the plants—to see the layering of materials and the visible root growth is the magic of water gardening. A glass soufflé dish, a fish bowl, a large brandy snifter, a photo display cube—use your ingenuity. (For details on Water Garden Culture, see the section Getting Potted and Repotted.)

The water-garden method is unique and particularly adapted to smaller plants and smaller space. The plants grow in water with liquid plant food added. Care is simplified because you only need to make a note to keep the water level at the same height and plan to change it about once in four to six weeks. You might decide to plant a stone kitchen crock, an old enameled coffee pot, even a row of mugs which will fit a windowsill, but it is more a guessing game about the critical water level. Stay away from anything copper, brass, lead or tin lined; the fertilizer salts may produce a harmful reaction from metal to plant.

Plant a single plant or a small jungle in one container which you can watch close-up. The windowsill has always been a handy place to start a geranium cutting or an avocado seed, but to peek at the changing life cycle of the following plants is fun for the child in you.

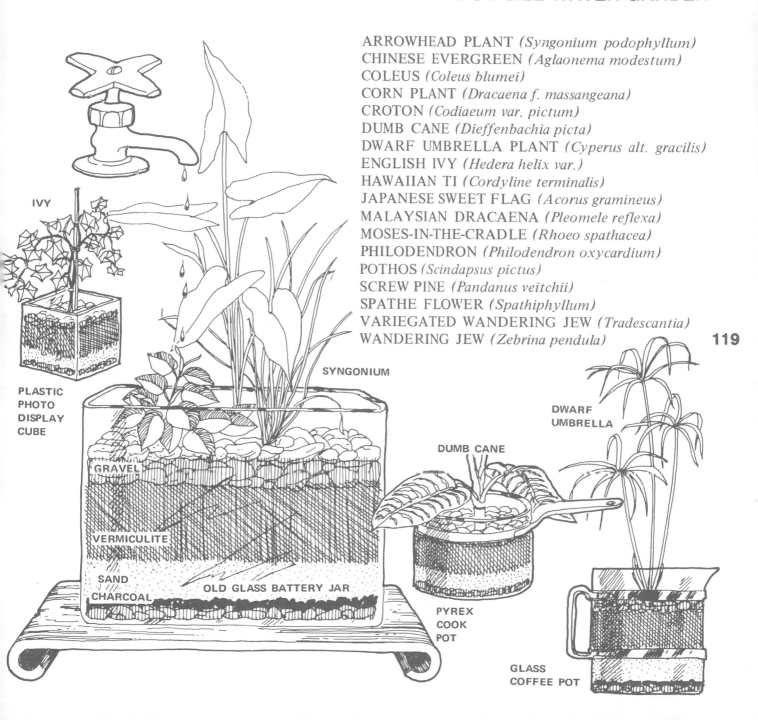

ARROWHEAD PLANT *(Syngonium podophyllum)*
CHINESE EVERGREEN *(Aglaonema modestum)*
COLEUS *(Coleus blumei)*
CORN PLANT *(Dracaena f. massangeana)*
CROTON *(Codiaeum var. pictum)*
DUMB CANE *(Dieffenbachia picta)*
DWARF UMBRELLA PLANT *(Cyperus alt. gracilis)*
ENGLISH IVY *(Hedera helix var.)*
HAWAIIAN TI *(Cordyline terminalis)*
JAPANESE SWEET FLAG *(Acorus gramineus)*
MALAYSIAN DRACAENA *(Pleomele reflexa)*
MOSES-IN-THE-CRADLE *(Rhoeo spathacea)*
PHILODENDRON *(Philodendron oxycardium)*
POTHOS *(Scindapsus pictus)*
SCREW PINE *(Pandanus veitchii)*
SPATHE FLOWER *(Spathiphyllum)*
VARIEGATED WANDERING JEW *(Tradescantia)*
WANDERING JEW *(Zebrina pendula)*

119

IVY

PLASTIC
PHOTO
DISPLAY
CUBE

SYNGONIUM

DWARF
UMBRELLA

DUMB CANE

GRAVEL

VERMICULITE

SAND
CHARCOAL

OLD GLASS BATTERY JAR

PYREX
COOK
POT

GLASS
COFFEE POT

SWEET POTATO
"GENII"

YOUNG SPROUTS

The "why-and-how" curiosity of a four-year-old or older is nicely adapted to plant life. From the first picking of a weed or the discovery of a live Christmas tree, children can be led into the magic of growing: grass seeds sprouting on a wet brick; a carrot top (allow at least an inch of a root vegetable for the experiment) sending out dainty fernlike growth when it is set in a half inch of water in a saucer; a sweet potato's first vining from its water bed in a fruit jar or in an old chipped gravy boat (stick toothpicks in the potato to keep it partially up for air).

Encourage the young gardener to learn the names of the plants he's raising. And let him give his personal names to his friends; carrots will always be a "Willie" to a child whose first try was called that.

The eat-now-plant-later methods mentioned in Vegetables and Fruits are good keep-em-busy projects. Grapefruit and orange seeds can be started in a half milk carton with holes punched near the bottom and a good soil mix; soak seeds overnight, plant and keep in a shaded place, water daily, and fertilize after the first month. The avocado seed, like the sweet potato, is toothpicked to hold the pointy end above water in a fruit far—the beginning of a real tree; once it has six leaves, whack it back to two so it won't become Jack-and-the-beanstalk skinny. Root vegetables like beets and turnips will perform like the carrot tops.

Lentils will start sprouting in a saucer of water. Cress (not the true watercress, but still edible) will grow on a turkish towel kept wet in a cookie sheet, as will alfalfa, also a good additive. A bryophyllum leaf, tacked to a windowsill, will start leaflets at the edge, and of course the pick-a-back plant is a good sturdy kid's subject.

Lettuce will sprout out of the mouth of a small frog made by the southwest Indians. Dyed eggshells cracked in half and emptied can be made into miniature hanging baskets for alyssum or petunia seed which will blossom into Easter gifts.

YOUNG SPROUTS

VENUS FLYTRAP GROWS BEST IN TERRARIUM, JAR

MARANTA FOLDS ITS LEAVES AT NIGHT

BRYOPHYLLUM: PIN A LEAF ON THE SILL & LEAFLETS APPEAR

1 PLANTS THAT DO SOMETHING

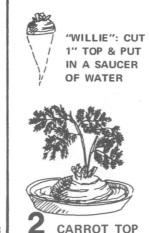
"WILLIE": CUT 1" TOP & PUT IN A SAUCER OF WATER

2 CARROT TOP

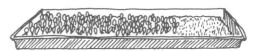
SPREAD AN OLD WET TERRY TOWEL IN A COOKIE SHEET AND SOW LOTS OF SEEDS & SUN; KEEP WARM, MOIST. WATCH FOR A SALAD HARVEST

3 WATERCRESS GROWS ON A TOWEL

SPROUTING SEEDS INCREASE FOOD VALUE (VITAMIN C, 4 TIMES; B_{12}, 13 TIMES); COMPLETE PROTEIN FORMS IN GRAIN. TRY BARLEY, LENTILS, SOYBEANS: SOAK 8 HOURS, COVER WITH LOOSE CLOTH, RINSE & DRAIN 3 TIMES DAILY

ALFALFA SPROUTS IN 3-5 DAYS

4 SPROUTING VITAMINS

PUT A SWEET POTATO ON AN OLD GRAVY BOAT, HOLDING IT UP WITH TOOTH PICKS; FILL BOWL WITH WATER TO TOUCH POTATO

5 SWEET POTATO

STORE ALMOND SEEDS A MONTH IN REFRIGERATOR (WALNUTS: 3 MONTHS); START NUT SEEDS IN PLASTIC BAG WITH MOIST VERMICULITE & WARMTH

6 "SQUIRRELING" NUTS

DYE EGGS, CUT IN HALF, REMOVE SHELL & FILL WITH SOIL, SEEDS; GLUE YARN HOLDER

PLANT SMALL CLAY FROG WITH LETTUCE

7 HOME-GROWN GIFTS

FIND A POROUS 1" UNPAINTED BOARD, SOAK IT; PLANT SEEDS, KEEP SHADED, WET

8 BABY TEARS GROW ON AN OLD WET BOARD

SOAK BRICK OR SPONGE, SPRINKLE WITH SEED, SOIL AND KEEP WET

9 GRASS GROWS ON WET BRICK

GRAPEFRUIT SEEDS: SOAK OVERNIGHT, PLANT & COVER WITH PLASTIC TENT

10 EAT NOW, PLANT LATER

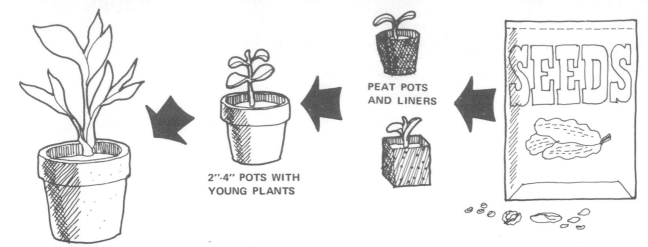

PEAT POTS AND LINERS

2"-4" POTS WITH YOUNG PLANTS

HAPPILY STARTED 6" OR LARGER POTS

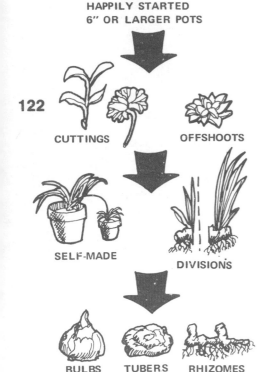

CUTTINGS

OFFSHOOTS

SELF-MADE

DIVISIONS

BULBS   TUBERS   RHIZOMES

122

WHERE DO PLANTS COME FROM?

BUYING PLANTS

People in nurseries who grow or sell indoor greens are a friendly breed of catalysts—eager to suggest, to help you find your way in the forest of house plants.

In this age of pick-it-out-and-lug-it-to-the-cashier, you can't expect much time of day from a supermarket checker who is thinking only of his next coffee break. The relaxed time of the past when salesmen could answer questions is gone; but, a nursery is still a place where people love the product they sell and are happy to talk about it.

Ask questions. Don't leave with your purchases without getting as much information as you can—the plant you save may be your own!

You'll find nurseries and garden centers have sections devoted to most of the plants identified in the Plants to Nourish and Cherish section. Florists have foliage ones, too, but may be a better source for flowering types. For the not-so-common varieties, try the mail-order growers; send for catalogs which will list available plants and information about their living habits, sizes and costs. There will be handling fees, but most plants are shipped to arrive about 10 days from time of order. They have to be certified by state agencies to be healthy, clean and free of bugs, so you're sure of getting the best the market affords.

If this is your first plant orgy here are some suggestions (which may be wasted on the more experienced—but won't hurt to review).

☞ Don't get carried away. Don't buy too many at once.

☞ If you can't afford one big plant, buy three of the same variety in smaller size, and repot them into one big pot when you get home; in six months the new triple-stem pot will expand your mind even if not the size you couldn't afford. Most plants are sold in garden centers by the size of the pot—two inch, four inch, six inch, etc.—rather than the size of the plant itself. A 10-inch pot is an older well-started specimen and is priced to repay for the months of care and the several repottings which have taken place.

☞ Check the color of the leaves. If they show signs of yellowing, steer clear. However, don't be upset when you take home what looks like a happy plant and it sheds a leaf or two in the first week. This isn't necessarily a trend, but only a matter of the change-of-location blues. If more start giving up the host in the next couple of weeks, it's a sign to move it to another spot. More light? More humidity? Watch daily for evidence of stabilizing.

☞ Check the foliage for silhouette and for a distinctive leaf shape. If it's a fern, it should be full and crisply green. If it's a schefflera, it would have those thin handsome arms outstretched straight or upwards, each with its umbrella of big, healthy, dark-green leaves. Don't take the first one you see without looking at all available. It's like choosing the best apples in the supermarket bin: be fussy.

☞ Plant forms, particularly the larger ones, must be chosen to relate to the space they'll occupy. You ask: how can I tell? Well, frankly, most of us, even with experience, make some bad choices, so you can't expect certainty—except for fundamentals like daylight and darkness! For instance, if you have a taller-than-average ceiling and not enough furniture to pull the eye down, try a mass of hanging gardens to create a lowered feeling. If you wish your ceiling to be lifted, paint it white or sky blue with clouds and add seven-foot tubbed trees with low pots of flowers nested at the base.

Norfolk pine will do nicely for a Christmas tree—if kept cool, and not weighted with heavy ornaments. Stake tree to keep its trunk properly straight.

123

Don't forget catnip as a house plant. The family pet will seldom disturb other greens when it can nibble its favorite. Try growing in an east-window exposure.

Mistletoe fig (Ficus deltoideae), will sometimes grow horizontally, a self-made bonsai with tiny non-edible fruit that ripens to pink in fall. Leaves are round but with old age may revert to elliptical. Look for mistletoe— very durable.

☞ To repeat, watch out that you don't plant yourself into a corner: keep large types pinched or pruned back to manhandling size. By the same measuring stick, do not limit yourself to a lot of small plants all the same size—that's a boring windowsill cliché which went out years ago. Do repeat one plant if it's particularly attractive to you, but plan to add one or more that are taller with a different leaf texture or color to give the I-planned-it-all-this-way look.

☞ Check the bottom of the pot for a good drainage hole. The best way to know if a plant has a good root system—the key to long life—would be to knock the plant out of the pot and examine the ball, but you can't very well do that without getting bounced out. So you'll have to rely on overall healthy leaf shape and the fact that the leaves stay on the stem right down to the soil in a young plant. (Older established big specimens rarely have those bottom leaves, but the size and health of the plant indicate adequate root support.)

☞ No house plant will keep on growing all 12 months. They need rest periods. The deciduous trees outside know when leaves start falling that it's time to knock off until spring. Inside greenstuff has similar cycles too. They simply stop growing or blooming; some rarities, like the bonzai Japanese maple, will defoliate because they are really outdoor types. No food, little water while dormant.

☞ On page 54, there are recommendations for plant or seed suppliers of fine reputation. However, there *are* unscrupulous firms that advertise in national magazines, offering banana trees that promise more than any plant can possibly produce, or shrubs that will grow indoors with the speed of Jack's beanstalk. Beware of overblown claims. Don't ever trust that get-rich-green-quick scheme; buy from reputable sources.

☞ Look for signs of insects. Beware of caked soil around the pot rim—that plant is susceptible to inadequate watering and root problems. If there's heavy dust on the leaves, the plant hasn't had proper care lately. Do not try to rescue a droop even if it is a fantastic bargain—it's like trying to reform a bubble-gum addict.

NEW PLANTS FROM CUTTINGS

The word "cutting" implies a way to grow new plants from older ones (they used to call this "taking a slip"). This is in contrast to starting from scratch with seeds; it may take anywhere from six months to seven years for seedlings to mature into flower-bearing adults. Using the cutting method, plants are formed in much less time, and you know beforehand that the new baby will look just like mother.

Cuttings made from stems are probably the most satisfactory for propagating into new plants. Some leaf cuttings prove out well. But in any method, be prepared for a few failures. The trick is to try several sections at a time and hope you'll get rooted results from each, depending on the fickle thumb of fate.

When you admired a friend's favorite plant in the old days you might automatically be offered a slip to take home. Today, if you see something you're wild about, it's possible to ask for a cutting; if you feel generous, offer to trade one of yours.

HOW CUTTINGS ARE ROOTED

There are two kinds of stems, soft and hard. The hard woods, like dracaena and podocarpus, may take two months to root. Summer is the best time for taking cuttings because this is the natural growth time. Plants which have been put out for summer may put on too much size to be welcome back in the house; September is still not too late to try cuttings from those plants which will benefit from the fall-winter spell to take hold.

The simplest rooting method is the soft-stem slip put in water. Take three- or four-inch lengths from the tip of the stem; flowering ones like impatiens, coleus and wax begonias root in two to three weeks. Simply put the stem into an empty bottle with a modest neck so the whole cutting doesn't slip down below water level and drown

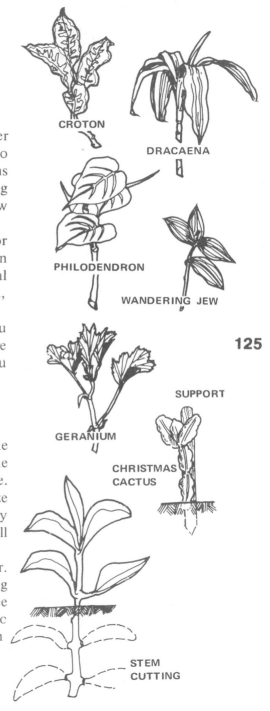

CROTON

DRACAENA

PHILODENDRON

WANDERING JEW

GERANIUM

SUPPORT

CHRISTMAS CACTUS

STEM CUTTING

CUTTINGS

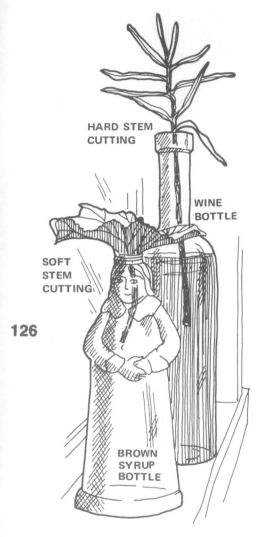

HARD STEM CUTTING

WINE BOTTLE

SOFT STEM CUTTING

BROWN SYRUP BOTTLE

FOLD LEAF AND CUT A TRIANGLE

Remove all but the two or three tip leaves and any blossoms, and fill the bottle with water. Brown or amber glass containers like syrup, liqueur or wine bottles hold back the amount of light in the stem area but let the leaves get it good. Geraniums take longer this way and you may want to try the sandbox. Ivy is a water-root cinch.

It is obvious that you must start with healthy plants which show vigorous growth. You can't make a scrawny sow's ear into a silk oak (*Grevillea robusta,* an Australian 100-foot flowering tree which stays a neat ferny five-footer indoors). Cuttings taken from the older part of a plant, but green growths of the current year, are more apt to respond to rooting. Make sharp cut just below the place where the leaves are fastened to the stems, they're called "nodes"; at least two of these nodes must be below the water level.

Direct sun is not good; in fact, shade the cuttings for the first couple of days to keep leaves from wilting. The rooting process moves faster with warmth; a kitchen windowsill over the sink where moisture from steam and natural kitchen temperature work hand in hand is a fine place for bottle rooting. Add a small piece of planter's charcoal to keep the water "sweet."

The sand method calls for clean sharp builder's sand or half sand, half peat moss in a shallow box or container with drainage holes so the water won't stop to rot the stem. Place a large tray underneath.

Dip the newly cut stem end in a rooting hormone before inserting it in the sand or mix. This compound is available either as liquid or powder at any garden supply store. If the leaves left on the slip are large, they may demand too much moisture to root well; fold them carefully along the main vein and with a sharp knife trim off the edge to leave a triangle. Cuttings which have never had buds will make the strongest new plants, but if you can't get yours without, remove flower signs as with any rooting system.

Bury only enough of the stem so it will stand upright. Small plants like neighbors, so try several at a time—and they don't have to be the same varieties. Keep the leaves from touching one another. Water the medium—but don't soak it. Adding an improvised umbrella of plastic over the top makes a kind of terrarium so that the recycled water will be trapped. After two weeks, remove the plastic and see what has happened. If there are no roots, stick the cutting back in the soil and wait and wait. If the plants don't wilt now, leave the roof off.

Sand doesn't furnish any nutrients so this is first-stage living only. Once signs of roots appear it is time to get pots ready for the new tenants. These should be tiny pots filled with a purchased mix. The new plant needs all the help it can get and the prepared mix will be a light well-balanced formula. New roots are tender and even shifting them from stage one to stage two can be ticklish. Once they're transferred, put a couple of wood clothespins on opposite edges of the pot to hold up a plastic sandwich-bag tent. A week with this cover and the little one is on its way.

LEAF CUTTINGS

The succulents are almost impossible to keep from rooting. They make new leaflets on their tips if you use the leaf-in-sand trick. However, a whole rosette of leaves set in moist sand will shoot off faster. The Christmas cactus and epiphyllum stems should not be buried, but be treated with hormones and held upright with the end just touching the sand; prop them with two popsicle sticks until the new plant can stand on its own feet.

Succulents can be multiplied by the cutting routine, but because they're another breed and the stems store water, a slip should be allowed 24 hours in a nice dry spot after it has been taken from the plant with a sharp razor.

Gloxinias and African violets, which are sort of semisucculents, can be started by leaf slips. They like to live in a double layer of special

PLASTIC CAKE COVER OR UPSIDE-DOWN PUNCH BOWL TO MAKE A MINI-GREENHOUSE

LARGE PIE TIN

CAKE-COOLER RACK LIFTS POTS ABOVE DRAINAGE WATER

127

FOR OUTDOOR ROOTING

INEXPENSIVE PLASTIC UMBRELLA WITH HANDLE REMOVED

CUTTINGS

VIOLET LEAVES: INSERT AT AN ANGLE

SINGLE LEAF IN A WATER GLASS

128

SPIDER-PLANT RUNNER

BEGONIA LEAF WITH KNIFE CUTS ON MAIN RIBS

mix with an inch or more of sand on top. The leaf end gets the hormone dip and then is inserted at a mild angle into the sand. The angle business keeps the moisture from sitting on the stem end where it bleeds. Succulents don't require the sandwich-bag routine, but a week or so for the gloxinias and violets will speed up rooting. They get the same kind of watering as the soft-stem plants, and once they leave the tent, light watering is all that's necessary. The use of artificial light will really give them a boost, particularly the violets.

Violets will also root in water; the stems should be threaded through holes in a wax-paper cap held on top of the glass of water with a rubber band or sticky tape. This keeps the leaves dry, the stems wet. When rooted, they are ready for a two-inch pot filled with rich leaf mold or special African violet soilless mix which you can buy; later, when potbound, move them into three- or four-inch pots where they will start flowering.

OTHER OFFBEAT LEAF TRICKS

Some of the plants which take dry conditions, like the sansevieria, can be multiplied by taking a leaf and slicing it into sections about two inches long. Dip the cut ends in hormone powder and set them in the sand and potting mix; they will form roots and the roots will grow "runners," forming new plants a short distance away. The spider plant sends out long arms with plantlets that increase the population; plant the little one in a pot placed next to the big one, and as soon as signs of new roots show, snip the umbilical.

Rex begonias can be tricked into producing their young by making several cuts at the junction of veins on a healthy leaf. Pin down the leaf on moist sand with wire hairpins so the bruised area contacts sand; new plants will appear on the top. (This is a long, long process and you may get bored and agree it's simpler to buy a new rex.)

The success of any cutting is dependent on constant moisture and temperature control. Mini-greenhouses made of plastic can be bought. A terrarium box with glass sides and top or an old aquarium will make excellent nurseries for the new babies. For trying just one or two, use the sandwich-bag cover over a small pot and set where it will get even room temperature—put it on a counter or shelf.

Some plants reproduce without any midwifing from you: kalanchoes and a few other succulents develop tiny new plants as do strawberry geraniums and the candle plant. Wait until you see the complete plant before you sever relations.

AERIAL ROOTS

Philodendrons, the arrowhead and some others sometimes get leggy. One answer is to repot the culprit into a much larger pot, leaving at least an inch of new soil mix at the edge. Take the viny stems and wind them around and around; use a vine staple or a paper clip cut in half and cinch down the stems to force them to stay in the top of the mix. As you do this, deliberately bruise the outside tissue of the stem—this is where the new roots should start poking out. This repotting takes the curse off straggly ends and gives the plant a new lushness.

Plants which throw out too many aerial roots like the monstera and some of the philodendrons can have them barbered back. If the whole plant is getting too big for its niches, cut back a section with aerials attached. Plant the section (get rid of some of the leaves so the demand isn't too much for the new plant) in a good-sized pot, winding the roots around inside in the soil mix. It won't take long for the underground action to get real roots going. Give the young vine a stake support until it learns to stand up for its rights.

**PLASTIC
SANDWICH BAG**

129

No flowers on the bromeliads? Place a pot in a plastic bag with an apple and presto! The apple produces a gas which turns on the bromeliad and speeds up its blooming.

Another preschool project: Root the leaf of a jade tree. Place a leaf on top of the soil, face up. Press into soil so the stem is lightly covered. Water carefully; set pot in filtered bright light. Within two weeks, a new plant will start (and the mother leaf won't be needed).

LAYERING

Finally, one mention of another method of rooting: "layering." This is a complicated method of forcing a plant to grow roots midsection on a stem which has been notched or shafted and then wrapped in damp moss and plastic until the new roots appear. Then you cut the stem below the roots and pot in the proper method.

Layering is better left for advanced gardeners and professionals who use it to root plants for increasing their collections or for controlling overgrown plants. For most of us, it's easier to go out and buy what we want, so I won't take space for details here; if you're an experimenter, look further in horticulture books for proper recipes.

Begonia cuttings: Always take young shoots from the base of the plant; two inches is a good length.

130

STARTING FROM SEEDS

You had better be both young and patient to try growing house plants from seeds, for it can take anywhere from six months to seven years before you reach the size plant you want.

So, you can readily see it's part of the *now* living to go out and buy the plant in the market place. You can choose for form and foliage, aware of the true color of the flowers. (I remember a "white" Chinese wisteria planted against a yellow house turning out to have Italian pink blossoms when it bloomed.) You also know when you see the plant if you have the variety which will look best in your chosen location.

Black-eyed Susan is an annual that makes a gay hanging basket for a summer room, is moderately easy to raise from seed. Thunbergia germinates when planted directly in basket or in peat discs and transplanted later. Give lots of sun, air motion to keep basket cool.

Seed growers are an exclusive breed and prideful of their prowess. One success may turn *you* on to trying all sorts of rare and nutty plants you can't find any other way! For instance, many large trees make superb household specimens if started from seeds and kept restricted so they don't outgrow you. "The coffee tree has been a trustworthy and rewarding foliage," to quote John Brudy (Florida) in his fascinating Rare Plant catalog. But where can you find this plant? You send for a packet of coffee seeds.

Each seed has its own idiosyncracies and most catalogs give you the dope on how to get the most results. To repeat, don't expect 100 percent of a package to take hold; nature cops out now and then, too.

Keep in mind these factors if you get into the seed-propagation trap: temperature, moisture and light are all-important. The rule of bottom heated, top cool and light bright is unchallengeable.

You can put together a wood box with a couple of two-inch holes in the bottom. Turn it upside down with a 40-watt light inside (place the bulb so it won't overheat the table or the box). Then set the seed container over the holes and you've solved bottom heat.

Seed babying is a daily job. The soil mixture must be kept moist but not wet. Small seeds need a very weak addition of food; some soilless mixtures have nutrients added and this will be adequate. Larger seeds should be placed very carefully so the root end is down—it will make for stronger seedlings.

Never water with a strong stream; a misting daily will do the job. And a cover glass will hold in the moisture. New seeding needs protection from the sun and bright light. Transplanting of the new plantlets should be into individual tiny pots as soon as they can be handled without damage. Remember, don't be impatient.

Some seeds must be soaked before they can be planted; others should be nicked in the seed coat and soaked. Some take very hot water. Check the catalog for proper handling.

When propagating seeds of rare and unusual plants, it's a good idea to add one heaping tablespoon of a powdered fungicide to each two gallons of planting mixture. Mix well before setting seed.

OFFSHOOTS

The aloe, agave, cyperus, bromeliads, some begonias and banana produce side plants on occasion and these can be cut off with a sharp knife without disturbing the parent plant to form new pots. Offshoots make good gifts, as do your extra rooted cuttings and slips from violets, gloxinia, strawberry geranium and episcia.

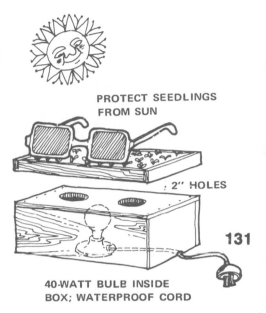

PROTECT SEEDLINGS FROM SUN

2" HOLES

131

40-WATT BULB INSIDE BOX; WATERPROOF CORD

DIVIDING PLANTS

Removing an offset shoot is one form of dividing; this is fairly easy because you can see the separate plant. Some plants, however, form multiple sections which can be safely operated on to repot as singles. This is really a job for advanced gardeners and, like layering, is best left until you know whether surgery is your bag.

Single-stem plants like the palm or dracaena cannot be taken to the operating room, nor can woody-stemmed ones like fuchsias, or any of the vining plants. Succulents which store water cannot be divided.

BULBS

Probably nowhere else in the plant family has there been so much hybridizing (making a new offspring from two different relatives) which produces better strains. Each improvement means more beautiful blossoms or longer flower time or healthier bulbs.

So, the first order of business when you decide to try growing these beauties is to buy the biggest, fattest of each variety. Tender "precooled" bulbs are intended for early indoor bloom, before the regular outdoor season. Because it has been forced, all of the plant's power goes into this one big push and when it's all over, the poor bulb is exhausted and must be replaced with a new one next year. This is particularly true of paper-whites and little hyacinths.

Select bulbs with smooth onionskin look, with an unbruised and healthy "plate" or bottom where the roots start. These bulbs are ideal for starting in bowls with nothing but pebbles and water: the bowl should be twice the depth of the bulb, and the pebbles deep enough so the points of the plant are halfway above the top rim. Keep the bulbs close together and plant as many as possible for a happy cluster. Bring the water level to the bottom of the bulbs.

132

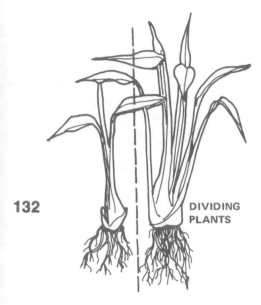

DIVIDING PLANTS

PLATE

Set them in a cool dark place until root growth is obvious before bringing them out to a sunless window. Once blooms start, keep them out of the sun. House-grown narcissus need a ring of yarn to keep the slim stems vertical because they have a tendency to plop over.

If you would like to go for a series of bloom periods, buy a larger number of bulbs all at one time (they may have disappeared from the source if you want more later) and let them hibernate in a cool, dry, perforated plastic bag in the refrigerator; keep them away from moist vegetables and don't freeze them. Start new bowls of bulbs at two-week intervals. Count on six to seven weeks from start to bloom.

Hyacinths and daffodils grow best in a special soil mix you can buy; they must have their noses visible above the mix. Tulips and smaller bulbs are strictly undergrounders. After planting store the pots in a cool dark place for two to two and a half months until there is sign of growth. They need moisture but never sogginess.

Once the growth process has started, keep them out of bright sun but in a warm room in daytime, a cool room at night. When the bloom is over, give the leaves time to cool it. Then put pots outside or give them to a neighbor.

You've probably seen the specially designed hyacinth-bulb glass. It has a narrow neck and a kind of half-cup top where the bulb perches. You fill the glass with water to the base of the bulb, add a few bits of charcoal to the water and keep the level as nearly the same as possible. Give it the dark room treatment, or even the back of a shelf of the refrigerator (*no* freeze, please), until roots show; then, out to a sunny window. Give it a slight turn each day so the leaves and blossoms don't lean toward the light.

HYACINTH-BULB GLASS

133

A bulb is neat. It's an all-here-in-one-package plant, with its own food supply. After blooming, energy is low, so it is your job to start feeding with a high phosphorus formula, 5-10-5. Cut off bloom as soon as it fades so it won't go to seed. Never cut the green foliage; snap or break off only when it turns yellow.

TUBERS

TUBER

134

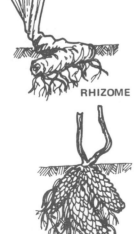

RHIZOME

ACHIMENES
RHIZOME

TUBERS

Begonias make up the most important indoor plant in this pack. You can buy the tubers, sometimes with the stem buds showing. There are several schools of thought about planting, but double-planting seems to be the safest way.

Begonias can be started in a shallow planter with the round side down in a very loose rich soil or peat moss. The main objective is to keep the tubers moist but not waterlogged as the rot problem rears its ugly head. This is a prerooting period where they begin to show life, and they too, love bottom heat and artificial light until the stalks show leaves of uniform size.

Cut a block of the soil mix around the tuber and repot it, hopefully without disturbing the roots and tuber, and place it in very rich soil with the top exposed. Continue the overhead light and add some good fish emulsion. Watch for curling leaves—sign of too much food; also check circulation of air; tubers are willing hosts to mildew. Like most tuberous plants, begonias need to rest in the winter and can be put to bed in a dark closet or the basement until wake-up time.

Plants like the achimenes, or widow's tear, grow from rhizomes, which are rootlike stems, thicker than those above ground. They plant best in a mixture of two parts peat moss and one part each soilless mix and sharp sand. Keep them moist, warm and in bright light. After flowering, the plant will seem to expire, but again it is dormancy time and you store the rhizomes in plastic bags with a little peat. It is possible to divide rhizomes in winter to increase the pot population.

PROPAGATION BY SPORES (FERNS)

This reproduction process is not difficult but it is a very long one and calls for patience.

Most fern fronds are fertile in the midsummer months, from June to September, and the little dots under the leaf in neat rows are the spores or mature "sori" you need. Cut the frond and let it dry out in an envelope for about a week, or until it releases the spores. Remove the debris and there's powdery stuff left in the bottom of the envelope.

Small refrigerator dishes are ideal starter places; wash with very hot water and fill one-third to one-half full of damp vermiculite. Add boiling water to the same depth and fill the dish to within one-half inch of the top with very fine leaf mold or special rich soil mix. Press down and make smooth. Let the mixture stand for an hour until saturated through and cool to room temperature. Then sprinkle the spores onto the moist surface and cover tightly; maintain the same warmth and in a week or two you should see the first greening. *Don't* peek under the cover because constant conditions are essential. Be warned, too, that staghorn ferns may take as long as a *year* to show their color!

Once there's sign of life, gently add fertilizer, and give the little ones up to 20 hours daily of fluorescent light; keep temperature at 70° and the surface sprayed wet. With the cover off, put the dishes into a larger terrarium atmosphere with glass or plastic cover. The original green will disappear when the real fern appears. This is where patience counts: it may be ready for potting within a year.

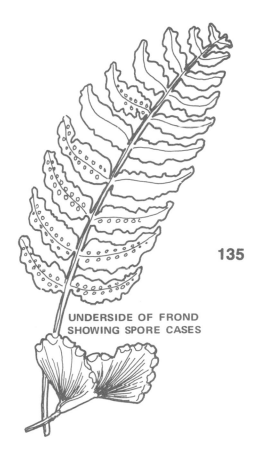

**UNDERSIDE OF FROND
SHOWING SPORE CASES**

135

GETTING POTTED AND REPOTTED

Drainage is a most critical factor. If the soil is too fine, or if it compacts, the new rootlets can easily drown and the plant dwindles down to a sad end. When a plant has been in one pot too long, it can become almost solid roots, also denying water to the center of the root ball.

LET'S GET DOWN TO EARTH

It's elementary: if you're on to house plants, you'll need soil sooner or later. Every advanced gardener has his (or her) recipe for how much leaf mold and how much sand you mix together with the dirt to pot up a plant.

Genuine soil from a garden (today, you have to keep in mind that plants grow in *non*-soil, too) provided it is nice, loose and loamy, comes first to mind. But if you live in California where clay was born, or in an apartment in Chicago miles from the nearest truck garden, *then* what?

INSTANT SOIL

Making soil is as simple as making a package cake to which you add water. Your supermarket, the nursery, even discount drugstores have packaged soil-substitute mixtures for every plant you want to pot.

These formulas are put together scientifically so there's a proper balance of growth elements. Not soil at all, but a blend which allows good drainage, charcoal to keep it fresh and neutralize alkaline water, and nutrients for early growth encouragement.

There are packages specifically plotted for potting African violets, others with compatible bark-type stuff for orchids, something for cacti and succulents and even an acid trip for azaleas.

Problems can result when you use soil from the garden, too. There are nasty little nematodes infiltrating: there is that dread damping-off threat (rot at the soil level because the drainage is poor) and fungus. So, many hobbyists have taken to baking soil to sterilize it. This has always been a smelly mess—until a smart cook came up with a new wrinkle: the "brown-in-bag" oven sack, filled with soil to which you add water. Bake with same timing, temperature as a turkey. Use the bag to store extra soil, too. Here's a tested formula:

    2 parts garden soil

    1 part leaf mold (decayed leaves)

    1 part sharp sand

    1 teaspoon bonemeal fertilizer to each 5 gallons of mix

The drawback is that you spend a lot of time getting it all together—and who has time? Our lives are complicated anyway; don't let guilt spoil your thing. Use the packaged mixes and leave the baking to the organic gardener.

ADDITIVES TO HELP THE SOIL BREATHE

Peat moss is the most common soil improvement because it absorbs water and lightens the soil. It is not a fertilizer and plant food must be added separately. Peat moss insures good drainage conditions which bring a "warming up" of the soil; wet soil is considered "cold" and slows up root growth. Coarse texture peat is best.

In the section on Plants to Nourish and Cherish, you will read the

No shards to place over the hole in the pot (to insure hole will not become clogged)? Try a washed seashell, the bent lid of a frozen juice can; carefully break an old cracked cup and use the curved pieces.

137

**BROWN-IN-BAG
SOIL STERILIZER**

words vermiculite and perlite over and over. These derivatives of mica mineral are readily available in package form. They keep the soil aerated: for rooting cuttings so that the tiny new roots don't rot, as a growing medium to aid in transplanting new plants without damaging roots and for plant germination under light. Vermiculite and perlite also hold the moisture in sandy soil, reduce need for watering as often, have no weed seeds, are great for storing bulbs and are inexpensive. They are the first purchase you make, along with plant food, if you expect to overcome purple thumb.

Wood shavings add humus value to larger house plants, but you may find shavings only in large quantities. Orchids like something called osmunda fibre, consisting of roots of cinnamon and interrupted or royal fern; it contains all the essential food for two years, but added drainage is necessary. Fir bark, coconut husks and gravel have been tried with orchids but have no available plant food. Peat moss and sphagnum combination have been used for many years with good results. Safest rule with orchids is to stay with the material the plant is in when you start being its parent. As the potting medium breaks down, watering is more critical—and the problem is how much, not how often.

Saline or alkaline soils will be helped by the addition of granular redwood sawdust which is high in acid reaction; it also reduces speed of water evaporation from the surface, and is used by growers of nursery stock to give young plant roots more air space for moisture and oxygen. Sawdust creates a nitrogen "draft" on soil, and added bonemeal is required when it is used, about an ounce for each inch of depth.

THE CONTAINER

A pot is clay, plastic, styrofoam, glass, wood, ceramic, an old teapot, an empty coconut, an enameled coffee can, a half milk carton, a hanging basket, a window box, a terrarium—anything which has sides and a bottom.

Clay pots, the most common of all house-plant containers, come

RUMOR HAS IT THAT CLEAN **CAT LITTER** IS A WORKING SUBSTITUTE FOR VERMICULITE TO AERATE THE SOIL

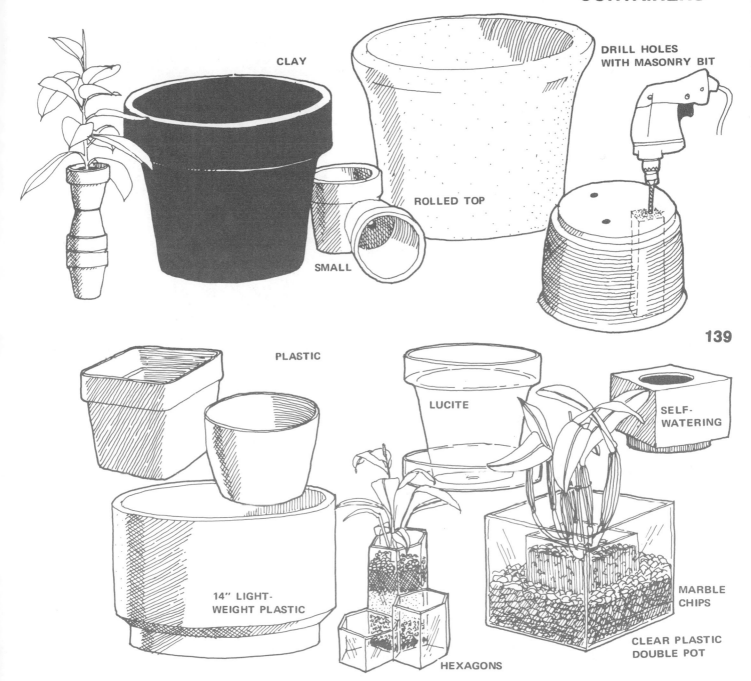

CLAY

ROLLED TOP

SMALL

DRILL HOLES
WITH MASONRY BIT

PLASTIC

LUCITE

SELF-
WATERING

14" LIGHT-
WEIGHT PLASTIC

HEXAGONS

MARBLE
CHIPS

CLEAR PLASTIC
DOUBLE POT

CONTAINERS

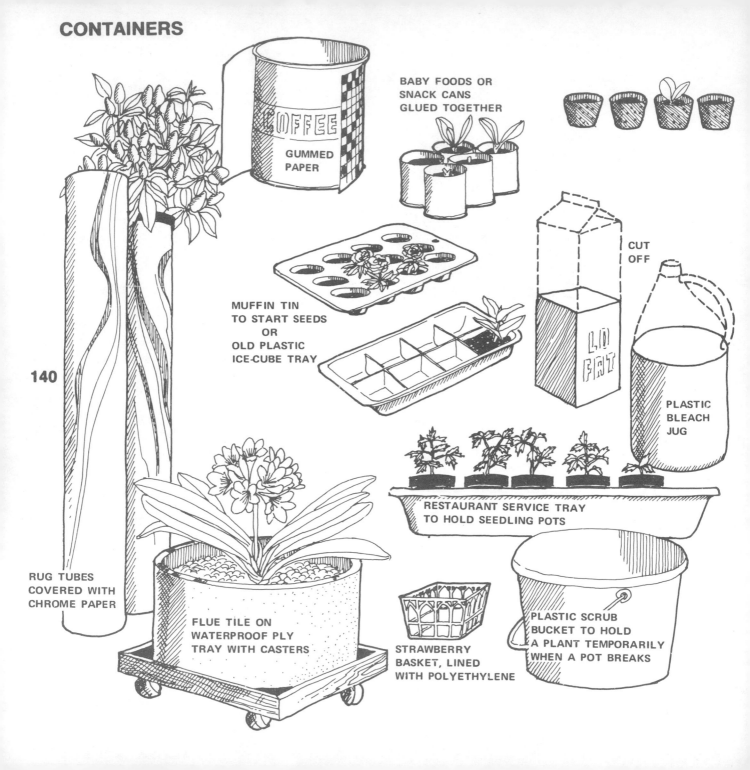

BABY FOODS OR
SNACK CANS
GLUED TOGETHER

COFFEE

GUMMED
PAPER

CUT
OFF

LO
FAT

PLASTIC
BLEACH
JUG

MUFFIN TIN
TO START SEEDS
OR
OLD PLASTIC
ICE-CUBE TRAY

RESTAURANT SERVICE TRAY
TO HOLD SEEDLING POTS

140

RUG TUBES
COVERED WITH
CHROME PAPER

FLUE TILE ON
WATERPROOF PLY
TRAY WITH CASTERS

STRAWBERRY
BASKET, LINED
WITH POLYETHYLENE

PLASTIC SCRUB
BUCKET TO HOLD
A PLANT TEMPORARILY
WHEN A POT BREAKS

in a very wide range of sizes and heights. They let out the moisture and let in the air. They absorb moisture when you double-pot, that is, put one pot inside of another with a filling of moss between. The glazed pot works fine as long as there's a good drainage hole in the bottom. Clay pots can be set into a decorative glazed one, if you don't cotton to the clay's plain dull color; this works particularly well if the fancier pot has *no* hole and you can water with impunity and never worry about rings on the table (don't forget to fill the bottom with pebbles so the pot will not stand in water).

Plastic pots do not need watering so often because they hold in moisture. They are much cheaper to manufacture, weigh less and that's important to supermarkets. Plastic, however, does not allow air through the walls to aid in drying the soil. Traditional potters suspect the plastic also because once you inadvertently overfeed or overwater, it's *zap* for the plant. You don't have to let this bug you—just hold back your eager thumb. On the plus side plants in plastic make good weekend orphans.

No matter what you plant in, make sure it is clean. If the pot is clay, use steel wool and warm water to scrub out any old remains; then let the pot dry a little before you add the mix. Plastic and ceramics come clean easily. You probably won't reuse a styrofoam pot (watch for easy breakage of these; glaring white isn't very happy, either).

Pots which house orchids need particularly good drainage; some are made with larger rectangular holes in the bottom.

GETTING POTTED AND CROCKED

The English call it "crocking" and it's an old tried-and-true essential in potting. You take one or several pieces of broken clay pot, depending on the number of drain exits in the pot you're using, and set a piece over each one with the curved outside up to allow the water to drain down under and out without being blocked by the planting material. Root rot is a common cause of plant mortality. (If your

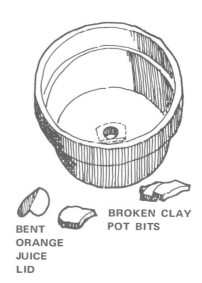

BENT
ORANGE
JUICE
LID

BROKEN CLAY
POT BITS

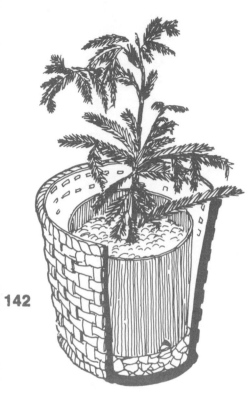

142

apartment living is minus broken clay pots, bend the lid of a frozen orange juice can to place over the hole.)

There are two ways to handle pots which have no drainage holes (well, three, if you drill the pot's bottom with a silicon-carbide-tipped electric drill bit—a long iffy job): either the pot-in-pot mentioned earlier or planting directly.

The first method is more efficient if you add a one-inch layer of pebbles inside the larger pot to stand the smaller on. This keeps the bottom of the planted pot from drowning in water (the shapes of some pots make it almost impossible to tell when water is collecting in the lower container). Pebbles and gravel work in many ways with house plants, so start collecting; bending over is good for the midsection, too.

If you decide to plant directly into the holeless pot, be prepared to revise normal potting techniques. Starting with a layer of broken crocking pieces and pebbles (again), add a half-inch layer of pea-sized charcoal. A pad of sphagnum moss or even some clean packing excelsior before adding the mix should bring the level up to about one-third of the pot depth. Complete the planting with packaged soil mix under and around the roots.

You may find the plants you buy have no crocking. Even with the new soil substitutes, drainage is vital so when you repot, crock.

THE MECHANICS OF PLANTING

Finding a place to do your gardening exercises is the first order of business. Ordinary single-family dwellings have many choices of spots to set up work areas—the garage, the basement, the laundry room and, if you're lucky, the kitchen-sink counter when there aren't too many peanut-butter-jelly-sandwich corps around. Emptying an old pot or even washing one can be a hassle in most apartments and mobile homes; you may find an ironing board with plastic sheet protection, or your incline exercise board bridging the bathtub will have to become the garden work center.

No matter where you work, a large piece of plastic (cleaner's bag or your Sunday Times plastic raincoat?) keeps the crumbs and water under control. Organize the tools, materials and The Plant, and you're ready to start.

Optional, but recommended for pots with holes, is filling the bottom of the pot with pebbles (did you crock it first?), a layer of sphagnum moss, which has been presoaked, or peat moss; this should bring the first level to about one-fourth of the way up the inside of the pot. Crunched peanut shells—*not* the salted type—can substitute for peat.

You'll need a large mixing bowl to thoroughly moisten the planting mixture. If you will be using the entire package, you can pour the lukewarm water right into the bag, knead it to a good consistency and squeeze the excess water out. If you don't have a handy drain, save the water in a bowl to use on other plants or flush it down the toilet. If you use ordinary garden soil, water after the planting is completed.

Then add some of the moistened nonsoil from that package, or garden soil. If the plant is a tender young thing, gently spread its roots over the mix; then slowly turn the pot, dribbling more mix. As you do this be a kindly gardener and hold the plant to keep it from bending at the waist. Just for good measure, give the pot a few spanks on the bottom (just as the doctor does for a new baby) to settle the contents as you fill. Keep the soil level the same as it was before.

Firm the mix around the plant (but not next to the stem) with your thumb—not too solidly, just enough fatherly pressure to let the plant know who is in charge. The woody types take a good manly push-down; softer young roots and tubers prefer the gentler nudge.

The planting mix should end at least a good half-inch below the rim of the pot to allow for watering. That first watering should be a thorough one, but added slowly so the roots and plant are not disturbed. Let the excess water drain off and add a saucer under the pot. Keep it out of the sun for a few days. If the plant looks a little wilty

What's my name? Always make little labels for cuttings—it's so easy to forget what is in the pot if you have a lot of babies in the nursery.

143

KEEP SOIL
1/2" BELOW RIM

SOIL MIX

SPHAGNUM

GRAVEL

CROCKING

A good mix for repotting gloxinia, Episcia, *violets: Sphagnum peat moss, vermiculite, perlite and a little ground limestone; moisten thoroughly. Use fertilizer with discretion each watering.*

Spotless pots: Always start with a scrubbed pot when planting or replanting. Nasty things like fungus spores can reactivate from a sick plant to the next tenant. To remove the excess salts of fertilizer or molds, soak pots overnight in a laundry bleach solution; neutralize by soaking a second night in two gallons of water plus one cup vinegar.

during that time you can try misting—but don't water any more. The plant will perk up in a week and be ready for more light.

Perhaps it is foolish to mention, but when you put a plant to pot, it should be centered; an offside play never has authority. The exception is the bonsai: these miniature breeds are nontypicals, planted in nontypical containers. They are not for beginners, or even some advanced gardeners. When you are tempted to try one, check your local library for special books on techniques.

REPOTTING

This is also called "potting on," but for sake of clarification, it is action forced on you when a house plant says "My roots are up tight!"

What are the signs? Plants which you have lovingly tended are bound to grow. The roots of outdoor plants can keep spreading in the ground; those in pots have no place to go except round and round into a tangled mess—which will become a solid mass unless you recognize in time and act.

Know the danger signs: plants which show signs of slight wilt hours after you water or whose lower leaves get sickly yellow (a plant shares what nutrients and water it can absorb with its growing tips first, and the older members suffer). If the leaf size gets smaller, it is a sure sign of a call for help. If you wait too long, the compression factor cannot be reversed and even repotting won't save that great beauty.

Some plants, however, prefer to be rootbound—in fact they blossom better in a tight girdle. And there are plants like the Christmas cactus which can live in the same pot for 20 or 40 years; it is anyone's educated guess. But the phrase *potbound* means the roots want out.

REMOVING PLANT FROM POT

There's a standard technique for getting a plant out to check for root problems, sick soil or whatever. Take the pot in your right hand, under the bottom, and place the open fingers of your left around the stem or stems at the top so that when you turn it upside down it won't all fall out (if you're a southpaw, reverse the hands). Carefully rap the rim on the edge of a shelf or table to loosen the plant *and* the contents all in one action. If it doesn't drop out into your hand, bring it upright again and run a kitchen knife carefully around the sides to release stubborn little rootlets which may have grown right into the pot; then try the upside-down rapping again.

If the root ball looks solid and you can see those strong white roots, you move to the next step. However, when the root ball smells sour and roots look brown and soft, get rid of the plant!

145

It some of the roots look spongy or unhealthy, cut them off with sharp shears. If the root mass is badly potbound and you can't bear to give it the heave-ho, you might try to loosen some of the roots all around the edge—no guarantee it will work, but again you won't know unless you try. If the crocking has grown into the mass, carefully work it loose. If this happens to be a dividable plant, you might consent to surgery and both plants will be refreshed.

The new pot size should be up to two inches wider in diameter (but no more because the roots won't grow fast enough to use the new material and they get sodden while the center of the pot isn't getting enough moisture). This additional space will allow about one full inch all around the outside of the root ball.

BIGGER POT

NEW SOIL

GRAVEL

CHECK CROCKING

Start with a clean pot and plan to use material similar to that which the plant resides in now. Switching brands puts stresses on an already troubled individual.

TOP DRESSING FOR THE BIG PLANT

If the instructions say that a plant needs acid soil and you don't have a gadget to measure the pH, try adding ½ tsp. of cider vinegar to a quart of water and administer to soil a couple times a year.

Repotting is fine for plants you can easily handle or lift. Repotting a tubbed plant which may weigh a hundred pounds is a nurseryman's headache. Ordinary folk resort to top dressing. This is a process of scraping away the top one or two inches of soil, working around the roots with a small spoon so you won't injure them. Then add a layer the same depth as that removed. It is a good idea to add a half teaspoon of bonemeal to the good new soil (or a soil substitute if that is what was used in the tub) as a pick-me-up. A little peat can be added too, to keep the soil airy. Then you do the usual thorough watering and let the plant begin to dry before watering again.

Top dressing is particularly helpful to older plants which were planted in soil which gets crusty on top or shows the white markings of watering or feeding which had too much saline for the plant to take. This top dressing chore may occur only once a year, preferably in the spring so the growing season coincides.

146

MULCHING

A suggestion from a favorite plant information source, the Avant-Gardener: *Dipping new and cleaned pot rims in a polyurethane varnish, or brushing it on, will later prevent collection of fertilizer salts that burn leaves when they touch rims.*

A mulch is a kind of blanket to cover the bare bosoms of soil around the stem. White marble chips come in packages (as do assorted colors, but these distract from the plant, I feel) and can be spread evenly over the pot area. Mulches hold in the moisture more, and white reflects warmth—both positive growth factors.

A layer of small polished stones found in Oriental stores makes for low-key elegance. Flat beach stones in grays and black, coarse-chopped redwood or fir-bark chips, even a planting of baby tears or wild strawberry are natural ground covers which say "I like this plant."

SUPPORT YOUR LOCAL PLANTS

Multiple-stem greenery suffers on occasion from middle-age spread. It starts flopping over in an awkward fashion and needs the support and comfort of staking near the center of the plant. A thin bamboo cutting, available from a hardware or nursery center and placed so it doesn't run into major roots, will do. Lengths of yarn attached to the stake from the runaway stems will bring the plant to stand-up attention again.

Newly potted rigid-stem cuttings with top-heavy leaf clusters are inclined to tipsy positions and need temporary correction. Vines, like ivy, anchor themselves to wire frames but they need a friendly hand to wind them up. The wax vine will be happier with a post or pole, secured outside the pot, to give its shoots floor to ceiling blast-off space. The monstera, huge split-leaf king of the jungle, depends on trees to climb to reach the sun; a long length of timber bamboo inserted in the container will be an adequate substitute with a few supportive ties. If you can't locate bamboo, use a six-foot closet pole or even a broom handle sanded smooth (remove all signs of paint: neatness counts).

Ties for these heavier plants should be inconspicuous. Patented Twistems, which are lengths of wire covered with a heavy green paper, are ideal because the paper protects the stems from metal contact. Raffia, macrame cord, jute twine—all will work. Care must be taken that the ties allow for growth of the stems.

Vines grown for window "curtains" can be held in place by putting vine staples at regular intervals on the frame, and tying black wrapping string from the staple to the vine.

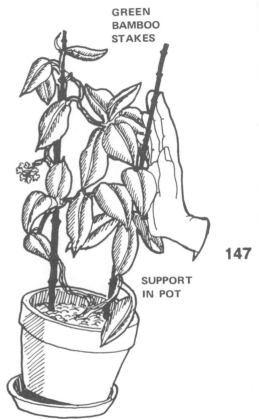

GREEN
BAMBOO
STAKES

147

SUPPORT
IN POT

Planting wire baskets? "Sheet moss," used by nurseries to line baskets, is hard to find. Instead, try clean burlap to hold soil; place so it extends above top and use thin wire or plant ties to hold securely.

148

CUT-LEATHER SLING

MEXICAN BURRO MUZZLE

GETTING THE HANG OF POTS

Plants which are swingers—hanging baskets and pots—need discipline and daily surveillance to keep them in line. Here are some thoughts about that.

Foremost, plants suspended from the ceiling or brackets on walls have air circulating around all sides, which means they dry out faster. The upper layer of air is warmer than that of their neighbors downstairs. Also, most of us start out with just one hanging pot—and plants *do* like company. Groupings thrive better than loners because they can transpire more efficiently. And several hung at different heights are more interesting than a single.

Be warned that hanging plants can be a darned nuisance to water properly—or even hard to reach to water. If you get hung up on hang ups, invest also in a lightweight aluminum stepladder, one which will elevate you three to four feet and bring your eye high where you can watch the watering action. Ordinary pitcher watering from floor level is awkward, with your sleeve getting most of the splashdown.

How much as well as *how to* water is critical. Clay pots dry out fast; if you can, take them down one at a time and submerge the whole pot to be sure moisture reaches the center. Plastic, ceramic and glazed ones hold in moisture, and once you've mastered the gymnastics, you'll find they are more satisfactory. The fact that these plants are hung at eye level makes you more conscious of the shape and imagination of the container and the gimmicks which hold them in suspension. Pots at low levels attract the eye *into* the plant, so the pot itself is less aesthetically important.

Taking down a plant daily to check water, particularly if it is heavy, is a hazard, so always move slowly and deliberately (and have a sheet of plastic or newspapers under in case of an emergency). Rigid wire hangers (the kind the planted pot usually comes with) are fairly easy to slip in and out of fixed hooks, but the rope, macrame and leather ones have a way of sagging just as you think you've got them hooked. So I vote for the ladder, a long-nose watering pot and a calm steady hand—and leaving the plant in place.

When watering don't forget the urgent need for a saucer under the pot to catch the excess before it spoils the rug and your day. The wire support normally holds only the pot, so a simple answer is to find a cork the right size to insert into the drainage hole before watering; then remove it after a few hours when the soil has soaked up the water. Plants have to be housebroken too.

Many contemporary containers are available with attached saucers; they are well worth the extra cost. Then, there is the pot-in-pot technique again where the outside pot holds the excess water (remember to put a layer of pebbles inside for the smaller pot to stand on so it stays above the water line). The space between the two pots will take a layer of moist moss to insure proper humidity.

An old-fashioned hanging "basket"—not necessarily a basket but any kind of open-work container—drips profusely, sheds moss and belongs in a greenhouse or hanging outside. These can be wire egg baskets, orchid baskets, open-slat wood squares built like Lincoln log houses or colanders. I suggest sticking with swingers in real pots.

Finally, because hanging plants lose their nutrients faster than their low-level brothers, they can use extra feedings while going through growing pains. Use a weak solution of liquid fertilizer.

Vine-type plants reach out for light so be kind and rotate them once in awhile to help them keep their shape. Keep a sharp eye out for bugs; if you suspect invaders, take the plant down, immerse the foliage in a big bucket of water and let it drain well before rehanging. If the bugs hang tough, take the plant outside and apply a garden spray. If you have a spare tree, hook the container on a branch so you can spray the underside of leaves more easily. A gentle misting with the hose outside refreshes foliage, too.

Succulents are great as hang-ups because they love the warmth and the dryer climate. The Christmas cactus and the burro tail sedum are likely tenants, both distinctive in leaf form and low care.

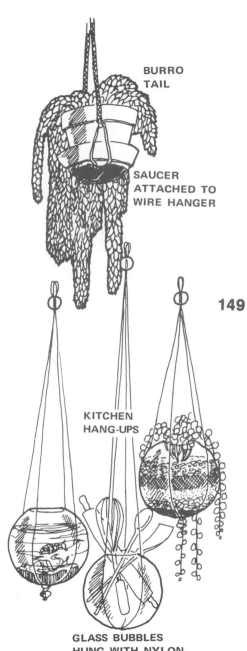

BURRO TAIL

SAUCER ATTACHED TO WIRE HANGER

KITCHEN HANG-UPS

GLASS BUBBLES HUNG WITH NYLON FISH LINE

149

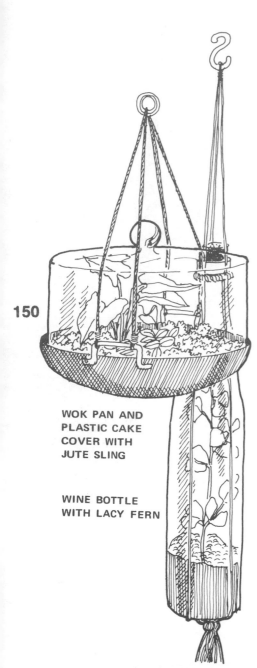

150

**WOK PAN AND
PLASTIC CAKE
COVER WITH
JUTE SLING**

**WINE BOTTLE
WITH LACY FERN**

PUTTING A TERRARIUM TOGETHER

Modern terrariums, those glass gardens which, once planted, take so little care because they are practically self-watering, are descended from something called a Wardian case. In 1842 a man named Nathaniel Ward stumbled on the covered-jar plant method: moisture evaporates from the soil and the leaf transpiration, rises to the top of the jar and condenses, sliding back down to recycle the moisture. He was so excited he built large glass cases in which he could try rare tropical plants. The Victorians went further and built huge glass hothouses, heated humid places, and thus began today's rage for indoor plants.

If your life is complicated, or your living area limited, the terrarium offers an ideal way to experiment with plants. If you are a heavy weekender, or want to ski for a week in the winter, terrarium plants will house sit themselves. They survive nicely in offices, too.

Practically any container in clear glass (stay away from color and ripples because you want to see what's inside) can be transformed with planting: an old aquarium, a brandy snifter or even one of the new package kits with terrarium, planting material and instructions.

There are completely enclosed terrariums like candy dishes and glass eggs which come apart in the middle. Large old battery jars and cookware are easiest to plant, but you will have to locate glass covers to promote condensation. The dish garden is a pot or deep ceramic planter with a glass dome to allow tall plants. And there are the inevitable bottle gardens which take an angel's patience.

TERRARIUM POTTING

The package mix is the safest material to use for this particular container: it is balanced, nutrimented and loosened with organic ingredients to give the best drainage—and blooms, if any. It has charcoal so the material doesn't get sour (it will help to add a layer of pea-sized charcoal on the bottom of any planter before adding the moistened mix: see Getting Potted). Depth of the planting mix should be about one-fourth the height of the container; it should never be flat straight across but have parts higher than others and small valleys.

The terrarium looks best with plants of several sizes and varieties (see Plants to Nourish and Cherish: Terrariums) which are of the same disposition. Some should be small and creeping, some medium size and dynamic and some tall with good profiles.

When you are ready to plant, arrange the plants (on that sheet of plastic for easy cleanup) in the most pleasant grouping; avoid indecisive fumbling inside the glass. When you think it looks pretty good, dig the first hole in the mix with an iced-tea spoon in the deepest layer, and plant the big plant first; spread the roots out horizontally and then cover with more of the mix. Tamping the stuff to hold the plant firmly in place is next, and a wine cork stuck on an ice pick will make a good stiff tamper. Add the medium-size plants next, keeping in mind their relationship to the large one in your original design. The creepers, together with some moss if you want, come next. Step back and have a walk around all sides to be sure you've made a little gem. If you still feel the need of a focal point, a few pebbles, some driftwood bits, a handsome miniature sculpture will give it your own signature.

BOTTLE GARDENS

The steady hand wins with bottle gardens. Keeping the glass clean is the most important part of the act. Cover the bottom with strata of pebbles, sand and charcoal, inserting each in turn through a funnel made of rolled-up note paper. The soil mix is tough to get in without smearing the glass—a wood chopstick to push it through the funnel-protected neck takes infinite patience.

You'll need one of those purchasable gadgets for planting bottle-aria—a long mechanical kind of finger for digging, handling, tamping. If

Add to the list of soil lighteners for the '80s: Commercial plant growers are experimenting with fine plastic beads of expanded foam to maintain even moisture in the pot; they are dust-free and do not compact.

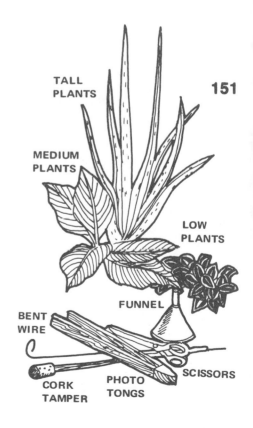

TALL PLANTS

151

MEDIUM PLANTS

LOW PLANTS

FUNNEL

BENT WIRE

SCISSORS

CORK TAMPER

PHOTO TONGS

What will clean the interiors of terrariums that have become stained, dull? For a tank, try an automotive glass cleaning solution on a cloth or paper towel. Sudsy ammonia may be even more effective. Glass in which liquids have been stored for years may become etched and impervious to correction. Soak bottles in a solution of household bleach to loosen algae and scum.

you are handy, you can improvise with wood photo pincers, bent coat hangers—and pipe cleaners to clean smears.

Plants should have pliable leaves to get them in the bottles and any pruning should be done before the plants go in. When you are ready to insert them, remove as much soil as possible from the roots, fold the leaves around the stem and slowly lower, with a nudge from the chopstick or a small wood dowel; you can get the plant in place and tamp with either of these, watching that you don't damage the foliage. The little plants go in last. If a plant doesn't make the descent and getting it out creates more problems, just take the dowel, dig a small grave, bury the victim—and try another!

Adding water to bottle gardens the first time can be messy with splashes. Use a funnel of plastic or metal with a length of narrow hose attached. Lower the hose down to the mix and add the water carefully. Water too much and the plants will drown; not enough and they look sick. Feel your way with terrariums because there is no set rule.

A FEW NOTES ABOUT TERRARIUM PECULIARITIES

☞ If you have trouble getting sand, watch for local home-building action; there's usually a pile at the street edge where you can talk the contractor into sharing a shoeboxful.

☞ Take a close look at the terrarium the day after you finish planting. It should have a slight mistiness around the top. High humidity, cool nights and warm days are ideal.

☞ If the cover is sopping wet, slip it back (or uncork, if it's a bottle) to let in more air. If a pall of mold settles over the soil and the plants and stems look droopy after a few months, you've overwatered. The best recommendation is to start all over with a carefully cleaned terrarium, new soil mix and new plants. Mold is contagious and you don't want to transfer the earlier false start.

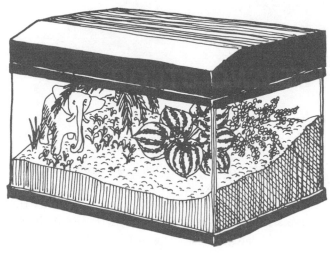

**LIGHT UNIT
ON TOP**

**RECYCLED
AQUARIUM
OR PLASTIC
PLANT BOX
WITH BUILT-
IN LIGHTING
SYSTEM**

☞ Never let the soil dry out completely. If leaves start getting brown and drop off, add water.

☞ Use lukewarm water; avoid any water-softened or heavily chlorinated water.

☞ Bottle gardens can live for months without additional moisture; however, watch ferns and moss for drying signs.

☞ For the first few days after planting, keep the container out of bright light. Then, up the wattage. Plants left in one position with not enough light, get leggy; move the terrarium around.

☞ Cut back plants which threaten to engulf others. If something is getting too big, take it out, pot it up for a friend, and plant a smaller variety in its place. (Do not try this with bottle gardens.)

☞ Keeping a glass house in a too cold room or one too hot will encourage buildup of fogging. Find a place where there's bright light and comfortable room temperature. Remove foliage which is rotting from excess moisture with tweezers or a wire hanger bent to go through a narrow-neck bottle.

☞ Cacti and succulents look great in glass houses. They take sandy mix (add a good portion of fish-tank gravel for variety) and very little moisture. Leave the top off and give the plants lots of warmth and light. If you feel the urge for a pet, invite a salamander into your terrarium; it would like a piece of desert wood or rocks to hide under.

153

Terrarium living is euphoria for most ferns. Here are a few takers: Mother, button, ribbon and Southern maidenhair, Polypodium, Davallia, *bird's nest, holly.*

WATER GARDEN CULTURE

Familiar small house plants and cuttings in readily available materials are planted into a see-through water garden, which you may enjoy at eye level.

Start with a deep, sparkly clean glass container of a size that will fit your windowsill. Buy small plants in two- or three-inch pots from garden centers, florists or sidewalk stands outside the neighborhood five-and-dime store; or take cuttings which usually root in water. The potted plant, however, will have a better shape and attitude toward the world than a cutting.

You will need marble chips or small bags of white terrarium rock. Wash the marble to remove dust and put a generous layer on the bottom of the container. Now add the next layer of packaged plant charcoal. Then add a layer of coarse sand.

Remove the plants from their pots and wash off all the soil under the faucet, being careful to protect the rootlets. With sharp shears remove any broken or decayed roots and arrange the plants on the sand, filling in with grey gravel around the roots and up the stem until it is at the original soil level. A single layer of polished Japanese mini-stones gives one more strata. If the plant wants to lean, give it a geode or mineral rock to lean on—and to catch the sparkle of window light. (The white-grey levels are propagation "chambers" and cause new roots to form when they reach down for the food and water.)

Now prepare a water "potting" mixture by adding to water one-fourth of the amount recommended on the bottle of a good liquid fertilizer. (Store unneeded amounts in a gallon jar for later replacement of the evaporated water.) Add the fertilized water to the window garden until it reaches one-half the upper level of gravel, where it must be maintained.

Check once a week to keep the right amount of water in the container. Change the water every six weeks by draining it in the sink or by using a basting tube. Prune a plant too tall for the window.

154

HELPING YOUR PLANT
DO ITS OWN THING

THE WATER PICTURE

By now you should be reassured that purple thumbers are not indelibly marked for life. Frustration *can* be hosed off with an enlightened attitude about watering.

No two plants are alike in their thirst, even plants of the same family. No two locations involving light and temperature are exactly the same. Not even green thumbers can make rules for watering.

What you and your plant have to do is compromise—there's no guarantee one way or another that what you do will be exactly right. But when you discover that plants give signals and you recognize those signs, it will be fairly easy to work out a nice coexistence.

Beginners usually overwater. That's Sin No. 1. What happens next is that the important little rootlets, or hair roots, which take in the nutrients, can't breathe because the water fills up all the air spaces and keeps out life-giving oxygen.

If the soil is allowed to dry out a little between each moistening, the roots work harder to reach that moisture and the plant flourishes. Saturate the mixture continuously and the rootlets rot. The victim shows no immediate signals but within a week some of the lower leaves get a jaundiced look and the plant looks miserable. Once root rot starts, there's little hope for salvage.

About underwatering: don't panic at the droop of a normally happy leaf. A potted indoor hydrangea or an impatiens laps up water and the first sign of sagging leaves calls for instant liquid. A plant can go through this wilt-down and pop right back several times, but it won't take too many neglects. Don't press your luck.

Cacti and succulents are desert rats, brought up on rationed water. They resent a Nervous Nellie with watering can and even the hardiest will flake out from an overdose. Some succulents, like the orchid cactus (*Epiphyllum*), need consistent watering if left in a sunny window, but revert to the dry routine during dormancy.

Keep jasmine cool; water well until it drains out, then none again until there's a slight drying of top surface.

Areca palm likes soil slightly moist all of the time. Feed liquid food monthly during growing season. Try east exposure light.

To repeat, there is no set rule. In Plants to Nourish and Cherish there are suggestions about what each plant likes. But "how much?" depends on the plant, where it is, how big it is, what kind of pot and soil it's living in and what the surrounding temperature and light conditions are.

WATER THERAPY

To help you figure out your general plan, here is a recap of suggestions which are sprinkled in other parts of this book.

☞ Soil is light in color when dry, darker when wet; but don't water just because it is pale—it could be sneaky wet down under.

☞ Watch crusty soil. Put your finger on the stuff and push down. Does it feel dry? If you scratch away a little (careful of those roots near the surface), is the next depth dry? A light pot means it needs water, a heavier one indicates there is still moisture inside. However, this weight gain or loss is tough to identify and if the container is a big one, impossible. The finger touch is still best.

☞ Try rapping the pot with your knuckles: a dry pot has a sharp sound, a full one sounds kind of dull.

☞ The surest way of looking at the root/moisture condition is to knock the plant out of the pot by turning it upside down with one hand holding the plant; hit the rim on a table edge so that it is released. If the pot size is over eight inches, skip it. Smaller pots are the critical ones anyway because they are quickest to dry out.

☞ Thick soil holds back water more than a loose soilless mix.

☞ The soil level in a big tub or container ought to be at least an inch and a half below the rim so you can give it a big drink at one time. Then let the plant rest until your finger tells you the soil is barely moist before you add more.

☞ Pots incorrectly planted with soil right up to the brim can be successfully watered by dunking them in a bucket filled to the midway

157

"KNOCK, KNOCK, WHO'S THERE?"

When misting, don't give a plant a shower; try to lay on a very thin layer of droplets that will evaporate quickly. Make it a regular habit, particulary in dry summer months. P.S. And don't forget to wash leaves once in a while (dust the hairy ones and leave the misting to the rest). Dusty foliage prevents carbon absorption through the foliage pores.

158

Watering rule-of-thumb (non-purple): Oftener if plant has large thin leaves, less if thick leaves or spines, more if a large plant in a small pot, more if pot is clay, less if plastic.

point. When water seeps through to the top of the soil, remove the pot and let it drain.

Newly planted? Add tepid water slowly so that the plant will not move or float. Let the soaked pot sit in a sink or washtub until the excess has left via the drain hole.

Cold water is injurious to roots. It should be room temperature or slightly warmer. Rainwater is fine; snow or ice must be melted to a comfortable degree. Save the water from boiled eggs for special treat to your small plants like shamrocks.

Lots of chlorine coming out of your pipes? Let the water sit overnight before using. Softened water is hard on plants, too, if there's sodium in its makeup.

If a plant is growing, it needs more liquid; if it is resting, less.

Small pots dry out faster than larger ones.

Greenery in clay pots requires more watering than that in plastic.

Hanging pots get all-around drying air; add water oftener.

Plants heavy with buds? Extra water at this time.

Fuzzy-leaf plants (African violets, etc.) must keep their heads above water; cold-water droplets on leaves cause discouraging brown spots. Irrigate by deep-watering. This is a lengthy operation—don't try it if you're rushed. For temporary relief use a kitchen baster. Water temperature of 70° is ideal. Cyclamen and begonias like tubs rather than showers, too.

Deep-watering, the submerging of the pot in a bucket or tub of water, lets the water get to the heart of the pot. Too often ordinary action doesn't soak through to the bottom roots. Once a week—you have to decide whether it's oftener—is better than mini-waterings several times in that same period. (It *is* easier to remember that Saturday is bath day.)

Higher room temperatures send out calls for more humidity.

When a plant looks sick, withhold liquids; water just enough to keep it alive. (And for heaven's sake, *don't* feed it to make it well—the plant has enough problems already without indigestion, too!)

WHAT TIME OF DAY DO I WATER?

Most reliable sources suggest morning watering so that it is absorbed by the plant for manufacturing oxygen before the temperature drops at night. Experimenters add water in the evening on the basis that dew falls then. But, rain falls *any* time, so I try watering when I have plenty of time to give it my full attention.

Spilled water on leaves makes them unhappy if there's bright sun. When you pour, pinpoint the water into the soil.

Misting of plants which like additional leaf-intake and humidity can be done anytime provided the plant is not in full sun.

To keep a single plant alive if you're away for a couple of weeks: Place water in an empty coffee can, punch a hole in the plastic lid and thread a yarn wick through; bury the other end of wick in the plant's soil. The lid slows natural evaporation.

THE MECHANICS OF WATERING

The common carrier is a pitcher or kitchen measuring cup from which water is poured into the top of the pot. These are basic the-only-thing-I-can-find tools; they aren't very satisfactory for finding openings in dense-foliage plants.

Once you decide to be serious about indoor greenery, invest in a simple tin watering can which will hold a quart and which has a long, slim no-drip nose. Some have a shower head on the tip to disperse driblets, but I like the plain narrow end which gets right into the jungle and the soil with a steady even flow. Move the watering can around the pot, sticking its nose between stems as you go to be sure the water gets distributed front and center, uniformly. With this kind of equipment you don't have to mop up after every watering.

The saucer-watering method can be done a couple of ways. First place a deep saucer or tray under the pot; it can be at least an inch larger clear around the bottom of the pot. Add water. Then with a kitchen baster, suck up the excess not drawn into the plant through the drain hole. No plant should ever be allowed to sit in a puddle—unless it is a true water-baby. Putting a layer of pebbles in the saucer to lift the

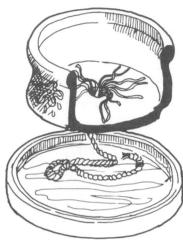

WATER-WICK POT

160

pot and keep it from touching the saucer will eliminate removal of excess water—and at the same time furnish a more humid condition as it evaporates.

The saucer filled with pebbles and watered from the top of the pot rather than the bottom is another method.

Then there's the water-wick, a tried and true answer for azaleas and violets. First make a wick from glass-fibre cord which can be unwound. Put the unwound end into the pot through the drain hole and arrange the single strands inside the bottom in a circle. Complete the planting and set it on a pebble-layered saucer with the wick coming out of the drain hole and inserted in the pebbles. By capillary action the water follows the wick up into the pot and provides constant moisture in a limited measure.

The kitchen baster is ideal for watering tiny pots because it gives out minimal amounts of liquid and is controllable. Clay "cones" and glass plant-quenchers which can be poked into pots before you vacation are now available in gift and floral shops. They become automatic plant waterers—and sometimes more satisfactory than the friendly neighbor who overwaters or forgets to check in.

The fog or mist sprayer is your good friend. There are small brass ones for less than three dollars. An ironing sprinkler with a squeeze handle holds more water but tends to drip occasionally. Rubber bulb syringes work too; and some beautiful metal pressure sprayers are appearing on the market which will delight gadget collectors.

MORE ON DRAINAGE

The pot with crocking, or broken bits of old clay pots over the drain hole or holes, should have no trouble. However, when the plant lives too many lives in one pot, it can fill the area around that drain with roots and finally close the exit. When you knock the plant out of the pot to repot, you will have to free the crocking and start with new. Uncrocked pots get clogged and make trouble for you.

Big ceramic pots and built-in planters with no drain holes depend on the gravel and charcoal layers to keep the soil from going bad. Watering and liquid feeding are ticklish, and you can only find the best routine by patience and varying your attention.

Pots-within-pots have drain headaches too. The water tends to collect in the larger pot and may attract mosquitoes, get smelly or creep up around the smaller pot. Keep a vigilant eye here and be sure there is space underneath the inner container—raise it on a pebble layer or in the case of huge plants put a brick underneath. (When you do double-potting, plan to keep the rims of both pots at about the same level for appearance; don't let the inner one disappear because the whole plant needs light and the drying action where air circulates.) When you fill the space between two pots with sphagnum moss and plan to keep it moist, there is still air circulation and the added humidity will cut down on watering action.

Wicking: Fiberglas netting, the kind used in building boats, moves water from one point to another as well as cotton does, never rots. It is especially efficient used in orchid pots which need more moisture because of their loose potting medium.

SPEAKING OF HUMIDITY

Humidity and temperature are relatives: the higher the temperature, the more humidity is needed. Low humidity, commonly found indoors in winter due to closed windows and blaring heaters, is seriously felt by plants. Greenhouses have similar temperatures, but their high humidity makes a plant thrive rather than be deprived. Air conditioners which operate with a moisture factor are a help, but some dry the air; check the action.

Plants grouped together tend to supply one another with a better relative humidity level. Putting them on one deep tray with bottom covered with gravel or small stones makes for easy watering and the moisture around the stones again keeps a happy humid level.

Even leaving a small pot of water near a plant will give it a boost. Portable humidifiers of acceptable size are now available and provide continuous steady results. And of course the misting process once a day is a plant-saver. Spray to add humidity but not saturate the plant.

Don't cut the growing tip of a palm—that's its only new growth hope.

Two final words about casting your plant on the waters. First, don't underestimate the power of the shower. Ferns and plants which truly enjoy water will come out clean and gorgeous. So, take a plant to bathe with you; they love the moisture of a warm damp room. And lastly, don't be afraid to let nature help you. In San Francisco's Chinatown, on any rainy not-too-cold day the curb is lined with house plants put out to catch the drops. One last word: water softeners contain soluble salts that may affect some plants adversely.

PRUNING

162

After a bromeliad flower dies, remove it. New rosettes form at the base that will make several new plants. Each common bromeliad blooms only once.

Some plants never need pruning or pinching back. But for the few radicals, you have to use a nonsentimental cutback constantly; wandering Jew, for one, gets leggy fast. Geraniums, Swedish ivy and fuchsias benefit from active pruning.

Pinching the soft stem between the thumb and forefinger will remove the offending straggler. A sharp knife or hand pruners are needed for woody stems.

Pruning indoors is similar to outdoor practice. Lop off a branch or stem just above a leaf bud which is pointed in the direction you want it to go. Stubs are ugly; if the branch has few leaves, take it off right back at the juncture to the main stem. Dead branches and stems must be removed to keep the plant neat, even if it leaves the plant slightly lopsided. If the plant is healthy it will pull itself together again. Woody plants take pruning after blossoming and the resting time that follows. Housekeep blooming plants daily as you walk by to remove deadheads.

KEEP IT LIGHT

Understatement of the year is to say most indoor conditions are not ideal for plants. Is yours an old house with small windows and dark wood-sheathed walls or a flat with limited light access? Do you slave away in an office without natural light?

Don't be discouraged: plants have been grown in dark basements by lamplight; vegetables rose up in the Polaris submarine, deep in the seas, under fluorescents; and scientists grew a carrot/marigold garden under ice at the South Pole using fluorescent and incandescent light together with controlled temperature. Gardening indoors with added artificial light is an everyday wonder. Marvelous results can be experienced with a little practical imagineering.

Fluorescent tubes give out red and blue rays, incandescents give red and far-red; this may not mean much to you but it represents what the plant asks of the sun. Blue rays excite foliage action, red plays on flower power. When you combine natural light with artificial, it increases the rays and the plant will really go all out.

Any additional man-made light will help a plant, but combining fluorescent and incandescent—one warm white and one cool white—is an ideal marriage. Two 40-watt tubes and one 25- or 30-watt bulb will take care of a fairly large family of plants. The fluorescent should be closer to the foliage; use longer tubes because there is some light loss at the ends. Keep incandescents at least 18 inches above the plant's top to minimize the heat from the bulbs.

If you use only one type, it gives the same condition as a shady corner of the garden. Use only tubes and you'll have to be satisfied with a piddling display of flowers. You can grow foliage successfully, however, with a cool-white fluorescent because the greenery can be as close as four inches to the light source and not get burned by the high intensity. Fluorescents lose efficiency with age (put date of installation on end of tube with a grease pencil) and replace as needed.

Both kinds of light are readily available and not too difficult to

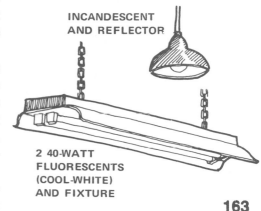

INCANDESCENT AND REFLECTOR

2 40-WATT FLUORESCENTS (COOL-WHITE) AND FIXTURE

163

164

install in a barren area where you otherwise couldn't garden. You need a handy outlet, a waterproof cord and a place to attach the lamp. Special plant-growth and wide-spectrum lamps let the plant's color appear more natural than under fluorescent (the greens and yellows of the spectrum have been minimized), and provide the wavelengths most closely approximating sunlight. Warning: use porcelain sockets for plant lamps. The new mercury vapor and halide bulbs give off ultraviolet radiation when broken. Handle very carefully and only when bulb has been turned off and is cool.

Your neighborhood hardware or lighting store can lead you to the proper fixtures. A common industrial fluorescent unit that holds one or two tubes is sturdy, fireproof (keep inflammables away from the fixture parts). Customizing a bookcase or a planter takes electrical know-how—don't borrow trouble by trying to jerry-rig it yourself.

Of course, there are several simple suggestions for adding more light on the subjects: reflective surfaces, like white walls and mirrors, lift up the amount of light from a window. Also, opening the window shades fully and pruning back any trees or shrubs outside that may be cutting out light give natural light its full effectiveness.

HOW MUCH LIGHT DOES A PLANT NEED?

A footcandle is electricianese for a measurement of light intensity. Up to 50 footcandles will not support house-plant life; 50 to 250 will do for foliage plants like the cast-iron aspidistra, the century plant (agave), baby tears, philodendron, dracaena, sansevieria or aucuba. Most plants need 250 to 650. But there are some which require 650 to 1400; this includes seed and cutting propagation, and kalanchoe, primrose, primula and calceolaria.

Borrow a friend's photographic light meter if you don't own one; it will be calibrated in footcandles and you can go all over your living space jotting down the amount of light wherever you might possibly try your new green thumb.

There is one critical bug in this measuring act: the light level changes drastically depending on the time of day and the time of year. On a brilliant day in summer the needle goes off the scale—10,000 footcandles' worth; a winter's grey day may shoot it down to 500. Also, this rather simple experiment does not give you critical information about light rays the eye does not see and so it isn't a perfect answer.

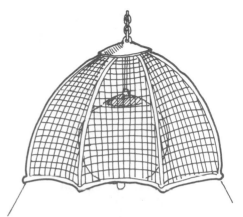

When determining a plant's light needs, you must also consider the length of time the plant needs that light. Some plants grow in cycles when 14 hours of light and 10 of darkness are right. Most bulbs like less—about 10 hours a day for daffodils, hyacinths and tulips. African violets, however, like 18-hour days (and at least 650 footcandles): putting their light source on a time clock will mean they bloom profusely and you don't have to get up at 3 a.m. to turn on the lights. Chrysanthemums need dark glasses in order to bloom. Poinsettias insist on a short day and won't give out with that red or pale-green crown unless they get a 14-hour night.

165

Luckily most plants are easier to get along with on average cycles of light. Vegetables are considered average, but they grow faster, fatter with longer day cycles and being foliage they can do without incandescent help. Grow them close to the kitchen sink where they are easier to water or to harvest for a winter's salad—and a light left on after hours won't upset the family.

As you can see, putting your plants together in simpatico groupings will simplify your life. They will be easier to tend and all will benefit from one artificial light installation. If one plant prefers less light, it can be put offside or in the shade of the greedier ones.

Place plants under existing incandescent lights—a centerpiece on the dining table under the main fixture, a small pot under a table reading lamp. Remember, though, that the light will have to stay on at least 10 to 12 hours a day.

The shelves of a wall bookcase/hi-fi/knickknack unit will take

LIGHT IN
SHELF
UNIT

166

several plants provided you attach a fluorescent light under the shelf above (the shelf should be adjustable to take care of changing height of plants). Room dividers, remodeled bathrooms, kitchen reshapings can become plant centers if you make plans before the carpenter is too far into the plywood.

Add the light of a 60-watt bulb to a window garden and lackadaisical greenery perks up and blooms as never before. The bay window which has its own shelf is a lucky break for plant-happy souls because the plants group easily, and get their light sides and back. Add an artificial light at the front and the leaves will stop leaning toward the window, and present you a better face to face.

Plants growing with artificial light transpire very much more than under ordinary conditions, so they must be watered more often.

If the cold light of the fluorescent offends, try setting your time clock so that it goes on at six in the morning. By the time you are ready for regular evening illumination, you can switch to incandescent until bedtime.

With light, the terrarium mini-greenhouse can be used to propagate seeds; added overhead lights will speed up nature's calendar. And your cuttings will show active growth in the humid warmth of a glass box, particularly if you can add heat from the bottom.

If you are experimenting with a few seeds, take an aluminum kitchen pot and find a clay planter which will sit on top of it (like a double boiler with part of the planter inside the pot). Attach a waterproof extension cord with light socket to a 7½-watt lamp which you put inside the cooking pot. Plant the seeds in the clay pot; put it on top of the aluminum one and cover the moistened seeds with plastic food wrap. This light gives bottom warmth, steady and gently, but don't let too much top light on the subject until the first green appears. Then remove it to a sunny spot, adding soluble plant food every two weeks. When the new plants begin to crowd one another, repot them.

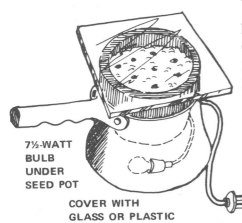

7½-WATT
BULB
UNDER
SEED POT

COVER WITH
GLASS OR PLASTIC

TO CONCLUDE ON THE LIGHT SIDE

One more use of light, this time for display and not to help growth: miniature lights make it possible to stage theatrical lighting on your plants in dark places or in the evening. The drama is heightened and the plants attract the eye. As when light is used at night to liven the outdoor garden, its source should be hidden.

If you are hooked on indoor plants and your footcandles are bare, choose cast-iron foliage and give up hope of flowers. But, if you want blossoms, add lights. Don't overestimate your power if you can't furnish the condition to match.

TEMPERATURE CONTROL

Higher thermometer readings rob plants of humidity. Greenery nearer the ceiling dries out faster because the temperature is higher up there. In an overheated room, a plant is naturally more content near the floor, but if you like plant-watching at the upper level, then give it ventilation (*not* drafts), and more misting and watering. Open a window slightly at the top, the one farthest away, to increase movement of warm air. When the surrounding air is too warm and dry, leaves will get brownish at the edges and lower ones will drop off leaving permanently bare stems.

Plants which get too great a variation of temperature (60° one day and 80° another) will be the first to show signs of wear. An unheated space, like a guest room, is a good vacation room for the plant which is resting; don't let temperatures go below 55°. A uniform 60° daytime will please most plant guests. Keep any plant away from an air-leaky window. Put a curtain or a plastic screen between to ward off cold. Pity the poor pot left next to a freezing glass window; it may just barely recover if you remove it to the bathtub or shower and spray with cold water, allowing it to unstiffen slowly in a cool spot.

African violence? Are the leaves of your violets thin, light green, with long stems? . . . flower poorly in winter? They need enlightening; 14 to 16 hours a day, either bright indirect sunlight or a south window in winter. Feed a half portion of high-phosphorus fertilizer at each watering for solid flowering.

167

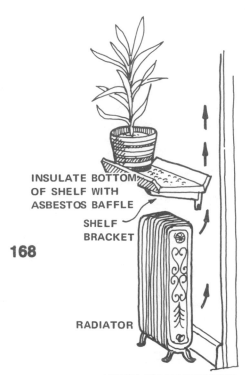

INSULATE BOTTOM
OF SHELF WITH
ASBESTOS BAFFLE

SHELF
BRACKET

168

RADIATOR

LEAVE SPACE BETWEEN
SHELF AND WALL FOR
UPWARD WARM AIR
MOVEMENT

Tropical plants adapt nicely to warmer positions, but must be deep-watered to make up for moisture lost to warmth. Big planter boxes filled with tropicals, like those in an office or studio, manage to provide extra humidity among themselves and combat some of the dryness of big-building heating systems.

Living in an apartment or flat where the temperature is dependent on a callous janitor can diminish your hopes for lush flowering displays. Incandescent lamps will help to keep the thermometer steady. And a heat lamp, placed to prevent overheating, may do the trick.

One warning about incandescent lights: a grouping of several can build up a heat imbalance; leave a small room thermometer at several checkpoints to be sure you're not toasting the foliage. And never subject a plant to the blast of the air conditioner.

Radiator heat can be death on vegetation. Too often the steam or hot-water unit is directly below a window where you might feature plants. By installing a kind of deflecting shelf over the radiator, covering it with asbestos insulation board (or even a stove-top tin-and-asbestos protector cut in half with tin shears), you can make a home for certain plants. The shelf needs to be six inches wider than the radiator and raised about six inches above the metal. Add a tray on top and an inch of gravel to set the pots on. Keep this tray always water filled, the bottoms of pots above the water. Check Plants to Nourish and Cherish for suggestions.

FEEDING: DIET AND THE GROWING PLANT

Green things which reside outside have unlimited room for roots to roam for the nourishment they require. Bring a plant indoors and confine its growth machinery to a space less than one-quarter of a cubic foot, and the miracle is that it grows at all.

Add ordinary or organic fertilizer to the garden and it breaks down slowly, releasing the nutrients. If you try to do the same for the potted plant, the reaction of the fertilizer is too slow, it offends the nose and most of the good is carried off in the watering before it can act. So here's food for thought.

When you pot up a plant, the soil mixture, particularly the packaged soilless variety, will have enough built-in food to carry it through the weaning. When you buy a young pot of foliage, it won't need a pick-me-up for at least three months.

You can tell fairly well by the slightest lightening of color in the bottom leaves when it is time to start shopping for indoor plant food. Formulas today come in liquid, powder, pill or pellet form. They contain balanced helpings of nitrogen, phosphorus and potassium—plants' three favorite appetizers.

Whether you use liquids, tablets, sticks to insert in the soil or time-release pellets, all have identifying numbers that indicate their composition, like 5-10-5. The first number tells the percentage of nitrogen, the second phosphorus (or phosphates) and the third potassium (potash). Select the large number for the job needed.

Nitrogen promotes good leaves, green coloring and adds to growth. If given too much nitrogen, however, a flowering plant will run to foliage, so the higher percentage should go to phosphorus which gets right into the sap stream and helps promote roots, flowers, fruits and seeds. Potassium balances the nitrogen by stiffening the stems and helping the plant resist bug invasions.

Organic buffs may still be tempted to make a weak "tea" of well-decayed manure, but its tardy action and the unlovely smell are

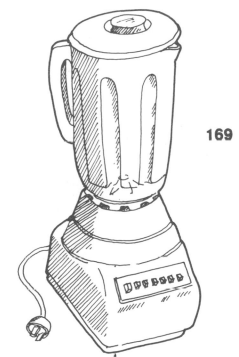

169

WHIP UP A JUICY HEALTH FOOD FOR PLANTS: ORGANIC "GARBAGE" LIKE VEGETABLE PEELINGS, LETTUCE LEAVES, EGG SHELLS, WITH TEPID WATER ADDED

Gardenia looks like the last stages of Camille? It may be hungry, particularly if leaves are yellowing. Add a steady diet of acid-type fertilizer and water-soluble iron.

170

Don't overfeed any member of the Crassula *family, including jade, silver dollar, silver beads, airplane, rat tail, rosary vine and Arab's turban. They're slow growers, so twice yearly is enough.*

even more reason to vote for odorless liquids, tablets or even plant sticks, which you just insert into the pot.

This is the place to sternly warn you: always water any potted plant thoroughly before adding fertilizer. When the soil is dry, it can be dangerous even to an old toughie.

To add liquid fertilizer by the watering method, use the exact measurements indicated on the bottle you buy! Don't throw in an extra spoonful for good measure; the formulas are carefully worked out and you are doing the plant no favor by going overboard. In fact, *less* than the recommended amount is a kindness to the vegetation. Once a month is plenty unless more is specifically recommended in the section Plants to Nourish and Cherish—and *none* during the months when the plant wants to rest for a while. Plants in northern areas take less food because of light levels.

Solutions made with liquid fertilizers (check the suggested formulation on the container) can be effective when sprayed on the leaves. For this action, you will need to take the plant out of doors or to put it on a large rug of newspapers so the residue won't mess up.

Dry powders have to be scratched into the surface of the soil, and to my thinking are the least attractive method of feeding your plant.

There are tablets and pellets for foliage promotion and for encouraging blossoms. There are some for African violets only, and plants like the azalea should have a high acid offering. The tablet routine is good in summer when you go vacationing and leave the family in care of a plant-sitter: no danger of overfeeding by a zealous but uninformed friend. The tablets are inserted once a month, at the outer edge of the plant where they can't burn the roots.

Don't feed a sick plant. If you do, it may just expire right now. Don't feed a newly potted plant; let it get used to its new home for at least three months. Don't add fertilizer just because the fancy hits you; if a plant is growing happily, leave it alone. Don't excite a small plant if you don't want it to outgrow its space. Most plants rest from September to March or April so let them alone.

SICK SICK SICK!

The major reasons for sick call are too much or too little of some vital growth factor: light, water, humidity, temperature, soil, feeding—and the obvious infiltration of insects and fungus. You can't ask the plant to open up and say "ahh-hh," but you *do* look at physical signs. And once you've effected a cure, the plant may live happily ever after—for awhile.

Overwatered? Leaf tips or margins brown, color is yellowing, leaves drop? Looking at the base of the pot, are there signs of sogginess? Root rot comes when water fills all the air spaces and the plant suffocates. (Azaleas have this particular weakness.) Is there a softening of the stem?

Need more light? Leaves too far apart, stems leggy? Yellowing leaves, oldest ones drop? Growth thin and weak, new leaves small, flowers fail to develop, color less intense, no bloom? Try more light, and quickly. If no window is available, try a 100-watt bulb 18 to 24 inches away from the nearest leaf. Leave the light on until 10 p.m. and it will give a big boost, particularly during short winter days.

Are the leaves brittle and unyielding? Perhaps the pot has been allowed to dry out too long or the atmosphere is too arid.

Leaves falling off? Overwatering or lack of water, too much fertilizer, too much sun, fumes or drafts.

Buds dropping before they open? Insufficient light, too low temperature, lack of food, compacted soil, drafts, length of daylight, too much sun and either too much or too little water for the roots. A budded plant doesn't like to be moved or turned; be patient.

Browning leaf edges? Too much sun and heat through glass, overwatering or lack of water, too much fertilizer toxic to roots, drafts.

Yellowing of the green plant? Lack of light, (particularly if the stems seem spindly), excess light too intense for some plants, high temperature at night, lack of food or overfeeding, tired soil (needs nitrogen fertilizer added) or dry roots the water hasn't reached.

171

If a big plant loses some of its lower branches or leaves, plant rooted cuttings of the same variety or four-inch pots obtained from your local nursery. They will fill in quickly, and being compatible, take the same watering pattern.

172

The wrong kind of mulch: Do not allow dropped leaves to remain on the soil. All dead material must be removed because soil pests may find a haven in decaying materials.

Wilting? This plant weakness can come from the pot standing in water, or from the other extreme—not enough moisture. Has the plant stood too long in the sun or near heat of stove or radiator? Did you add *cold* water? (Remember, it should be lukewarm.)

Are the leaves dusty? Sponging each leaf with water and gentle soap (*not* detergent) removes grime so the plant can breathe. A small plant can be dunked or misted, but never wet the leaves which are fuzzy (dust with a soft brush). Keep a washed plant out of the sun until it dries.

No blossoms? Insufficient light, too high temperature at night, overwatering or poor drainage; lack of food, compacted soil. Some plants are stubborn and will not oblige indoors. Gardenias and camellias drop their buds when the temperature is too high; cyclamen needs a low of 55° to set blooms; and geraniums dislike a warm kitchen. Poinsettias will not flower if there's more than 12 hours of light (turn off lamps, TV); kalanchoes, Christmas cactus and chrysanthemums are likewise frustrated.

Is the whole plant sagging? It may be growing too tall for its own good and needs a prop with a simple stake and a couple of ties. Little leaf ivy needs something to grow attached to; a two-by-two post or floor-to-ceiling pipe furnishes a leaning place for a tall dracaena or a climbing hoya. Turn the plant around if it leans toward the light.

Damping off? This pesky problem happens when the main stems seem weak at the soil level and the plant tilts; it could be fungus, but usually the first cause is water which stands on the upper soil and doesn't drain off (shamrock stems flop quickly with too much moisture). Or, the plant may have been caught in a draft; change the location, the watering habits. Check soil to be sure it isn't compacted; scratch the surface with a kitchen fork to loosen and aerate.

Moss on the top of the soil? Scrape it away; check to see if soil is compacted and apply a light top dressing of new soil or mix. Dry white areas may indicate hard water leftovers, or an accumulation of salts from the fertilizer which the plant can't use.

Fungus? Most house plants are home free from this growth because interiors are too dry and hot for it to flourish. If it is cool and they get excess moisture, yellowing and round brown spots appear on the leaves; pick off affected leaves and burn. Dust with a commercial compound which contains sulphur.

Mildew? A kind of white powdery stuff appears, resulting from too heavy a hand with water; try sulphur application here also and be sure the plant has adequate ventilation—but no drafts.

Does the soil look lifeless, sour? It should be crumbly and not a hardened mud pie. Look for drainage problems; if the water is readily absorbed and runs out the bottom, leave the soil alone unless it needs a top dressing. Big pots and tubs respond if you do this once a year.

Did you recently dose the plant with fertilizer? There *are* times when you hold back food:

The newly potted plant: give it three months' rest.

The dry plant: give it a good soaking and be sure the moisture has gone all through the pot before you feed.

The sick plant: just as you get the special diet treatment at the hospital, be sure recovery is a fact before starting regular feeding.

During winter months and on dark cloudy days, hold off; plants rest or hibernate in winter, particularly cacti and some succulents. Bulbs lie dormant, as do cyclamen. Give them time to finish their naps and they will perk up on their own schedules.

When flower buds start to color, slow feeding.

Although this age is into the organic, *don't* use fresh manure; it must be well decomposed.

**EROTIC EXOTICS, OR
A PAT ON THE BOTTOM
WORKS A MIRACLE**

173

A New Yorker lived with a pathological plant which refused to do what she expected a plant to do: bloom! One morning, before leaving for work, she snatched the pot in frustration and banged it on the kitchen counter, announcing in a loud voice the end of their relationship.

Two weeks later, the plant had new leaves, started signs of blossoms! Simple answer: its roots found new spaces to move around.

Scale on your banana? Add one tsp. of kerosene to one qt. of tepid soapy water. Wash each leaf and trunk with a soft sponge in hand, and then rinse with clear water. Use every three weeks until infestation disappears. (Scale: It's not a disease, but an almost invisible sucker which lives under a tiny brown or tan shell; the shells can be scrubbed off with an old toothbrush, but soapy water is needed to get the pest.)

When you prune a diseased plant, put all cuttings in plastic bags and tie securely before putting in trash can. Disinfect shears with household-bleach bath.

Now, for details of the battle strategy with those little things always waiting in line for their chance to chew new leaflets, to spit on the stems, curl the buds and mangle the roots. Specifically they are cottony mealy bugs, aphids, red spiders and white flies, mites, things with and without wings, and cowardly sucking types which hide under brown tents called scale. Tiny black ants move in to set up housekeeping, and before you know it are in the moving business transporting scale from plant to plant. Even a stray earthworm may slip into a pot if you use soil from the garden; he could disturb the crocking at the bottom and inhibit drainage. Itinerant caterpillars may also manage to come to dinner on your pet plant.

I have used the word "bugs" loosely in this book. Actually, bugs are a suborder of insects, destructive and difficult to control. Sprays work best on mowing them down, although if they are new to the scene, you might try picking them off with tweezers. If they have already laid eggs, sprays of a Malathion mixture and household bug bombs are your best ammunition.

Most home insect sprays are not injurious to humans and animals, but for extra caution should be used outdoors. Read the small print carefully before you put down your money for a can. Take a plant to the garden, a back porch, a fire escape, a garage or the sidewalk. If you are able to elevate it on a stool or box, spraying will be more efficient in reaching the undersides of leaves where the enemy is entrenched, and the crotches of stems and leaves which attract web-building mites.

Systemic protection eliminates the need to spray for aphids and leaf-hoppers: there is a granular product which you work well into the soil and water in. A six-week interval between applications and your friend will be home, bug free.

For the organic minded, nicotine can be injurious to the health of bugs too. Find a cloth package of cigarette tobacco, the roll-your-own kind, soak it in a quart of warm water until water is the color of dark tea, then pour it on plants like grape ivy and Boston fern.

But for small plants you can readily handle, try washing the plant under a gentle shower or dunking it in a bucket of soapy water to handle the first onslaught. Try a new wrinkle: your electric water-pik, the forced-water gadget for cleaning teeth, can be used to make obstinate bugs vacate fast.

If that doesn't wash the problem off, then resort to sprays.

Ants Look for them if there is any sign of scale or aphids; they go for the sticky-sweet droppings these pests produce. Apply a household insect spray, bait them with a commercial ant-trap, which comes in a small bottle or container, or an ant-stick from the hardware store. If ants nest they are capable of loosening the soil around the roots.

Aphids They float in on the breeze from outside and head for the choicest young leaf. Watch for leaf curl and check under the foliage for this sucker. These wingless insects are about an eighth of an inch long, pear-shaped and may come in several colors. Sticky stems and leaves (caused by the aphids' sucking action) attract ants, who in return carry the aphids from plant to plant. Sooty black fungus is also attracted to the sticky parts. Moisten soil in pot, cover with foil and turn the pot upside down so you can gently bathe the leaves in a tepid bath of Ivory suds or a mild dishwashing detergent (two teaspoons to one quart).

Mealy Bugs These are large enough to be seen without your glasses. They are grey-white oval shapes, usually bundled up in a wooly white jacket which defies water. They hide in joints and against stems, sucking the host's juices, and they multiply almost faster than a computer—600 eggs at a time. Watch for yellow specks and a general yellowing plus a deforming of the plant. The swab-with-alcohol treatment on each one is emergency treatment; dig out colonies around roots and where branches have been removed and soak well with the swab. Several applications are in order—keep constant vigil and handy alcohol. Mealy bugs yearn for African violet, fuchsia, coleus, wax vine and clivia, among others. Any badly infested plant should be destroyed because it will be almost impossible to save.

Mites Sometimes referred to as cyclamen mites, these are suckers which stunt the plant, cause leaves to curl and buds to stay folded. Use

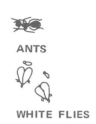

ANTS

WHITE FLIES

MITES

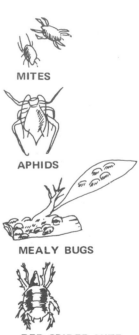

APHIDS

175

MEALY BUGS

RED SPIDER MITE

SCALE

Cyclamen mites feed on buds and cause flowers to be crippled. Submerge foliage in 115° water for 10 minutes. (That's the same temperature needed to dissolve yeast when making bread.)

Fungus gnats: When you find tiny flylike things hopping on top of soil or flirting with a nearby lamp, check all your pots for possible fungus gnats. For easiest cure, see pg. 19. Spray surface of soil with a pyrethrum insect spray, and you'll have finished off both the gnat and its larvae, tiny white worms in the soil.

household insect spray on the grey webs if you can't get it to a strong water wash. These microscopic troublemakers are tenacious. If the plant is neglected and gets too sick, get rid of it fast before the plague spreads. Wash garden tools and your hands to avoid passing on infestation; sterilize emptied pots before repotting with something else.

Red Spider These mites are so tiny you can't see them, so rub your index finger across the underside of a leaf, and if it comes up marked with a reddish stain, you've identified your man. These mites like hairy homes, will leave foliage mottled white and yellow; the mutilated leaves finally drop off. A bath in soft soapy water will drown them, but resort to spray if you are treating a big plant. Hydrangea is a favorite target, so is small-leaf ivy.

Scale A small insect, a crawler which grows a brown shell once it has found a juicy stem for setting up housekeeping. Sprays and dunking do little good, but a slow sponging with an oil emulsion on each leaf and each stem can dislodge that shell. A soft old toothbrush will work on hard stems, and particularly well on the veining of big leaves like the schefflera. Remember to support the leaf with one hand while you do your scrubbing.

White flies Another kind of leaf-sucker which leaves a trail of mold-attracting sweet stickiness. Because these 1/16-inch insects have wings, they flit about in clouds when the plant is touched and are easily identifiable. White flies are the bane of flowering types like geraniums, fuchsias and achimenes. Use a soapy spray or household insect bomb.

Keep all household sprays out of reach of children; they should be taught that this is a "medicine" and out of bounds.

Follow the manufacturer's instructions on any preparation you use: don't overdo the treatment and make the plant even sicker. And be reminded: never feed a sick plant.

MOVING AND VACATIONS

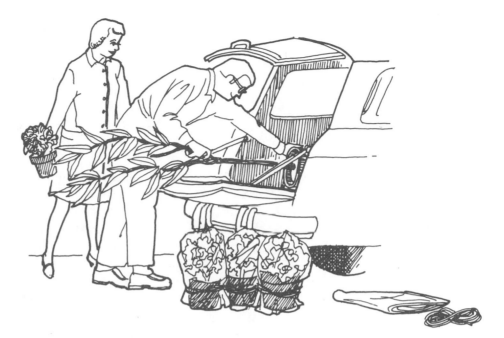

MOVING DAY

This is an aspect few people consider, but it is critical in the life of a plant, no matter what age. Moving from the nursery or plant boutique to the home, moving from one house to another, moving plants across town and across the country, in sun, wind and winter.

The simplest and safest move is the one you and your new green friend make the day you first meet. If it is a hand-carrying pot, common sense will tell you that you should protect it from windburn, or from the heat of a closed car on a hot day. But, if you buy a large specimen and the seller doesn't deliver, it's another haul game.

First, the weight: how do you get the plant into the house or apartment? Will you have to lift it up stairs or squeeze it into a tiny elevator? If it comes home in the trunk of your car or horizontal in the rear deck of a station wagon, how do you guard against damage?

When there is no way to get a delivery, a large container and plant can usually be fitted into the rear trunk of most cars (VW owners open the sun-roof). Wrap a thin plastic covering (the kind cleaners stash your clothes in) around the exposed foliage as a buffer against wind-whipping. Have some heavy objects ready to prop against the container to keep it from rolling around, and a piece of clothesline to secure the trunk lid from bouncing up and down.

178

Words worth: acclimatizing and acclimating say the same thing. Nurseries do this to adjust plants to home conditions before selling—if they're reputable. Unfortunately, you have to be on the alert for scalawags who offer big plants for bargain prices— plants dug out of the ground, stuffed into pots, with no time to adjust—sure way to quick and disappointing end.

Don't try to handle it all by yourself, unless you have had plenty of experience in deadweight lifting; no point in going to a hospital with strained back or muscle.

A two-wheel dolly, the kind of hand truck used for moving boxes and crates, is a great help; rent or borrow one on moving day. A piece of burlap or an old quilt well placed will save skinned stems and container. You also can make a two-man rope carrier with a kind of sling which allows you to set the plant down when your muscles scream, or to maneuver around corners and steps.

Once the container lands in the general area where you will leave it, slide the plant on the burlap or padded material, or a small rug, rather than lifting unnecessarily. A saucer or tray can be put in place underneath by tilting or by one final hoist. The addition at this point of a movable low stand with three heavy-duty casters is wise so that you can easily move the plant to clean it and to change its light direction.

This is a good time, too, to do any staking or pruning of broken branches before final cleanup. Don't put the big plant in bright light immediately; just let it get adjusted gradually to the new scene. If a leaf or two drops, it is the physiological reaction to being moved to strange conditions. And no feeding for at least three months, unless the nurseryman gives special orders.

FRIGID WEATHER MOVING

When you have to move in the middle of winter and the van will travel long distances, unload your plants on various friends and start a new collection at the other end. It *is* possible to have green things moved, but the expense is high and the chance of survival debatable. If the move is local, try to plan a day when the sun is shining and you can wrap newspapers around the plants as insulation. Lots of paper held in place with sticky tape will ward off injury, if you move fast.

For smaller pots, line a cardboard carton thickly with folded newspapers and fill a hot-water bottle. Wrap the plants gently by laying them, one at a time, on their sides on one corner of several layers of paper. Roll the plant diagonally, watching brittle leaves for possible cracking. (Don't risk moving a newly potted plant in cold weather; wait until it is firmly established.) Put the prewrapped packages around the outer area of the box and slip the hot-water bottle in the center.

MISCELLANEOUS MOVING NOTES

Speaking of shock, don't ship plants by air in any weather, even though commercial firms do this all the time. The cargo areas are cold up there, and if your plant is not properly packaged with insulation, you're likely to pick up an ice plant at the other end of the trip. Other hazards are time lags and overhandling.

Interstate shipments? Start with your county agent or contact the state plant quarantine division to arrange for fumigation, inspection and certification *before* you move a plant across a state line. Commercial movers recommend *not* sending plants on their trucks because the ordinary load will not fill one truck and they gang several shipments; also, they can't afford delays at checkpoints because of plant inspection. If you insist on using interstate carriers for plant shipments, they will take no responsibility for survival of your green friends. If you have valuable choice plants, carry them in your own car with proper labeling and filled-in certificates.

Transporting plants in the trunk of the car calls for some urgent precautions. Open the trunk to let in light and air whenever you stop. If the day is hot, get a block of dry ice to place near the plants; they thrive on the carbon dioxide given off by the ice as it melts and the temperature will be lowered considerably. Pack seedlings in a moss-filled box or terrarium. Always carry a supply of kitchen-size plastic food bags for packaging small plants and the root balls of defoliated ones. Plastic is ideal for moving greenery because it allows maximum light. Give any plant moved on a hot day a good misting both before and after the act.

The big moving companies advise "Move them yourself." They're primarily movers, not horticulturists. When they handle several loads, meaning several stops, in one big van, it may be weeks before the plants can be watered.

179

Transport pots in cardboard cartons; stuff moistened newspaper around the pots to keep them from rolling and to add needed humidity. Make sure they fit snugly. If being moved a long distance, be sure to leave a car window partially opened for ventilation. When unwrapping, do it quickly and place in modest light at first.

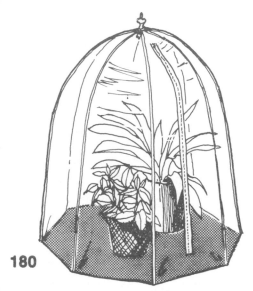

**36" CLEAR VINYL
PLANT-SITTER WITH
ZIPPERED OPENING;
FOLDS FOR STORAGE.
AVAILABLE THROUGH
MAIL ORDER CATALOGS**

WHEN YOU GO AWAY

Vacation planning is complex enough without having to dig up a temporary goldfish feeder who can also rescue newspapers you forgot to stop *and* who will be a knowledgeable plant-sitter. For some reason, house-plant care scares most people; if left to their own judgment, even with careful instructions they either overwater, forget to water or feed the goldfish food to the spider plant.

And so, here are a few ways to handle absentee-owner pots by yourself. Find a bright spot where you can store the plants with *no* sun at all. Using clear plastic garment bags salvaged from the clothes brought back from the cleaner, you can manufacture a kind of terrarium where moisture will be held in for long periods. Start by watering the pots thoroughly and then allow them to drain. Don't saturate the plant or mist the leaves or let water stand in the saucer; too much water and you invite root rot.

Add three or more bamboo plant sticks around each pot edge to support the plastic; these sticks are usually found in bundles at a hardware store. A couple of bent coat hangers will do for small pots, like the four-inchers. Tie a simple knot in the bottom of the bag and slip the plant or plants inside.

A little structural engineering helps at this point. Take a three-by-five-inch card, a blank recipe one will do, fold it lengthwise and tape it to form a 'T' at the top of each stake; this prevents the stake from making a hole in the plastic and gives added width to the top of the bag so it won't rest on the leaves. Close the top with a wire bag tie and your makeshift terrarium becomes the built-in plant-sitter.

If your vegetation is the giant expensive size in tubs or planters, slit the plastic bags to flat sheets, depending on how much area you have to cover, and plan a kind of tent to cover the soil area. Attach masking tape or electricians' tape to one edge all around the top of the container. Water the plant normally—don't saturate. Then gather the plastic together at the base of the stems and tape it so that as little air as possible gets to the soil. If it is an extra-big planter, you will have to build stake supports and buy a sheet of clear thin plastic to make a tent; packaged in a nine-by-12-foot size, it is available at discount drugstores or paint supply stores.

Small pots can be gathered together in the kitchen sink and watered; clear plastic is laid over the top and taped around the edges. Install a strong incandescent light and add a time clock so that the greenery gets a 10-hour rest.

The preceding treatment works for the bathtub or shower terrarium, too. Putting all your friends together and installing a plastic tent will take time, but once watered they will wait two to three weeks until you return, provided that they get good light, too. Drag a reading lamp into the bathroom, one which will give 150 to 200 watts of illumination. Keep the light bulbs at least a foot and a half away from the plastic and add a timer here also.

If you are going to be away during cold weather, leave the thermostat on at 60°, or slightly higher if it is freezing outside. Don't feed the pots before you go; a few weeks slowdown won't hurt them.

When you return, give the plants a chance to re-enter slowly. Open the plastic but leave the plant inside to ease shock. If the plant needs water add it right away, but wait a day or two before putting the pot back on its saucer and disposing of the plastic. After you get your bags unpacked, carefully check each pot for possible invasion of bugs.

Once you become a specialist or collector, there are specific answers for plant-sitting: check a phone directory in the yellow section for orchid and African violet societies which can direct you to trained people who will take care of a collection for long periods.

DRY BOUQUETS AND CUT FLOWERS

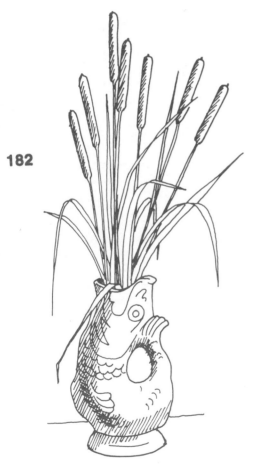

182

CATTAILS IN FISH PITCHER

This section has been added for people who may *not* want to brighten up every dark corner just to grow a house-plant collection.

Soft natural light won't support anything living, but it can revive a big old umbrella stand filled with pale weeds plucked on a walk in the desert. Their stiff but lacy bones are enhanced by adding milkweed to the arrangement (seal the stems by burning) and several stalks of tall teasel.

Or, an old stone bottle with a bouquet of salsify, picked on a mountain roadside, will be transformed from just pretty blue blossoms into giant dandelion-type seed globes. Keep them in water a week then allow to dry as the seeds appear. When all the leaves have dried and can be stripped off, spray the seeds with artist's fixative or a clear lacquer spray. Hair spray will do a good temporary job.

Most weeds and grasses are easy to dry—it's their natural destiny. And they will last indefinitely away from direct sunlight. The smaller ones are particularly beautiful when they are arranged under glass, in a bell jar or under a plexiglas cover. If the glass is airtight, the weeds will stay dust-free and the color preserved.

A large group of plants can be dried by cutting them and placing them in a waterless vase for a few weeks; then, they can be tied in bunches and hung upside down in a dark place, like a closet. Try this method with sea lavender, buckwheat, thistles, pearly everlasting, artichoke's lovely purple thistle, lavender, magnolia cuttings, century plant blossoms (agave), baby's breath, yarrow, goldenrod, dill, celosia and achillea. It is well to pick most flowers to be air-dried in the last stage of buds rather than fully blooming.

Straw flowers, perhaps the most common dried thing readily available, grow outside on an ugly plant; it is sprawly and only worthwhile because you can cut the two-inch yellow and orange blooms as they mature, without stems, and spread them to dry. Add wire stems to complete a sunny arrangement.

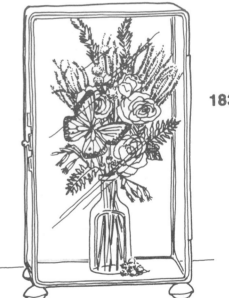

Flowers with fragile petals or bright colors have to be dried in something called silica gel, a chemical form of silica, a highly absorbent and dehumidifying agent. It is put into a cardboard box in a half-inch layer, the flowers are gently placed on this layer and more of the chemical dusted over so that all the petals are covered. Zinnias, larkspur and snapdragons can be preserved this way. When the blossoms are "crisp," they can be removed. Open one side of the box and let the silica gel sift out onto a layer of newspapers. (Save it in an empty coffee can for reuse; label and date the can.) Don't remove the flowers until entirely exposed. Different flowers require different drying times.

Some flowers and leaf stems are preserved by the glycerine method. Getting the preservative can be a problem—it is available from a chemical supplier (see the phone directory yellow section) and you will probably have to buy at least a gallon. Try pooling adventurous friends into sharing part of the cost, each trying something different. Make a solution of one part glycerine to two parts water (one to one and a half may do better for some plants). Slit stems and stand in at least five inches of the mixture; they should be ready to remove in about three weeks. Mildew may form on stems which still contain moisture so final drying will take longer to complete dehydration.

WEEDS AS DECORATION

Freezing herbs: Chop parsley and chives before freezing, package in small amounts. Basil can be frozen whole; select healthy leaves, wash thoroughly and shake off water. Place on a cookie sheet in freezer and when stiff (5 to 10 minutes), remove and store in freezer bags and return to freezer. Date and label. No need to thaw herbs before using.

Container and contents should never be the same size: a primary proportion is to adjust the length of the weed to one and a half times the greatest dimension of the container. Limit the variety to three or four species for simple naturalness.

When you get tired of the arrangement, the parts should be burned to prevent spreading of the weeds' seeds.

Some weeds cannot be preserved; others should not be picked or are protected by law: fritillarias, the Joshua tree, smoke tree, succulents, sunflowers, phlox, squaw grass, poison oak, desert holly.

CUT FLOWER CARE

Outside of little pamphlets and booklets prepared by women's garden clubs and horticultural societies for limited audiences, information is almost impossible to locate on this subject.

A purple thumb by any other name is still colored by the fact that most of us know very little or nothing about keeping flowers around longer. The blossoms we cut for the table, the bouquet which comes unexpectedly from the florist, a child's squeezed-stem bunch of posies stripped from a prized garden clump—these almost always just get put in the nearest vase or drinking glass.

There are a few classic tricks which will prolong bloom; these are results of the experiences of a great many people and may just catapult you out of purple-thumb brinkmanship.

"Hardening off" is a florist's phrase used to insure cut flowers' continuing attractiveness long after the surgery which separated them from the plant. One method is to give freshly cut blossoms a deep-water soaking for a couple of hours. Plants which take up a lot of liquid in this soaking, such as marigolds, ranunculuses and stocks will also use much water in the arrangement, and it should be replenished shortly after, within two hours.

Some, like flax, cattails and horsetails, require little water for hardening off; most succulents can do with little water and echeverias will keep for many weeks with just a little misting.

Heads and stems of flowers left wrapped in paper but with the lower stems free, benefit even more from deep-soaking; tulips and lilies will last longer treated this way.

Iceland poppies should be brought into the house as tight buds and soaked for a couple of days in a cool, dark place. They will stay in bud form until you bring them out into the light and bathe the stems in warm water briefly.

A quick plunge into boiling water, about three inches deep, will harden off most delicate stems if you follow up with deep cold water for two hours. The blooms should be wrapped in paper during this action. Woody stems can stand the hot liquid longer.

Denatured alcohol is a good preservative and a few drops in the filled vase will prolong life. A teaspoon will eliminate the odor of ornamental cabbage, wild onion and other members of the lily family.

Aloes, columbines and euphorbias benefit from having their stems dipped in salt right after cutting.

Branches of forsythias and almond, brought in for the first promise of spring, live happier when their cut ends are charred and then immersed in water for an hour. Misting helps also, once the arrangement is completed. Fuchsias, hellebores, bougainvillea and clematis also relate to this treatment. To char the ends, use a candle or a match; most plants are afraid of gas. If the branch shows signs of wilt before you can get it properly taken care of, wrap the cuttings, leaving stems free, and give them the two-hour deep-water treatment, after three minutes immersion of stems in boiling water.

Bringing dormant branches in, and watching them come to flower in the house is a Japanese custom and fruiting while still in water is

White flies love yellow. If they are moving into your area, find a bright yellow cardboard, cover with double-face scotch tape and watch the white flies collect. Any sticky substance will do, but the color must be yellow.

considered a great good luck sign. Barberries, flowering quince, cherries, peach and crabapple take slightly more than three weeks to open while the snowball takes as long as six weeks.

Camellias sprayed with a light solution of salty water will hold their blossoms extra days.

Dogwood picked in the spring gets the boiling-water/deep-water treatment. In the autumn, add a teaspoon of vinegar to the boiling water, and dunk the stems five minutes; then move to the cold. Do this with Oregon grape and nandina, too; or char their stem ends.

Gardenias have short stems and cannot be treated like others; just keep them as cool as possible and out of drafts. They like the refrigerator, but should be left in a box. Any bloom left in this cold condition should be wrapped in wax paper or plastic because there is too little humidity provided. Spray or mist the paper before wrapping the flower.

Flowers which have wilted because of careless handling can often be revived by dipping stems in boiling water. Woody stems can stay until the water has cooled; soft stems need cold water as deep as possible right after the hot dip.

Nearly all blossoms will keep much longer if soaked in deep water eight to 12 hours before being arranged; keep them in a cool dark place during the waiting period.

Cut flowers do not go for strong sun, or close relationships with gas fumes or radiators. A bowl of water placed on a radiator will add more humidity to a room of flowers.

Change the water of an arrangement frequently.

In general, remove as many leaves as possible from the stems which will be under water.

Blossoms picked should be cut on a slant with sharp knife. This allows more absorption of water. Never pick when the sun is shining directly on the flowers.

SPECIFIC CUT-FLOWER SUGGESTIONS

African Daisies: pick early bloom and keep them in a cool place, deep-watered for two days.

Agapanthus: peel the stem part way around on blossoms, leaves.

Anemone: cut before entirely full; recut stems under water and immerse for four hours; one-half cup vinegar to two cups water.

Asters: add two tablespoons sugar and one of salt to each quart of water.

Autumn leaves: two parts glycerine to one part water; add plain water as needed.

Carnations: give the cut stems a barbering each day; try a quarter teaspoon boric acid to each quart water.

Chrysanthemum: break stems instead of cutting; to revive, use boiling-water treatment or add 10 drops of oil of cloves to two quarts of cold water.

Dahlias: cut in full bloom; let stand in deep water for two hours with one and one-half tablespoons alcohol added for each quart.

Delphiniums: change water daily to eliminate odors.

Ferns: wrap in damp newspaper.

Grasses: dip in vinegar for a short spell.

Hydrangea: cut and put in water immediately; crush stem end.

Iris: cut at bud time—keep water away from petals and put them in shallow water; add three drops oil of peppermint to each quart.

Lilacs: crush the stem and remove as many leaves as possible, but always keep the green leaf near the flower head as it is the water conductor to the bloom.

Maple: one teaspoon alcohol to a quart of water; salt added helps.

Marigolds: (same as African daisies).

Orchids: split stem about an inch; to revive, put in refrigerator.

Peonies: scratch stems on two sides but don't cut into them; give them a deep container with most of stem under water.

Roses: buds cut best; split the stem, trim off leaves that might go in water, but leave ones near buds. Stand in lukewarm water.

Stocks: remove leaves below water line and change water daily.

Tulips: cut in early bud, wrap in newspaper and deep-water with only buds above the water line; avoid warm room—they will open in two hours if in overheated place.

Violets: baptize them completely in water for a few minutes, then wrap in wax paper and refrigerate; will last several days if cold boxed each night this way.

Yarrow: two tablespoons of salt to two quarts water.

Zinnias: pick full-bloom, strip leaves to be under water; boiling-water, deep-cold-water treatment.

P.S. You can help preserve our watersheds and prevent erosion by leaving lovely wildflowers right where they are. In most states there are already laws which say "Look, don't pick."

So much for purple prose . . .

INDEX

188

189

ABOUT THE AUTHOR

At age 16, Maggie Baylis was an architecture major at the University of Pennsylvania, but because of the depression she left school and went to work. By the time she was 23, she was advertising manager of a department store in Tacoma, Washington. Then in 1938 she came to California to join the public relations staff of the Golden Gate International Exposition, only to discover that the department head had been fired and there was no job. She stayed in San Francisco, working in advertising and copywriting for a number of years. Later she was assistant art director for Sunset Magazine.

In 1951 she joined her husband, the late Douglas Baylis, nationally known landscape architect, as his strong right arm for the next 20 years—draftsman, delineator, bread-baker, carpenter and house-plant tender. The Baylises were also active contributors and consultants to all the country's leading home and garden publications, concerned with the developing consciousness of environmental planning and fulfillment.

Mrs. Baylis continues to live and work in their nontraditional two-story studio at the end of an alley on the side of San Francisco's Telegraph Hill, surrounded by indoor plants, a big sunny deck and an ancient fig tree that survived the 1906 fire. She is the author of *Practicing Plant Parenthood* and co-author of *Real Bread;* she also illustrated *Greenhousing for Purple Thumbs* and *The Punctured Thumb.*